P9-DNF-330

1,628 COUNTRY SHORTCUTS
From 1,628 Country People

*The best tried-and-true
tips to solve everyday
around-the-house problems
...gathered from the 4 million
subscribers to Country and
Country Woman magazines.*

HERE ARE THE ANSWERS TO THE QUESTIONS ON OUR COVER:

How do you get a skunk out of the garage?
Put a good dose of household ammonia in a large flat pan, one with plenty of surface area, and set it in the garage. Leave the door open far enough for the skunk to get out but keep plenty of the ammonia in. It works, because skunks hate smelly things themselves. *—Bill McLaine*
Eugene, Oregon

How do you get onion odor off your hands?
Simply wet them and gently rub in salt. Then rinse and wash with your usual soap—the smell will be gone. *—Kathy Firmin, Baton Rouge, Louisiana*

How do you get tree sap off your car?
Just hold a cube of ice on the sap till it gets hard, then peel it off.
—Jim Phillips, Harrisburg, Pennsylvania

How do you keep gophers from eating your tulip bulbs?
Put two or three mothballs in each hole when you plant tulips and other bulbs in the fall. This works for me! *—Martha Goessling*
Red Bud, Illinois

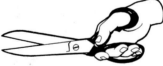

And that's just the beginning—there are more than 1,600 shortcuts and suggestions spread throughout this book.

1,628 COUNTRY SHORTCUTS
From 1,628 Country People

Editor: Roy Reiman

Assistant Editors: Kristine Krueger, Julie Schnittka, Joe Kertzman, Mike Beno, Henry de Fiebre

Art Director: Vicky Wilimitis

Illustrator: Jim Sibilski

Production Assistant: Ellen Lloyd

© 1995 Reiman Publications, L.P.
5400 S. 60th St., Greendale WI 53129

International Standard Book Number: 0-89821-148-4
Library of Congress Catalog Number: 95-68774

All rights reserved. No part of this publication may be reproduced or transmitted in any form or by any means, electronic or mechanical, including photography, recording or any other information storage and retrieval system, without the written permission of the publisher.

Notice: The information in this book has been gathered from a variety of people and sources, and all efforts have been made to ensure accuracy. Reiman Publications assumes no responsibility for any injuries suffered or damages or losses incurred as a result of this information. All information should be carefully studied and clearly understood before taking any action based on the information or advice in this book.

For additional copies of this book or information on other books, write: Country Books, P.O. Box 990, Greendale WI 53129. You can also order by phone and charge to your credit card by calling toll-free 1-800/558-1013.

FOREWORD

MY DAD would have liked this book. He was one of the most practical men I've ever known. Give him a piece of baling wire on the Iowa farm where I grew up, and he could fix just about anything.

Being isolated as we were, several miles from the nearest town, his knack of fixing things was born of necessity. You didn't just call a repairman or "serviceman" in those days when something broke down. Instead you just stood there, stared at the problem awhile as you scratched your neck, then found a way to "make do" and get things going again.

I inherited a bit of this knack from my dad. I'm not too adept at anything involving electrical wiring or gas heaters, but beyond that, if I scratch my neck long enough, I can solve about any household and outdoor fix-it problems.

That's why I really enjoyed assembling and editing this book. It allowed me to "get acquainted" with a lot of folks just like myself, only many of them are a lot more talented and clever than I am when it comes to practical, ingenious "shortcuts".

In fact, sometimes after editing a chapter, I couldn't wait to get home and try one of the tips shared by our readers. For example, last week I edited an item on how to get rid of those "dents" left in carpeting after you move furniture.

Sampling the Product

My wife, Bobbi, had moved some of our living room chairs and a coffee table about a month earlier, and about a dozen dents were *still* in that carpeting. They bothered me every time I saw them. (I'm such a nit-picking perfectionist I can't stand pictures hanging crooked in *other* people's houses. I've actually straightened a few of them when the host stepped out of the room.)

The handwritten tip from Sally Clark of East Bradenton, Florida contended anyone can clear up that problem by placing an ice cube in each dent and leaving it melt there overnight. Next morning, the carpet will be damp, Sally advised, which will cause the fibers of the carpet to swell. Then you simply use a towel or your fingers to scratch and fluff out the dent.

I decided that tip was worth trying. That evening, just prior to bedtime, when I walked into the living room with the ice cube tray, Bobbi looked at me like I'd "lost it". But I told her what I was doing and why, and though her eyebrows arched up kind of high, she went along with it.

Next morning, I was surprised to find a dozen small, clear "puddles" in each of those dents. The nap of our carpeting is apparently quite tight.

But I got a towel, soaked up the moisture and then used the other end of the towel to rub out the dents. *Presto!* Those dents were *gone*, and they still are. Thank you, Sally!

Here are three other "Gee, why didn't *I* think of that?" tips I particularly liked among the hundreds I edited for this book:

1. When washing windows, to tell if the streak is on the outside or the inside, wipe the outside of each window horizontally, and the inside vertically. Why, sure!

2. When painting stairs, paint every other step so you can continue using the stairs. Put a bold piece of tape on the "dry" steps so the family will know which ones they can step on. When dry, paint the alternate steps. Of course!

3. To save time, when you place a new garbage bag in the wastebasket or trash container, store several additional bags, folded flat, at the bottom of the container. That way you won't have to run for a new bag every time you make the change.

Now, why the dickens didn't I think of that garbage bag step-saver before? That simple idea is so good we're doing exactly that in all the wastebaskets around our offices now.

That's Just the Beginning

You'll find simple, practical ideas like these all through this book. While it may take you only a few hours to read it from cover to cover, it will result in saving you an amazing number of hours the rest of your life.

What's more, I'm sure you're going to thoroughly *enjoy* reading this book. You're likely going to find yourself smiling broadly again and again, not just because the shortcut or tip is just so down-home and clever, but because I didn't edit out all of the humor accompanying the tips.

I so much enjoyed reading all of the subscribers' "side comments" about how they came up with these ideas and/or how they went about doing them that I purposely left in some of those comments. (I can just picture Bill McLaine easing into his garage in Eugene, Oregon with that pan of ammonia to drive out the skunk that was staring at him from the other corner!)

You'll find reading this book is sort of like sitting down in a large room with more than 1,600 friendly, willing-to-lend-a-hand country people, and then having each one stand up and tell you their best tried-and-true time- or money-saving shortcut.

They wrote this book. All I did was edit it...and I enjoyed the task immensely. What's more, I'm already *using* many of these shortcuts.

— Roy Reiman

'A Practical Book Written By 1,628 Practical People'

AS IS usually the case at Reiman Publications, the best ideas come from our readers. The idea for this book, for example, came from Eleanor Weisshaar of Bellflower, California.

"One of the first pages I turn to in any of your company's magazines is your 'helpful hints' section," she wrote. "I've started a file on the ones I find particularly relevant. But you really ought to consider gathering all these down-home tips into a book.

"I'm sure I'm not the only subscriber who feels I've missed out on hundreds of good tips over the years. If you could categorize them, it would be even more helpful. So a book, please?"

Well, Eleanor, we've gone and done it, just as you (and many others) asked. We sorted through all of our back issues of all of our magazines, and pulled together the best "Country Shortcuts" for this first book of its kind.

The result is a very practical book written by 1,628 practical people. That's how many of our subscribers sat down and wrote (in many cases by hand) their one tried-and-true, "works for me" tip that ended up in this book.

From hints on an easy way to keep the bathroom mirror from steaming up...to a slick trick that'll prevent potted plants from falling off the porch railing...to getting gum out of Billy's hair, the solutions are all here...solutions that did the job for a country friend somewhere, and who was happy to share it with you in the following pages.

We sincerely thank each of these "editors", and hope these 1,628 work-saving, time-saving, money-saving tips make life just a little easier for you.

—The Editors of *Country* and *Country Woman* magazines

CONTENTS

CHAPTER 1
HOUSEHOLD REPAIRS & MAINTENANCE

Who wants to wash and wax floors more often than you have to? My floors used to get scratched from chairs sliding back and forth, so I cut little pieces of carpet and glued them to the bottoms of the chair legs. The chairs are much quieter, and I'm much happier not to have my floors scratched. I used indoor-outdoor carpet, but I'm sure any kind would do the trick. —*Mrs. John Krull*
Worth County, Iowa

To avoid clogged kitchen drainpipes, pour a cup of salt and a cup of baking soda down the drain, followed with a pot of boiling water. Sure makes the grease let go.
—*Helen Wilhelm*
Chillicothe, Illinois

A hanging pocket-style shoe bag is a great addition to any hallway for storing winter gloves and mittens, rubbers, scarves and caps. Put it where the children can reach it so they can be responsible for find-ing and putting away their own things.

To be even more orderly, you might want to label each pocket with a family member's initials.
—*Rachel Siegrist*
Lititz, Pennsylvania

Coil the ends of your rubber bath mat toward the center, and stand it on end in the tub to drain. If the mat doesn't stay coiled, snap the rolls together with a clothespin. Draining the mat will keep it from mildewing.
—*Mrs. Don Fimion*
Alma, Wisconsin

I needed large quantities of varnish remover to refinish portions of a wood floor and the woodwork. I found this recipe for varnish remover inexpensive and less dangerous than commercial products when small children are around:

Mix 1 cup cornstarch and 1/2 cup cold water. Add 1 quart boiling water, 3/4 cup sal soda, 1/2 cup ammonia and 1 tablespoon vinegar. Apply with a brush while hot. Rewarm if necessary. After varnish loosens, wash off with hot water and a cloth. If you don't have soft water, it will work better if you add a softening agent to the rinse water.

—Mrs. Wesley Doerr
Bloomfield, Nebraska

Don't throw away a garden rake just because the handle is broken. It can be used as a convenient rack to hold small tools such as hammers, screwdrivers and wrenches. Just attach the rake section to the wall with the tines out and hang the tools between the tines.   —Helen Patzlaff
Alexandria, South Dakota

Make an attractive doorstop easily if you have an old purse with a beautiful tapestry design that you no longer use. Cut and sew the material to fit over a brick.

—Elva Pate
Williamston, North Carolina

After the thin material around the sides of my mattress pad was worn beyond repair, I sewed the top of the pad to an old fitted sheet that was wearing in the middle. It's easiest to attach the two if you pin the top of the pad to the sheet while it's on the bed and then take it off to stitch on the machine.

—Mrs. Pat Wilkinson
Center Point, Indiana

To store dresser scarves wrinkle-free, I place them on a hanger that has a cardboard roll across the bottom. A rolled magazine securely

taped will serve the same purpose.

—Mrs. Kenneth Bordner
Morrison, Illinois

I found that revarnishing with a small soft lint-free cloth is twice as fast as using a brush. You can rub in any direction, and the varnish goes into the wood better. There will be no splatters and no brushes to clean out. Throw the rag away if it gets too dirty. Clean your hands with paint remover.

—Mrs. Ralph Albert Jr.
Ladora, Iowa

Use a coffeepot brush to clean your sewing machine. It will be long enough to poke into even the farthest recesses and narrow enough to fit into those thousand-and-one crevices where lint clings.

—Margaret Shauers
Great Bend, Kansas

Put whole cloves in pockets of woolen coats or in bags with sweaters when storing for the off-season. They prevent moth damage and leave a spicy clean aroma. Also place them in dresser drawers with socks and everyday work clothes.

—Mrs. Dennis Danzinger
Durand, Wisconsin

A discarded clothes hamper makes a good storage place for rubbers, overshoes and boots. It is ventilated and you can repaint it to go with the decor in your porch or hall. Put one near the doorway and your family will no longer have an excuse for leaving their footwear strewn all over.　　*—Helen Daley Parker, Colorado*

Use worn pillowcases as dust covers for clothing stored on hangers in a closet. Cut a small hole in the center of the seam and slip it over the hanger hook.
—Renee Johnson, Pierpont, Ohio

My husband turned one of my long-handled, two-pronged forks into a jack-of-all-trades by bending both prongs until they were perpendicular to the handle. I use this tool for pulling hot pans of food, cakes or baked potatoes from the oven. It al-so comes in handy for reaching articles on high shelves and for fishing things out of narrow spaces.
—Wilma Shauers, Beeler, Kansas

Do members of your family wear mud-collecting waffle-soled boots and shoes? Try spraying these muddied soles with Pam, let the mud dry and then hit the shoes together. Soles will come clean every time.　　　　　*—Carol Paul St. Joseph, Missouri*

Save the water from your dehumidifier for your steam iron and machinery and car batteries. It's convenient, and you save money.
—Mrs. Larry Jessen, Zion, Illinois

Coat brass fixtures with hair spray after polishing them, and they will remain tarnish-free much longer.　　　　　*—C. Peterson Imperial, Nebraska*

IT WORKED FOR GRANDPA!
Some "seasoned advice" from Grandpa Zeb:

NEXT TIME you need to move a big heavy box, chest or piece of furniture, don't strain your back lifting, pulling and pushing.

Just lift the front edge of the item and slip the straw part of a flat broom underneath. Then get a helper to push from the back while you pull on the broom handle and guide the heavy item.

It's one way to make a clean sweep of a tough move.

Here's another moving tip: Before you try to slide a refrigerator, washer, dryer, etc. on a smooth hard surface, put a small dab of shortening on the floor in front of the forward feet. It will then slide easily.

But don't get your shoes in the shortening, or you'll be "spinning your wheels" all day!

To keep your collectors' silver spoons from tarnishing while on display, wax them with two or three coats of liquid floor wax. They won't need polishing for a long time. —*Mrs. C.J. Adams*
Arlington, Iowa

I don't buy white shelf paper anymore. Instead, I line my shelves with heavy freezer wrap, with the waxed side up. It can be wiped off with a damp cloth and outwears regular shelf paper. —*Josie Wautlet*
Algoma, Wisconsin

While ironing starched clothing, some of the starch may transfer onto your iron. Should this happen, run the iron over salt sprinkled on the end of the ironing board until the starch comes off. —*Nanci Howard*
Cedar Lake, Indiana

Here's a way to deal with plastic knobs on appliances, drawers, etc. that repeatedly work themselves loose: Pull the knob off and apply three or four drops of lacquer thinner inside the knob and on the screw that holds it. Wait a few seconds so the lacquer can begin to set and then screw the knob back on. This time it will stay put for good. —*Sally Clark*
East Bradenton, Florida

In your bathroom, keep those odds and ends of pins, clips, rubber bands, etc. in a plastic silverware tray. —*Rachel Siegrist*
Lititz, Pennsylvania

Refrigerators are hardly ever destroyed in a fire. So, whenever you go away from home on a trip or vacation, store the file box containing your valuable personal papers—birth certificates, deeds, insurance policies, wills, etc.—in the refrigerator! —*Mrs. Pat Rodeffer*
Ferris, Illinois

This hint is for filling feather pillows. You need an upright vacuum cleaner. Remove the throw-away bag and attach the pillow ticking to the top end of the stationary bag, or completely remove  the bag and attach ticking to the nozzle end of the vacuum. Take out the roller with the brushes from the bottom of the cleaner. Put the feathers on a clean floor, start the vacuum cleaner—presto, the ticking is full of feathers in minutes! —*Mrs. Arthur Mentzer*
Ericson, Nebraska

To separate two glasses that are stuck together, put the bottom glass in warm water and pour cold water in the top glass. The two will pull apart easily without breaking.
—*Marcella Giebler, Hays, Kansas*

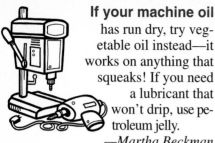

If your machine oil has run dry, try vegetable oil instead—it works on anything that squeaks! If you need a lubricant that won't drip, use petroleum jelly.

—Martha Beckman
Granada Hills, California

To clean a steam iron, fill it with vinegar and place over a pan on a metal rack. Set the iron on high and let it steam until it's empty. Repeat with water. Wipe dry and your iron will work again.

Keep the sole plate clean by running the iron over a square of wax wrapped in an old cloth.

—Mrs. Nels Sorensen Jr.
Dagmar, Montana

When your hammer or ax heads begin to loosen, soak the top of the wooden handle in a solution of glycerin and water. Reinsert the handle in the head while still wet and the wood will swell to give a tight fit.

—Julie Klee, Streator, Illinois

The next time you're out of kindling wood, improvise. Stuff empty paper milk cartons with newspaper and poke holes in the side of the carton. Place them under your wood and ignite as usual.

—Mrs. Fred Leick
Waukesha, Wisconsin

You can sharpen a dull pair of scissors, easily, by cutting through several thicknesses of aluminum foil.   *—Helen Huska*
Lebanon, New Jersey

To get rid of the leg dents that heavy furniture leaves in your pile carpeting, place an ice cube in each dent and let them sit overnight. The next morning, use a towel or your fingers to scratch and fluff out the dent until it's the same level as the rest of the nap. The water from the melted cube causes the fibers of the carpet to swell.   *—Sally Clark*
East Bradenton, Florida

To seal cracks in china, ceramics, etc., place the damaged piece in a pan of milk and boil for 45 minutes. The milk not only forms a tight seal, it covers the crack, making your broken dish as good as new.

—Mary Jane VanWyk
Monroe, Iowa

When it's difficult to get a nail started in an awkward place, put a

---

Since we don't have an air conditioner at our place, we rely on electric fans to cool things off in hot weather. To do away with the noise that a vibrating fan makes, we place a piece of foam under the fan. Everyone sleeps cool and undisturbed.

—Elsie Bauer
Greenleaf, Kansas

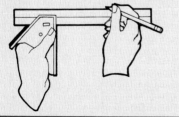

ball of putty on the tip of the nail to hold it in place while you drive the nail in. The putty is easy to remove once the hole has been started.

—Mrs. Harvey Muller
Danboro, Pennsylvania

Wooden frame windows that do not slide up and down easily may be in need of some lubrication. Dry soap, wax or paraffin rubbed in the tracks will usually solve that problem. *—Mildred Sherrer*
Bay City, Texas

Wallpaper scraps (washable *vinyl* especially) make great liners for both drawers and shelves.
—Jan Newman
Burlingame, Kansas

Instead of folding your linens, roll them up tightly before putting them away. You will fit more into your cupboards this way. Remember this space-saving trick when packing a suitcase, too.

—Maureen Beaver
Sparta, Wisconsin

Dip a new broom in hot salted water before using. This will toughen the bristles and make it last longer. *—Margaret Lozier*
Lockbourne, Ohio

You'll never misplace road maps if you file them alphabetically by state in a record file (we use the accor-dion-pleated type) or three-ring binder. No last-minute hassle looking for a map before you start off on a trip. *—Margaret Lewis*
Sioux City, Iowa

I run all my heat and air-conditioning vent covers through the dishwasher every spring and fall. It saves lots of time and does a better job than doing it by hand.
—Marge Grandy, Flippin, Arkansas

I made a little skirt to go around the bottom of my bathroom plunger. Then I stood the plunger in the bathroom and put several rolls of toilet tissue on the handle. Now the plunger—plus extra tissue—is always handy! *—Rhonda Boswell*
Holly Springs, Mississippi

To make a neat thread-spool holder, you need a stand-up photo frame, a piece of plywood cut to the size of the frame, a colorful piece of self-adhesive paper and some square hooks.

Remove the glass, if any, from the frame and take out the back. Lay the plywood (cut to the correct size) on the front of the frame. Smooth a piece of the self-adhesive paper on the plywood, leaving a 2-inch surplus all around. Snip the paper diagonally at the corners and stick down on the frame edges and back.

Screw in as many hooks as desired on the front, leaving enough space for the spools of thread.

You can make handy holders like this for bracelets and necklaces, too.
—Mrs. Ernest Ross
San Bernardino, California

If you use a wood-burning stove, you can make your own sweet-smelling "humidifier". Fill an old coffee can two-thirds full of water…add cinnamon sticks, cloves and orange peel…and place on the stove. When the water gets hot, it gives off a pleasant scent—*and* gives the house extra moisture.

—*Therese DeVlieger*
Davis Junction, Illinois

If you're always a mitten or a glove short at your house in winter, try this: Hang several pant or skirt hangers in the hall closet. Ask family members to clip pairs together on the hangers when not in use.

—*Liz Grove, New Carlisle, Indiana*

Tired of ending up with scratched, ruined china and porcelain when you scrub coffee cup stains with cleansers? Immerse your mugs for 5 to 10 minutes in a sink filled with water and laundry bleach. Remove them, *rinse well* and rub with a sponge. They'll be just like new.

—*W.H. Phillips*
Magalia, California

I'd often pull the wrong cord as I went to open or close my venetian blinds, so I tied a short piece of col-ored yarn around the cord that closes the blind. Now I know at a glance which one to pull.   —*Harold Kunz*
Lancaster, New York

An easy and effective way to remove the indentations left on carpets by heavy furniture is to use a steam iron. Just set the iron on the lowest steam setting and iron away.

—*Allison Tilley*
Manchester, Tennessee

Use two old towels as slings to easily move large household items such as mattresses and dressers.

—*Maggie Glassoff*
Concord, California

As soon as camping season ends, tuck a fabric softener sheet into each sleeping bag before rolling it up. The bag will smell fresh as can be for the first camping trip next season!

—*Gail Weightman*
Gills Rock, Wisconsin

To organize kitchen and other drawers, use boxes of various sizes to put things in. That way, there aren't loose materials scattered all over the drawers. I use empty cereal boxes that I cut open lengthwise.

—*Barb Aasheim*
Fargo, North Dakota

Use vinegar as a cutting agent for drilling holes in metal. It really extends the life of drill bits.

—*Sam Raley*
Lebanon Junction, Kentucky

You can dry wet boots, hats and mittens by placing them on a standing shoe rack and setting it over or in front of an out-of-the-way heating vent. —*Debbie Bosley Brodbecks, Pennsylvania*

Ever have trouble putting sheer curtains on a rod? Cut a finger off an old glove and put it on the rod—the curtain will slide on easily.
—*Mary Ault, St. Helens, Oregon*

Tired of splattering and spilling ingredients all over your cookbooks? Once you've turned to the page you want, slip the book inside a large plastic food storage bag to protect the pages. —*Rosa Graber Odon, Indiana*

When putting up new clothesline, attach each end to a short length (6 to 8 inches) of lightweight chain. Then when the line needs to be tightened, move the chain up a notch or two. —*Jean Lutz DeWitt, Michigan*

Looking for a homemade solution that cleans windows, glass doors and mirrors? Mix 2 ounces of rubbing alcohol, 2 ounces of ammonia and 12 ounces of water.

Add a drop of blue food coloring and mark it clearly to distinguish it 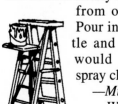 from other cleaners. Pour into a spray bottle and use it as you would a purchased spray cleaner.
—*Mildred Zuercher White Bear Lake, Minnesota*

COUNTRY TRIVIA

IN THE 20-mule teams famous for hauling wagonloads of borax, there were really only 18 mules...the two animals closest to the wagon, the "wheelers", were horses.

To mend a leaking vase, coat the inside with a layer of paraffin and allow it to harden. The paraffin will last indefinitely and the vase will not leak. —*Leona Harris Joliet, Illinois*

To make a fitted sheet out of a plain sheet, tie a knot in each corner, lay the sheet on the bed and tuck each knot under a corner of the mattress. —*Mrs. Stanley Sundet Brookings, South Dakota*

When thawing a frozen water pipe with a torch, start at the faucet end. If you start in the middle of the pipe, the expansion pressure is likely to burst the pipe—and leave you with an even bigger mess!
—*Sally Clark East Bradenton, Florida*

Remove sticky price tags from glass by spraying with WD-40. It works well. —*Herman Ensey Scottsbluff, Nebraska*

If grease is clogging your kitchen drain, try this trick: Heat a pan of water and hold it up to the trap under the sink. When the grease

clog warms up, it will melt and un-clog the drain. Run warm water for a few minutes to rinse the trap thoroughly. —*Marian Smith*
Lake Placid, Florida

If you have trouble keeping a fire going in a wood stove, try this: Throw an old candle into the fire when it's burning nicely, and the wax will keep melting and burning.
—*Angie Saul, Dora, Missouri*

To keep bed linen sets together and organized in your linen closet, fold the top and bottom sheets and one pillowcase, then store them all inside the remaining pillowcase.
—*Mrs. Walter Streifel*
Esmond, North Dakota

Tuck a few pieces of charcoal into your toolbox. It will absorb any moisture that gets in and keep your tools from rusting.
—*Julie Klee, Streator, Illinois*

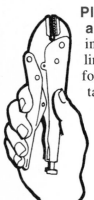

Place silver in an aluminum pan or in your kitchen sink lined with aluminum foil. Sprinkle with 3 tablespoons of baking soda and cover with boiling water. Let stand for 10 to 12 minutes.
—*Lois Kreider*
Lebanon,
Pennsylvania

To keep kitchen chair pads from sliding, buy a yard of rubber carpet padding at a carpet store, cut out small squares and put them under the chair pads. —*Ida Wing*
Monument Beach, Massachusetts

To speed up slow drains, pour in a cup of baking soda followed by a cup of vinegar. After a few seconds, rinse it down with a quart of hot water. This works well and leaves the sink smelling fresh.
—*Thelma Huttula*
Gladstone, Michigan

To remove hard-water buildup on your shower head, pour some white distilled vinegar in a plastic bag and place it around the shower head so the head is completely submerged. Tie the bag around the pipe and leave it overnight. You'll find the shower head will spray like new again the next morning.
—*Jennie Krell*
El Cajon, California

Arm protectors of fabric tend to mat or wear the fabric on the furniture. To avoid this, I attach plastic wrap to the inside of the protector with double-stick tape. The protector also stays in place better.
—*Mrs. Arnold Fahrenkrog*
Walcott, Iowa

To stop throw rugs from slipping around underfoot, glue some nonskid rubber strips for your bathtub to the underside of the rugs.
—*Melinda Neal, Muncie, Indiana*

Here's an easy way to expand the size of your dining room table: Cut a piece of plywood the shape of the table but larger and put on top

REPAIR

of the table. The plywood can be put under a bed when not in use.
—*Ruth Smith*
Buxton, North Carolina

When your hand-held can opener gets balky, use a toothbrush, hot water and dishwashing detergent to clean it. After cleaning, lubricate the opener with vegetable oil and set aside for a while. Wipe off excess oil and it will work like new. —*Ruth Brennan*
Tuscaloosa, Alabama

To color in nicks or scratches in wood-stained furniture, cabinets, trim, etc., rub with a pecan nut. The oil of the nut will "restain" the wood. —*C. Clingingsmith*
St. Bonifacius, Minnesota

When glue thickens in the bottle or you must remove a spot of it, use a little vinegar. It's a good glue thinner or remover. —*Mary Yoder*
Montezuma, Georgia

Which hinge is the culprit? When a door squeaks, remove one pin at a time and coat it with any all-purpose oil, then replace the pin. If the door still squeaks, do the same thing to the next hinge until you find the culprit. This could save you time: Since the top hinge of a door is most likely the squeaker, start with that one. —*Bill Reinhart*
Livonia, Michigan

Save time by keeping your folded, unused trash bags in the bottom of your wastebasket. When you take out a full trash bag, the next one is waiting right there! —*Betty Kolacz*
New Carlisle, Indiana

If your cane chair seats show signs of sagging, just wet down the seat and let it dry. Repeat several times. The drying process will cause the cane to shrink and tighten up again. —*Natalie Southland*
Buena Park, California

Stainless steel lost its luster? Place your flatware in a pan and cover with bubbly carbonated water, soda water, seltzer or club soda. Let set until the fizz has fizzled. Your stainless will shine like new!
—*Pat Peters, Matteson, Illinois*

To install or remove light bulbs in hard-to-reach places such as hallway ceilings, put the upper half of a round, pint-sized rubbing alcohol bottle on the end of a wooden mop handle, with the neck of the bottle on the handle and the bulb upside down in the bottle.

If you are

careful, you can screw or unscrew the bulb this way.

—*John Blatchford*
Port Orange, Florida

Do you have a tough time cleaning wicker items? Just spray your favorite furniture polish onto an inexpensive paintbrush. It makes getting to the hard-to-reach spots easier and takes a lot less time.

—*Sherry Hearn, Trego, Montana*

Use a discarded toothbrush to clean the carvings on furniture. Spray the brush with furniture polish and brush the dust out.

—*Rubie Gantt, Andalusia, Alabama*

To repair a scratch or blemish on varnished furniture, rub with cooking oil and a soft cloth. Also, rubbing alcohol easily removes ink from clothing and crayon marks from woodwork or wallpaper.

—*Claire Utt, Winfield, Kansas*

You don't need to purchase expensive tarnish remover…simply rub ordinary toothpaste with a paper towel on silver, then wash.

—*Sharon Moerman*
Redwater, Alberta

Here's a solution to a sticky situation—if you find the tops are sticking to your tubes of glue, try rubbing a little petroleum jelly around the rim. Works with paint can lids, too. —*Lola Finley*
Fresno, California

I keep a piece of fine sandpaper in a catchall drawer. It's handy to touch up the edge of a dull knife until I can get it sharpened properly.

—*Aurvilla Luko, Newton, Iowa*

To remove candle wax from carpeting, place a brown paper bag over the wax and gently run a warm iron over the bag.

—*Audrey Thibodeau*
Fountain Hills, Arizona

To remove old self-stick shelf paper, use a warm iron.

—*Marion Baker, Sterling, Illinois*

Use a discarded soft toothbrush to clean the filter on a handheld vacuum cleaner to make the filter last longer. —*June Ward*
Peru, Indiana

When you're applying varnish, you'll get a smooth finish if you do

NIP OF NATURE
How can flies walk on the ceiling?

BECAUSE they have little suction cups on their six feet. The cups are hollow inside and slightly moist, and when they're pushed against a flat surface—like a ceiling—most of the air is pushed out. Then the moisture seals the edges and keeps air from getting back in the cup. That helps the suction cup hold on to the ceiling.

it this way: First brush it in line with the wood grain, then brush the same coat across the grain. Finally, brush in the direction of the grain again. This results in three brushings per coat, but the result is worth it!
—Bill Gleason, St. Joseph, Missouri

If your wood furniture has a water stain, rub mayonnaise on it and let it stay there overnight. Wipe off in the morning and the finish should be restored. *—Florence Modica*
Port St. Lucie, Florida

To sharpen scissors, simply cut through a sheet of sandpaper a couple of times. It does wonders!
—Auton Miller
Knoxville, Tennessee

Put old socks on the legs of your furniture to prevent floor scratches when moving furniture.
—Julie Klee, Streator, Illinois

Missing some tools? It won't happen as often if you used the method my dad used with us kids. He had a "sign-out" sheet hanging on a clipboard in the workbench area. We'd sign out a tool when we took it and sign it back in when we returned it. It made us kids more responsible and kept Dad from losing tools! *—Phyllis Donahoe*
Sacramento, California

To keep drains running freely, pour baking soda into the drain and then pour in a little vinegar. Let sit for about a half hour before flushing the drain with hot water.
—Carolyn Pickard, Columbus, Ohio

When putting loose knobs back on dresser drawers, first dip the screws in fingernail polish or shellac before resetting them. This makes them stay tight much longer.
—Della Whitesell
El Dorado Springs, Missouri

Bore a hole in broom handles and slip a string through it so you can hang the broom up. The bristles won't curl and they will last longer that way. *—Abbie Thomas*
Lubbock, Texas

Cold undiluted white vinegar can accomplish a lot of things. It removes coffee, tea and wine stains from linens, it loosens stubborn nuts and bolts, and it removes old glue and price stickers. Try it, you'll see.
—Rosie Atkinson
Port Orchard,
Washington

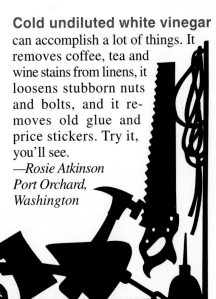

CHAPTER 2
OUTDOOR FIX-UP, TRIM-UP IDEAS

For your picnic tablecloth, hem a piece of inexpensive material. Then make pockets in each corner into which you can slip small stones. This will keep the tablecloth from blowing around.

—*Mrs. Roy Lairmore*
Beatrice, Nebraska

Place some nonslip strips, normally used in bathtubs, on painted porch steps to give your family and visitors nonslip safety in wet weather.

—*Mrs. Pat Rodeffer*
Ferris, Illinois

Those of us who have the metal-type, storm-screen windows all know the struggle of getting them up each year. To end all the pushing, tugging and broken fingernails, spray Pam (vegetable spray product for baking) along the metal frames. They'll simply glide up!

This may be repeated in the fall if they're stuck again, but mine haven't needed another treatment for two seasons now. Stuck or hard-to-open-and-close drawers respond to this treatment, too!

—*Marilyn Lanpher*
Trenton, Missouri

I painted and decorated two 5-gallon cans and placed them in the yard for the kids to dispose of soda cans and wrappers from candy and other junk food. It sure keeps the yard tidy.

—*Maureen Boe*
Polk County, Wisconsin

Stock water tanks will stay clean of scum and insects if you place several goldfish in the tank.

—*Mrs. Harvey Muller*
Danboro, Pennsylvania

Prepare your snow shovel for winter with a coat of floor wax. The wax helps prevent the scoop from rusting and also makes the snow slide off without sticking.

—*Mrs. Ronald Williams*
Stockton, Kansas

Try using some fertilizer to melt the ice and frozen snow from walks and porches. Salt kills the grass onto which the snow is shoveled, but the fertilizer will feed it.
—*Mrs. William Cosman
Garden Prairie, Illinois*

If your evergreen shrubs, cedars, etc. get bent out of shape from being weighted down with snow and ice, try this: In fall, tie fishing line around the bottom of the bush, spiral it around and around to the top, then tie it. The line isn't noticeable unless you are up close, but it'll keep your shrubs standing tall. In spring, snip and remove!
—*Inga Kolke, Waterloo, Ontario*

To add traction to an icy wooden deck, sprinkle on some cornmeal. It can later be easily swept away, and it won't damage the wood, plants or lawn.   —*Ethel Williams
Lawrenceville, Pennsylvania*

Paint the lower step of your basement stairs with white enamel. It can be easily seen and may prevent a bad fall.   —*Rosalee Zipp
Grand Junction, Colorado*

To protect my outdoor padlocks from rain, snow or frost, I put a piece of rubber inner tube over them. It works especially well in the winter.   —*Paul Wollenburg
Portland, Oregon*

Do your snow shovels and garden tools eventually come apart where the wooden handle and the metal implement "head" meet?

Here's a suggestion: Next time you change your crankcase oil, save a little and "paint" the juncture of wood and metal.

Apply liberally and periodically and tools will last forever! (Unused motor oil also works.)
—*Douglas Southworth
Waterford, Connecticut*

To make fast work of filling bird feeders in chilly weather, I pour birdseed into an empty 3-pound coffee can. Then I cap the can with the plastic lid, from which I've cut a small triangle-shaped notch for a no-mess spout.   —*Diane Johnson
Hutchinson, Minnesota*

A metal clothes hanger makes a nice hook for hanging suet bags or birdseed balls from trees in winter. Just cut off the hook, straighten the hanger and bend each end for hanging. These also work nicely for hanging flowering baskets from trees in summer. —*Kathy Primeau
Curtiss, Wisconsin*

My dad has a neat workshop. He uses baby food jars to hold nails, nuts and bolts. First, he nails the lids of the jars underneath the tool cabinets. Then he screws the filled jars into the lids. This way, he can easily see what's in all the jars.
—*Nelson Hearn
Vicksburg, Mississippi*

I recently bought some foam weather stripping tape. After putting it on, the door wouldn't close because the weather stripping was too thick.

I replaced the new weather stripping with felt that I cut out myself. I added as many layers of the felt as needed to keep the air from coming in.

It worked so well I used felt under other doors and windows, just sticking it on with glue. It really works…and the house is a lot warmer! —*Caroline Pfeiffer Boring, Oregon*

To clear soot from your chimney, save potato peelings until you have a good amount of them. Dry them, then burn them in your fireplace or stove. They burn with such a fury that they carry the soot right up and out of your chimney.

—*Ellen Wilson St. Paul, Minnesota*

Outdoor Christmas lights won't be gone with the wind…if you attach them to your trees with pincher-type clothespins! They're easy to both put on and take off, plus they don't harm the trees. Just paint the pins green, and they'll "hide" in the branches. —*J. Baley Lena, Illinois*

Sprinkle baking soda on your car's upholstery and carpeting before vacuuming to remove smoke and other odors. —*Sally Tilson Davison, Michigan*

Bringing home groceries in the pickup doesn't have to be a "rush job". Take along a cooler and a filled hot water bottle to store fresh fruits and vegetables so they won't freeze on the return trip.

—*T. Tripp, Granger, Wyoming*

If you hate grease under your fingernails from working on engines, scrape your fingernails on a bar of soap before beginning the greasy work. —*John Blatchford Port Orange, Florida*

Tired of "ice skating" back and forth to the barn in winter? Try on a pair of "ice grippers". They're simply serrated metal on a

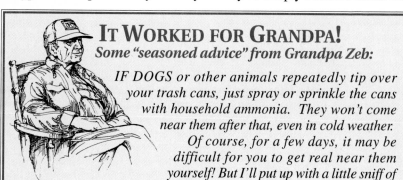

IT WORKED FOR GRANDPA!
Some "seasoned advice" from Grandpa Zeb:

IF DOGS or other animals repeatedly tip over your trash cans, just spray or sprinkle the cans with household ammonia. They won't come near them after that, even in cold weather. Of course, for a few days, it may be difficult for you to get real near them yourself! But I'll put up with a little sniff of ammonia rather than clean up garbage.

wide rubber band that slips right over shoes or boots. I bought a pair last winter, and they *work*!
—*Mary Sader, Winchester, Indiana*

If your car door locks are frozen, heat your key with a match or lighter. Insert the warm key in the lock and leave in place for 20 to 30 seconds. Be sure to wear gloves.
—*Phyllis Berenson*
Cincinnati, Ohio

If you get pitch on your hands while chopping or stacking wood, rub your hands with petroleum jelly. The pitch just disappears!
—*Lois Bethea*
Quilcene, Washington

Here's an Rx for rust in the garage or toolshed. Apply iodine to nuts or bolts, wait a few minutes, then apply more if necessary. Wait 15 minutes longer before loosening. (For easy application, keep an extra medicine dropper with the iodine.) —*Vera Laubscher*
Lock Haven, Pennsylvania

Keep your farmer field-safe in summer by checking over his on-the-job "wardrobe". Remove anything that can catch in machinery—such as the string on hooded sweatshirts and hammer loops on bib overalls.

Also, check with your county Extension service for a handy booklet about laundering clothes that have been exposed to farm chemicals.
—*Julie Holmes, Cambridge, Idaho*

If the thought of raking a yardful of leaves in fall leaves you weak in the knees, try mowing them instead! A finely shredded leaf mulch will protect your grass all winter and still disintegrate by spring.
—*Lyla Moore, Nashville, Tennessee*

To feed calves and colts easier, I built a shelf just the right height for the buckets to be lined up for them to drink from. I can feed several animals at a time with this method. —*Ruby Neese*
Liberty, North
Carolina

It's easy to read a rain gauge if you put a few drops of food coloring in the tube. Even if the colored water dries up, there is enough residue to help read the next rainfall. —*Frances Rueter*
Winchester, Illinois

Put a bit of petroleum jelly on the base of a light bulb before turning it into an outside light fixture. This will make it easier to remove when it burns out. —*Al Glidden*
Portland, Oregon

Can't cope with lost soap at your outdoor faucet? Try this. Tuck a bar of soap in the toe of a nylon stocking and tie to your water faucet. Soap will suds right

through the hose!
—*Marjorie Little*
Sarasota, Florida

Store your folding lawn chairs
in a large plastic trash or leaf bag. They won't need scrubbing in spring.
—*Peg McQueen*
Endicott, New York

This cleanup trick works
while you sleep! Lay a barbecue grill rack on the lawn overnight—the dew will combine with enzymes in the grass to loosen any burned-on grease. Try it with messy oven racks, too!
—*Nancy Merica*
Ripley, West Virginia

In a bind trying to loosen tight hay bales?
If you don't have a knife handy, just rub the string vigorously over the bottom edge of a scraper, shovel or other "bladed" barn tool that's within easy reach.
—*Betty Blasel, Medford, Wisconsin*

If your area gets snow and ice
in the winter, carry a few rough, sandy roofing shingles in the trunk of your car. If your car gets stuck, place the shingles beneath the tires to help you get going.
—*Avis Reese, Hallock, Minnesota*

Simplify snow shoveling
by pouring a little cooking oil on your shovel before you start—snow will slide right off while you work!
—*Amara Hammer*
Pittsburgh, Pennsylvania

To free up frozen car
or truck locks, blow warm breath directly onto the lock through a drinking straw.
—*Joanna Maness*
Reagan, Tennessee

When an umbrella
is worn out, don't throw it away before you remove the ribs. When used as stakes, they make wonderful supports for flowers. They're strong, yet can hardly be seen.
—*Shirley Patrick*
North Cape May, New Jersey

Rust stains
from metal outdoor furniture can be removed from concrete by using lemon juice and rubbing with a soft linen cloth.
—*Anne Norstram, Clinton, Iowa*

A great homemade bug killer
can be made in a plastic milk jug by mixing 1 cup sugar, 1 cup vine-

---

During the winter, padlocks freeze
and keys twist off inside of them. Here's a solution:

Dip padlocks in radiator antifreeze. Not only will the rust boil out...the locks won't freeze as readily. This treatment is good for about 6 weeks if you use pure antifreeze.

Be sure to keep the antifreeze away from kids and pets!
—*Dick Moon*
Franklin, Pennsylvania

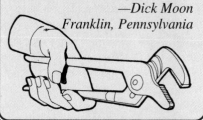

gar and a banana peel. Hang the open jug in a tree or place it in the garden to attract the bugs that are eating your prized fruit and vegetables. This really works! —*Anne Alt Caledonia, Illinois*

To kill cigarette odor in a car, leave a shallow pan of ammonia in the vehicle overnight or all day. Then remove the pan, roll down all the windows and allow the car to air out before driving.

We did this when we bought a used car from a smoker, and it cleared out 90% of the odor. It was a *vast* improvement.

—*Ralph Heider Brainard, Minnesota*

Use the caps from plastic liter soda bottles as coasters on the legs of your porch furniture. The caps fit nicely and can be replaced anytime you finish another bottle of pop. The caps help protect both the furniture and the porch.

—*Paula Barnhart Olive Hill, Tennessee*

To keep mice out of your garage or attic, place mothballs around the perimeter. This works well for us. It also seems to discourage spiders.

—*Jan Stepper, Dayton, Ohio*

Don't throw away old baskets. Bushel baskets make great space-saving containers to grow potatoes. Simply cut out the bottoms of the baskets and set over the potatoes. Place sand and compost on top of the plants every few weeks until the baskets are full. You'll be amazed at the growth of your potatoes with this method. —*Bill Vanscoy Nemaha, Iowa*

During winter months, when you check your young fruit and ornamental trees for damage from mice, stomp the snow around the trunks after each snowfall. This will discourage the mice from tunneling around the roots. —*Al Odendahl Lansing, Michigan*

To keep slugs away from your buildings or garden, fill shallow pans with beer and place them with the rims flush with the ground. When the slugs climb in for a sip, they'll drown. I read this somewhere, tried it and it works well.

—*Nels Stangard, Salena, Kansas*

Curb flying insects by encouraging swallows to live in your area. They eat a tremendous number of insects every day. So if you have a lake, pond or stream on your property, consider erecting swallow houses. They're some of the best "insecticide" you can use on your place! —*Roy Engle Columbia, Missouri*

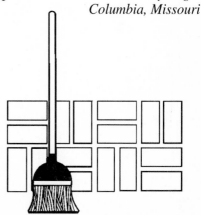

27

CHAPTER 3
HOUSECLEANING TRICKS & TIPS

For dusting under furniture and hard-to-get-at places, I slip an old sock onto a flyswatter and sew it securely into place. It's very handy.
—*Deanna Thomas*
Hollister, Missouri

Yellow stains can be removed from your sink or bathtub with a thin paste made of three parts cream of tartar and one part hydrogen peroxide. Spread this over the discolored areas, wait for it to dry, then just wipe with a wet cloth.
—*Leona Weber*
Markesan, Wisconsin

When I defrost my refrigerator, I save time by placing several layers of newspaper on each shelf. These sop up the water and eliminate a lot of time-consuming sponging later.
—*Ellen Wilcox*
Jones County, Mississippi

Here's a trick I learned by "accident". My son tipped a glass bottle of cooking oil off a grocery store shelf. The clerk quickly opened a 5-pound bag of salt and poured it over the oil. In a matter of minutes, he was able to sweep away the salt and oil with no stain. Works well for eggs, too.
—*Mrs. Lee Hoyer*
Lewiston, Montana

Don't throw away lemon halves after squeezing out the juice. Dip them in salt and rub on the bottom of a copper-bottom pan for a few minutes. The pan will shine like new. If you then scour the bottom of the pot lightly with a soap-filled pad, this will help prevent further accumulation.
—*Mrs. Orlin Petersen*
Utica, South Dakota

Instead of trying to press velvet, hang it in the bathroom with the hot shower running and the door closed for about half an hour. All of the wrinkles will be steamed out.
—*Mrs. David Guhde*
Auburn, Nebraska

Wipe even stubborn finger-prints off of light switch plates by using a slightly dampened soapy washcloth. Hand soap works best!
—*Linda Letterfield*
Marlette, Michigan

Next time a plastic bread wrapper melts onto the toaster or coffeepot, try this. Rub some petroleum jelly on the spot, reheat the appliance and use a paper towel to rub off the plastic and the printing.
—*Mrs. Gary Christopher*
Shipman, Illinois

To clean grease from the filter above the stove: Put the filter in an automatic dishwasher with an extra amount of detergent and run the full cycle. It comes out looking like new. If it hasn't been cleaned in a long time, you may have to run the cycle again.
—*Ruth Jackson*
Dresden, Tennessee

Fingertips from old cotton gloves slipped over each side of clothespins will prevent snagging when hanging hosiery on the line.
—*Mrs. Howard Fish*
Fedora, South Dakota

I clean men's felt hats with a mixture of half salt and half cornmeal, mixing up a cup of each at a time. Put in a jar and shake until mixed.

First, brush the hat. Then rub the cornmeal mixture into the hat thoroughly with your hand. Soiled spots may need a second application. Brush the hat again. If nap looks pressed down, steam it over the spout of the teakettle and brush. The hat will look like new.
—*Mrs. John Lewis*
Thayer, Kansas

Add a little witch hazel to the water in your steam iron. Your clothes will smell sweet and fresh.
—*Mrs. Harlin Jacoles*
Foley, Minnesota

When silk flower arrangements look old and dusty, dip them gently and quickly in warm water with detergent in it. Then place them on a towel to dry. They come out looking new!
—*Menno Erb*
Sugarcreek, Ohio

Clip a clothespin to the ironing board cover when ironing shirts and long-sleeved blouses. You can clip the sleeves together so they won't drag on the floor.
—*Mrs. Adolph Peischel*
Unityville, Pennsylvania

Patent leather handbags and shoes can be quickly brightened with a polish of milk. Apply with a soft cloth and rub into a shiny new-like finish.
—*Mrs. L.E. Ford*
Portland, Oregon

When you think a pan is scorched beyond saving, try this: Fill it with ordinary mud and let it sit for a day or so. Then scrub it vigorously with the mud. This will often save the pan when nothing else will.

—Mrs. H.D. Fountain
Iowa City, Iowa

For those down-on-the-knee chores, sew 6-inch x 8-inch pockets on the knees of your most comfortable pair of jeans and insert a 5-inch x 7-inch foam sponge into each pocket. Happy kneeling!

—Ruby Wybrant
Parthenon, Arkansas

I was unhappy with the method I used to polish our furniture. I felt I was just polishing the polish, to copy a phrase.

Now I take two used tea bags, add 1 quart water, bring to a boil, cool to room temperature and use that cooled tea water to wash furniture. Then I wipe the furniture dry with a soft cloth wrung out in the tea solution, let it dry and polish with my favorite brand.

This tea water does not harm the furniture, but it does remove all the old polish and any dirt and grime. Try it, and your wood will sparkle again! *—Mrs. James Jones*
Ogle County, Illinois

My laundry marking system is made-to-order for large families. One dot from a permanent felt-tip pen marks the oldest child's clothes; the fifth child has five dots, etc. When it's hand-me-down time, all I do is add another dot. No color codes to change, no name tapes to sew and no shirts with a half-dozen confusing initials inside the collar!

—Mrs. Robert Olson
Taylor, Wisconsin

I make my own cleaning solution for washing windows. It's easy and much less expensive than the commercial solutions. Add 1/2 cup rub-

IT WORKED FOR GRANDPA!
Some "seasoned advice" from Grandpa Zeb:

I HAVE a sure cure for hiccups. To help someone stop hiccuping, just say, "I'll give you every bit of change in my pocket if you can hiccup three more times."

It interrupts the body rhythm that causes hiccups, and for some reason, when they want to hiccup, they can't.

Give it a try, you'll see. Just offer someone a quarter or a dime, but always say it's for the next three hiccups. Because if you say "for the next one", the person may quickly hiccup before they've had time to think about wanting to.

bing alcohol to 1 quart water and use it either in a pail, or pour it into an empty spray bottle.

—*Mrs. Clifford Johnson*
Steele County, Minnesota

I use a small brush-type hair roller to clean radiators. Stick a pencil into the brush, making a handle, and it's a wonderful brush for hard-to-clean places. —*Mildred Sherrer Bay City, Texas*

If you have a problem with black heel marks on hardwood floors, apply a little toothpaste to an old toothbrush and give it the old "one-two". Then wipe with a damp cloth. The heel marks will be gone, and your floors will be shiny.

—*Mrs. Dewey Crank*
Lafayette County,
Arkansas

Since some commercial cleaning products are high-priced, I have found an excellent "recipe" for cleaning wood paneling, dark wood cupboards, furniture, etc. Wipe the surface with a soft cloth wrung out in a solution of 1 quart warm water, 1 teaspoon vinegar and 1 teaspoon olive oil. Polish with a soft dry cloth.

—*Mrs. Roy Noreen*
Hawley, Minnesota

For faster ironing, put a sheet of aluminum foil under your ironing board cover. Clothes absorb the heat held by the foil, thus speeding up the ironing task. —*Mrs. Harvey Muller Danboro, Pennsylvania*

Your bathroom mirror won't fog up if you clean it with canned shaving cream. It works on eyeglasses, too. (That means no more sudden "blindness" when you're unloading the dryer or checking the roast.)

—*Mrs. Roy Lairmore*
Beatrice, Nebraska

To clean your oven racks, place them in the bathtub. Fill the tub with hot water until the racks are covered. Pour automatic dishwasher detergent over the racks. Use a cloth to swish the water around, since the water will be too hot for your hands.

After the racks have soaked for a while, the burned-on matter will wipe right off. (If it is very thick, you may have to scrape it off with a knife.) If you continue to use this method, the racks should clean more easily each time.

—*Mrs. Glenn Walter, Wharton, Ohio*

The window on my oven gets hopelessly spattered and yellowed from broiling and baking. I found that baking soda on a damp cloth cleans the window easily and with no scratches.

—*Mrs. Bernard Schwenk*
Hebron, North Dakota

A child's wagon can be a mini-moving van around the house. It's great for moving baskets of wet or dry clothes, heavy boxes and even

small pieces of furniture. As an added plus, your child will love helping with this moving game!
—*Maureen Beaver*
Sparta, Wisconsin

Make a holder for a toilet brush by cutting out one side of a 1-gallon plastic jug. Leave the neck on, but cut it out enough to hold the brush.
—*Mrs. Elbert Austin*
Coffeen, Illinois

A handful of salt added to the last rinse water will keep clothes from freezing to the clothesline.
—*Mrs. John McSloy*
Havre, Montana

To keep lint from clinging to dark garments, add 1/2 cup vinegar to the last rinse. —*Mrs. Carroll Karch*
Birmingham, Alabama

To remove the soap and hard-water film that accumulates on plastic shower curtains (and won't come off with any amount of elbow grease), take the curtain down, place it on a flat surface and wash it with a solution of 1/2 cup ammonia to 1 quart warm water. The film just vanishes.
—*Sandra Weix*
Elmwood, Wisconsin

Clean the "wheel" of your can opener often with a sponge or brush dipped in a solution of hot water and baking soda. —*Mildred Sherrer*
Bay City, Texas

Fill a paint roller with your favorite wall washing solution and use a clean paint roller to wash your walls. Rinse with clear water. It goes much more quickly than sponging!
—*Milton Olson*
Klaten, North Dakota

With eight children at home, the biggest laundry saver I've discovered is this. When I buy socks, I pin them together with a little safety pin. When a child changes socks, he removes the pin from a clean pair and puts it on the soiled pair. From there, they

When I clean a room, I never walk into it without a large paper sack in hand. I put the sack right in the middle of the room when I start cleaning. I'm continually amazed at how many steps I save by carrying the sack from room to room with me. I use it for trash, or to carry things to the rooms where they belong.
—*Mrs. M. Tennyson*
Grafton County,
New Hampshire

go to the washer and dryer and back into the drawers with no sorting or searching for the missing sock.

—*Mrs. Rex Bills*
Fairview, Michigan

When you accidentally get hair spray on a mirror, make the glass spotless again by simply rubbing the mirror with a sponge or cloth soaked with rubbing alcohol.

—*Ann Peardot, Tomah, Wisconsin*

To give hardwood floors a new or antiqued look, add brown shoe polish to the liquid floor wax. This is particularly useful in areas where the floor has worn or faded because of heavy traffic.

—*Mrs. Ronald Longnecker*
West Plains, Missouri

When a shag rug goes limp from too many washings, I just lay it right side down on a flat surface after washing and brush strong liquid starch onto the backing over the entire rug. I let it dry, and the rug is practically like when I bought it.

—*Mrs. Ted Porter*
Okaloosa County, Florida

A soft drink carton makes an excellent carryall for assorted cleaning supplies, such as your furniture polish, window cleaner, spray for the dust mop, upholstery and rug cleaner and a clean cloth or two.

—*Marilyn Srp*
Ladysmith, Wisconsin

When cleaning plastic wastebaskets, try using some rubbing alcohol. I discovered quite by accident that rubbing alcohol cleans with a minimum of rubbing. At the same time, the baskets are being sanitized.

—*Mrs. Lawrence Walther*
Denver, Iowa

Before washing walls or windows, wrap absorbent cotton around your wrist. Hold it in place with a rubber band. The cotton catches the uncomfortable trickles that run down your arm. —*Mrs. W.A. Sears*
Hutchins, Texas

All you need is a plastic pail with a lockable lid to make a portable "washing machine" for road trips. Half-fill the pail with hot soapy water, place the soiled clothing inside and secure the lid. Wedge the pail in a corner of your camper, trailer or car trunk.

Once you have hit the road, your automobile will take care of the agitation. (Heavily soiled clothing might need a few extra rubs to come clean.) When you stop for the day, rinse and dry the clothes.

—*Clair Thelen, Fowler, Michigan*

That glove with the fleece side turned out makes a wonderful dust cloth for venetian blinds.

—*Mrs. Herman Helmke*
Lake Wilson, Minnesota

For easy cleanup after a spill in the oven, pour a small amount of water on the spill while the oven is still

warm. Allow it to stand for 30 minutes and the spot will wipe up easily.
—*Gloria Andrews*
Nenzel, Nebraska

Here's a homemade brass and copper polish for you antique collectors: 2 ounces oxalic acid (available at drugstores), 2 ounces Lux or Ivory flakes, 1 gallon water, 1 quart  ammonia. When stored in a tightly closed glass jar, this solution can be used over and over again before it loses its strength.
—*Mrs. Wendell Kreider*
Palmyra, Missouri

When I'm washing windows at the top of a ladder, it really bugs me when I drop the drying cloth. Finally, to save myself the trips up and down the ladder, I made a hole in the drying cloth and put one of my fingers through the hole. It saved me many a trip down the ladder, and the cloth stayed cleaner by avoiding contact with the floor or ground.
—*Mrs. Glenn Ballinger*
Pike County, Illinois

Make your own window cleaner by mixing equal parts of vinegar, ammonia and water. Put in a spray bottle, squirt on windows and wipe off with newspaper or towels.
—*Mrs. Joe Gerheardt*
Wilber, Nebraska

Dislike breaking in new jeans and overalls? I put the new garments through the regular wash cycle (soap included). Then I put them through another rinse cycle to which I have added an ample amount of fabric softener. When dried, the garments are soft and have fewer wrinkles. Only one treatment is needed.
—*Mrs. Gordon Boy*
Syracuse, Kansas

I save my coffee grounds and use them as a sweeping compound for the concrete floors in the basement and garage. It works great.
—*Mrs. Paul Lang, Remsen, Iowa*

The long-handled brushes meant for sweeping snow from car windows work great for cleaning out lengths of stovepipe in a wood-burning stove.

For those of you who use a wood burner, remember it's important to clean the pipe periodically.
—*Mrs. Richard Thayer*
Auburn, Maine

Striped denim makes a perfect ironing board cover. The stripes serve to line up edges of jackets and pleats of skirts and curtains.
—*Mae Ellen Walton*
Marengo, Illinois

"Coming clean" at harvesttime is easier if you get a head start on dirty field clothes —by hanging them on the clothes-

line and hosing them off. They'll be easier to wash...and you'll be watering your plants and lawn at the same time!   —Freda Lane
Walla Walla, Washington

I like to open basement windows for fresh air, but dislike the dust that blows in the window along with the breeze. So, I sew a piece of cloth over the screen and then reinforce it by hand-sewing a piece of lightweight flannel on the inside. (This way mice can't chew it off.) The air circulates dust-free and strong winds are cut down as well.
—Roxanne Fuhrman
Larslan, Montana

To keep shower doors shiny and clear, use a soft cloth moistened with baby oil. It prevents scum buildup from dirt and soap. And hard water spots won't appear for several months.   —Mildred Sherrer
Bay City, Texas

I spray the grill with oven cleaner and let stand according to the directions on the can. Then I put it in my dishwasher and run it through the full cycle. The grill comes out sparkling clean without any scrubbing. Works great for my oven racks, too.
—Mrs. J. Delmar Ebersole
Mt. Pleasant, Iowa

If you wash windows when the sun is shining on them, the glass will streak.   —Mrs. W.A. Sears
Hutchins, Texas

To save wax and time, use an old wet mop to wax your floors. The

COUNTRY TRIVIA

THE total land area in the 48 contiguous states is 2.3 billion acres, and agriculture accounts for almost two-thirds of it.

wax will go on smooth and even. Wash the mop in warm soapy water, rinse and let dry.   —Marilyn Srp
Ladysmith, Wisconsin

When it's time to clean underneath kitchen appliances, I move them easily by mopping the floor around it with soapy water. The soap makes even a heavy refrigerator slide across the floor and gives you a head start in cleaning your floor, too!   —Helene Levin
San Jose, California

Wadded-up aluminum foil makes a great kitchen scrubber. Use it to clean film and dirt off the chrome on your appliances, sink, etc.
—Maureen Beaver
Sparta, Wisconsin

If you need to remove candle wax from candle holders, freeze them! The wax will pop out easily.
—Elsie Charabin
North Battleford, Saskatchewan

You don't have to buy fancy copper cleaners to keep your copper-bottomed aluminum pans shiny clean. Just combine equal parts of salt and flour and add enough vinegar to make a thick paste. Rub this

To clean my windows inexpensively, I add a small handful of cornstarch to 3 to 4 quarts of water. Wash the windows with this solution and dry with a paper towel. Works great! It cleans and dries them faster than anything else I've used. —*Mrs. William Drury Mineral Point, Wisconsin*

paste into the copper using a soft cloth. Let it sit a few minutes, rinse and look at that shine!
—*Vera Wakeman Union Mills, Rhode Island*

Yellowed lace can be whitened again by soaking it in sour milk.
—*Mrs. John McSloy Havre, Montana*

Your ironing will go easier if you starch your ironing board cover. This also helps keep the cover clean longer. —*Mildred Sherrer Bay City, Texas*

Whenever I run out of kitchen cleanser, I go to our wood-burning stove for a scoop of ashes to sprinkle on the porcelain. Scours my sink nice and clean.
—*Mrs. Clarence Tills Highwood, Montana*

If you have willing little "dusters" around the house but don't want

them using spray cleaner, try this: Put old soft socks on their hands, and then spray the socks with cleaner. They'll enjoy dusting even more—and you'll find this method works so well *you'll* use it even when the kids or grandkids aren't around. —*Dorothy Hallaian St. Helens, Oregon*

To clean and condition suede garments, sponge them with a soft cloth dipped in vinegar.
—*Reta Robertson, London, Ontario*

I use an inexpensive paintbrush sprayed with furniture polish to dust model cars, picture frames and hard-to-get-at nooks and crannies. —*Mrs. H.J. Braddock Syracuse, Kansas*

Defrosting a freezer is not much fun, but here's a way to make the job easier. After you defrost next time, dry the interior and then spray it with vegetable cooking spray. The next defrosting job will go lots faster. —*Thelma Mappes Weedsport, New York*

When washing windows, wipe from top to bottom inside the house and from side to side on the exterior. That way you'll know whether a streak is inside or outside.
—*Linda Rae Faro, Phoenix, Arizona*

When you have merchandise such as glassware that has a price sticker glued on, simply put Crisco or a liquid shortening on it and let it sit for 15 to 30 minutes. Then rub and the sticker will come off without any scratches. If not all the glue or sticker comes off the first time, just repeat the process.

—*Christine Rupert*
Palmyra, Pennsylvania

To preserve the bright shine of brass, clean with Worcestershire sauce. It does an unbelievably good job! —*Lucile Trent*
Waverly, Missouri

Can't figure out how to clean the vents on your small pressure cooker? A pipe cleaner does a great job!
—*Fay Agnew, Lubbock, Texas*

I liked using metal scouring pads, but hated how quickly they rusted out. I solved this by putting baking soda in a small dish on the sink. Now when I'm through with the scouring pad, I put it on the bed of baking soda. The pad doesn't rust, and I can use all of it.

It helps to not dip the pad in water—just wet the utensil being cleaned, and that will activate the soap in the pad enough to do a good job. —*Mrs. L.C. Marshall*
Osage City, Kansas

After washing a cast-iron skillet, wipe around the inside with a wad of waxed paper while it is still warm. This will prevent troublesome rusting. —*Maureen Beaver*
Sparta, Wisconsin

Want to give limp curtains a crisp new look after laundering? Wash and rinse curtains as usual. Then, in a sink or large tub, dissolve 1 cup of Epsom salts in water. Dip curtains in this solution and hang to dry. No ironing's needed. Your curtains will be as crisp as when new.

—*Mrs. John Glithero*
Solana Beach, California

When spring cleaning, don't forget farm vehicles' cab windows. Every spring, we wash our windows thoroughly inside and out, then keep a magnetic broom (with handle removed) in each cab to simply brush off dust as it collects.

—*Elsie Charabin*
North Battleford, Saskatchewan

Baking soda mixed with ground cinnamon or cloves makes a great carpet freshener. —*Donna Hendry*
North Windham, Connecticut

Here's a way to save money on cleaning supplies: Use a wet sponge and baking soda to scrub your kitchen sink, bathroom and even tile floors. You get a nice shine!

—*Anna Huckaba*
Jackson, Tennessee

When your rubber gloves get a hole in them, cut 1/2-inch bands across the cuffs and palms to use for large rubber bands. The thumb and finger portions may be recycled, too—slip them over broom ends and mop handles to avoid scratches and marks on walls and woodwork.

—*Mrs. Harvey Darnall*
Harrisburg, Nebraska

If something spills over in the oven, sprinkle salt on it right away and finish baking. When the oven cools down, the spill will have turned to ash and can be removed easily. —*Gail Pitt* *Jacksonville, Texas*

Ketchup does a great job polishing copper. Just rub a small amount on the bottom of discolored pots or pans, let stand for a few minutes, rub again and rinse. —*S.N. Downs* *Annandale, New Jersey*

To clean mini-blinds or slats of shutters, use a clean paintbrush. It's a lot cheaper than buying expensive blind-cleaning tools! —*Mrs. Karl Streed* *Waukegan, Illinois*

To clean bathroom drains of hair and kitchen drains of grease, pour 1 cup of baking soda into drain, then 1 cup of vinegar. When it starts to foam, flush the drain with hot water. —*Mrs. Edwin Hill* *Santa Barbara, California*

When washing windows, pour a little vinegar into the pail of warm water. The glass will clean brighter and you won't have streaks. —*Annette Oppegard* *St. Paul, Minnesota*

Are there places in your house that you don't dust because they are too far underneath something for you to reach? Here's a way to get to those places, and—if you live where there's snow—also get year-round use out of your snow brushes.

Just go out to your car or garage and get the brush with the stiff bristles and long handle that you use to brush snow off car windows. The handle will let you get to those hard-to-reach places in your house...and the bristles will get into the cracks. —*Brad Wesner* *Windsor, Missouri*

To keep spiders out of your house, take a tomato plant at the end of the season and hang it in your basement. Let it dry there. I found spiders frequently before someone told me to try this, and I now have little or no spider problem. —*Frances Sears* *Ronks, Pennsylvania*

Use those plastic grocery bags with handles as liners for small wastebaskets. —*Betty Champagne* *Morrisonville, New York*

To clean pewter, rub the item with the outer leaves of a head of cabbage. Then buff with a soft cloth. —*Mrs. H.F. Busse* *Fort Wayne, Indiana*

Can't get the inside of your glass fireplace doors clean? Spray them with oven cleaner...wait a minute, then wipe off with paper towels. Works beautifully. —*Dora Otis* *Isle, Minnesota*

One way to keep plastic cups and dishes from getting knocked around in the dishwasher is to use rubber bands to tie down anything light. —*Mrs. Jimmie Short* *Baldwyn, Mississippi*

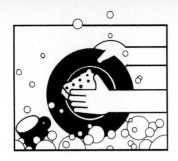

To remove lime deposits from jars, glasses, vases, etc., soak in a solution of vinegar and water. Lime deposits will float away. Soak longer for more stubborn stains.
—*Dora Jean Haynes*
West Plains, Missouri

If your oven racks need cleaning, slide them into a large plastic bag. Close the bag tightly with a rubber band, but leave a hole through which you can spray oven cleaner. After spraying, let stand overnight. If the racks don't come clean, another treatment should do it.
—*Mrs. Ted Eberlein*
Angwin, California

To clean under a dresser with no bottom panel, remove the bottom drawer so you can reach the area with your vacuum cleaner nozzle. Cover the nozzle with an old nylon stocking to vacuum away dust from the top of dresser and inside drawers.
—*Mildred Sherrer*
Bay City, Texas

If you button shirt cuffs to the front of a shirt before putting it in the washer, the sleeves won't knot and tangle in the wash.
—*Katherine Kalmbach*
Selby, South Dakota

Save all the big powder puffs from boxes of bath powder. They're excellent for dusting and polishing. They also make great "knee pads"— tie one to each knee when scrubbing floors.
—*Sallie Bristow*
Mattoon, Illinois

Cut your steel wool pads into four pieces; usually a quarter piece is enough to do the job and the pad will last four times longer.
—*Mrs. Joe Marz, Cascadia, Oregon*

An easy way to remove sticky price tags from new utensils and glasses: Pour fingernail polish remover onto a small cotton swab, then rub over the label. It will come right off.
—*Caroline Cheselka*
Spokane, Washington

Adding rubbing alcohol to any window cleaner will result in a cleaner, brighter shine. Used alone, it is great for cleaning chrome or brass, too.
—*Lorraine Roppe*
Fargo, North Dakota

Badly discolored aluminum pans can be brightened by boiling apple parings in them for a short time.
—*Ruby Shelton*
King, North Carolina

To wash shower curtains, fill washing machine with warm water and add two large bath towels, 1/2 cup detergent and 1/2 cup baking soda. Run through entire wash cycle. On rinse cycle, add 1 cup vinegar.

Do not spin-dry or wash out the vinegar. Hang curtains immediately. Wrinkles will disappear once the

curtains are dry. Note: This won't work without the bath towels!
—*Leona Harris, Joliet, Illinois*

Black scuff marks on a floor are instantly wiped away with a small amount of baby oil or petroleum jelly on a cleaning rag. Afterward, be sure to wipe the floor thoroughly with a spray cleaner, or it will have a slippery spot. —*Helen Menard Rayne, Louisiana*

After thoroughly cleaning your tub or shower walls, apply car wax and buff. Then you'll only have to wipe down the tub or shower instead of scrubbing. (But be careful when using the tub or shower afterward, since it may be slippery.) —*Marcia Mooney Bend, Oregon*

To remove burnt food from the oven, place a small cloth saturated with ammonia in the oven overnight. The next morning, the food will be easy to wipe out.
—*Kay Ware Apache Junction, Arizona*

For better control while pouring bleach and cleaners, punch a small hole in the inner seal rather than removing it. You can then gently squeeze the container for a controlled flow without splashes or waste. —*Helen O'Key Litchfield, Connecticut*

Clean up slivers of shattered glass without cutting yourself by pressing a slice of fresh bread lightly over the area, then immediately disposing of it.—*Carolyn Robinson Lawrence, Mississippi*

Wash the blades of wooden ceiling fans to remove dust and grime. Then cover the blades with a thin coat of floor wax and let dry. After that, dusting is all that's needed to clean them.
—*Mildred Sherrer, Bay City, Texas*

Here's an easy way to get rid of the gummy residue left on bottles and other items when you remove a price sticker or label. Warm a small amount of vegetable oil and rub a little on the spot. It works nicely.
—*Pauline Mucciaccio Brooklyn, New York*

I buried my oven racks, which were badly in need of cleaning, in the snow! When I dug them out the next day, it took very little scrubbing with a scouring pad to completely clean them up.
—*Mrs. Sherwood Dieter Allentown, Pennsylvania*

If you scorch a saucepan, just fill it halfway with water and add 1/4 cup of baking soda. Boil until the burned material loosens and floats to the top. —*Anna Yoder Hemingsburg, Kentucky*

I recycle my used dryer sheets by soaking them in fabric softener. When I need them, I squeeze out the fabric softener and place the sheet in the dryer along with the other wet items. —*Lenna Lambert*
Ikes Fork, West Virginia

Keep your stainless steel flatware looking shiny and new by soaking it in warm soapy water with bleach added. After a half hour or so, remove, rinse thoroughly and dry.
—*Geri Armstrong*
Aston, Pennsylvania

If your waxed floors get dull between waxings, just mop with 1 cup of fabric softener in a half pail of hot water. —*Sally Tilson*
Davison, Michigan

Don't throw away those foam dryer sheets after they come out of the dryer! They're good for brushing off lint, dust and hair from almost anything. —*Karol Mesna*
Nampa, Idaho

Use a dryer softener sheet to wipe your television screen to remove static electricity.
—*John Blatchford*
Port Orange, Florida

To clean your microwave, place a wet paper towel in the oven and microwave for 4 minutes. The oven will easily wipe clean with the towel after a minute or so.
—*Irene Sipes, Franklin, Kansas*

The best window washing mixture I've ever used consists of 1/2 cup rubbing alcohol, 1/2 cup of household ammonia and 7-1/2 cups of warm water. Mix the alcohol and ammonia first, then add the water and transfer to a spray bottle.
—*Beula Warden, Carlotta, California*

Slipcover a yardstick with fabric and use for cleaning hard-to-reach places, particularly underneath appliances. Then just remove the fabric to wash or shake out the dust.
—*Grace Varda*
Weddington, North Carolina

The easiest and best way to shine stainless steel or chrome—like the faucets in your sink—is to use a soft dry cloth sprayed with WD-40 (the lubricant). The metal will shine like a mirror.
—*Julie Frantz, Durham, Kansas*

Tired of your scouring pads rusting? After each use, put the pad in a plastic bag in the freezer. When you're ready to use again, run warm water over the pad until it thaws. Repeat this until the soap is used up and you won't get any rust.
—*June Lawing, Murchinson, Texas*

To easily clean glass fireplace doors, spray the glass and saturate a paper towel with any commercial glass cleaner. Use the paper towel to blot up cold white ashes from the

bottom of your fireplace; don't absorb the scratchier grit below the ashes. Then rub on the doors—the dark char will come off easily. Spray the door again with glass cleaner for a nice shine. The key is the soft white ashes. —*Beatrice LeVan*
Wilmington, Delaware

If you have a small plastic wastebasket in your bathroom, empty it and use it as a bucket when you clean your bathroom so it gets cleaned, too. —*Marge Harrold*
Greensburg, Pennsylvania

To easily clean your microwave oven, place 1 cup of water and 2 tablespoons lemon juice or baking soda in a bowl and place in the microwave. Heat on high until the mixture boils, then let it boil for 5 minutes so that steam accumulates on the walls and door of the oven. Remove the bowl and wipe down the interior.
—*Mary Alice Warren*
Waco, Texas

To remove labels that are stuck on glass jars, briskly rub on mayonnaise, then soak the jar in warm water. The label will peel right off.
—*Bessie Howard*
Yucaipa, California

Dry clothes outdoors even on windy days by stringing a plastic-coated chain link between poles as you would a clothesline (or even on the same poles that you have your clothesline on). Place clothes on hangers and hook each hanger in a link—they'll blow in the breeze but not fall off. —*John Baglama*
Glen Burnie, Maryland

When washing corduroy garments, add 1/2 cup of vinegar to the rinse water. The fabric will be brighter and lint-free.
—*Melinda Neal, Muncie, Indiana*

To help with making beds, I have stitched a thread at the center top of my sheets, blankets and bedspreads. When all the threads line up with the center of the headboard, I know I've "got it made".
—*Inez Upham*
St. Anthony, Minnesota

Protect the kitchen timer and buttons on the blender from messy fingers and spills by covering them with plastic. You can even keep the timer in a plastic bag!
—*Irene Best, Hood River, Oregon*

Candle wax can be removed from table linens by rubbing the spots with a generous amount of vegetable oil. Wipe off excess oil with a paper towel, and then wash as you normally would.
—*Mary Lindeman*
Fulton, Mississippi

If you run out of fabric softener liquid or sheets, substitute hair conditioner. For a full laundry load, try 1/4 to 1/2 cup. —*Mary Gray*
Marlett, Michigan

To remove soap scum from glass shower doors, apply lemon oil furniture polish with a soft cloth. This makes the doors sparkle for several showers.

—*Jean McCullough*
Emporia, Kansas

When we returned home from a recent trip, we found that our refrigerator had stopped and now smelled of spoiled food.

After trying everything we could think of to get rid of the awful smell, a friend suggested that we crumple brown paper grocery bags and pack them into the refrigerator, changing them for fresh ones whenever they began to smell.

We did that, and in no time the odor was gone. It really works!

—*Mrs. Dan Russell*
Miami, Florida

To brighten dull silver, rub it with a piece of potato dipped in baking soda. And to *really* get rid of grease in your disposal, 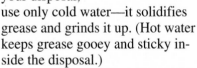 use only cold water—it solidifies grease and grinds it up. (Hot water keeps grease gooey and sticky inside the disposal.)

—*Mrs. Claude Sites*
Manheim, Pennsylvania

Outdoor work and play will often leave a "ring around the bathtub" at cleanup time. There's no need to

COUNTRY TRIVIA

TODAY, each American farmer feeds 128 people in the United States and abroad.

stoop or kneel to scrub, though. Just wet the tub, sprinkle with cleanser… and sweep with a child-size broom. The stiff bristles will have the tub spotless in record time!

—*Mary Egyed, Prewitt, New Mexico*

Clean the drip pans from your electric cooktop by spraying them liberally with oven cleaner and placing in a plastic garbage bag overnight. In the morning, take them out and wipe with a paper towel. Then wipe again with a damp rag.

—*Tena Atford*
New Market, Alabama

Use baking soda to polish the chrome fixtures in your bathroom. Put a small amount on a wet cloth, rub the fixtures and dry with a soft cloth. They'll look like new.

—*Mrs. Melvin Sisler*
Mountain Lake Park, Maryland

When you wash curtains, also wash the rods, then wax them. That will make the curtains slide more easily. —*Jean Tuten*
Easley, South Carolina

To clean wood wall paneling or wood mouldings, furniture and doors, try this homemade solution

my mother passed on to me: Add 1 cup boiled linseed oil, 1 cup turpentine and 1 cup vinegar to 1 quart of water. Mix in a pail, use a rag to rub into the wood and watch it work! —*Carolyn Keen*
Imlay City, Michigan

Don't discard empty feed and seed bags—they make fine winter "floor mats" in your mudroom for catching whatever sticks to the bottom of boots. And keep your pickup prepared, too, by stashing some there for bundling stray baby calves. —*Linda Melton*
Stockton, Kansas

To absorb carpet odors, sprinkle the area with baking soda, then wait about 15 minutes before you vacuum. If you're dealing with really tough odors, let the baking soda remain overnight before vacuuming.

It's a good idea to first test a small hidden area of the carpet for color fastness before you apply the baking soda to your entire carpet. And the carpet should be dry before you start. —*Alice Hentges*
Denver, Colorado

Salt can be used to accomplish a number of things:

Salt thrown on a fire will extinguish it quickly.

Salt will quickly clean a discolored bathtub or enameled utensils.

A lump of salt placed in the sink will clear the drain.

Salt mixed in water will prevent colored borders in towels and other fabric from running if the towels are soaked in the solution for 24 hours. —*Jean Steingold*
Chesapeake, Virginia

To remove soot and smoke stains from a marble fireplace, make a paste of baking soda and water. Apply it with your hands or a rag. The stains come right off with no rubbing. —*Marjorie McKinsey*
Miami, Florida

NIP OF NATURE
Why do ranchers build zigzag fences?

IF YOU'VE ever driven through Western ranch country, you likely noticed a lot of zigzag fences. Ranchers build them that way for two reasons:

1. A zigzag fence is sturdier than a straight one since each angled section adds to its support.

2. The land in some of these areas is sometimes so rocky that it isn't easy or practical to dig holes for posts in a straight line, and most zigzag fences use no posts at all.

When ants are a problem, sprinkle powdered chili pepper, paprika, dried peppermint, damp coffee grounds or borax where the ants are coming in. Lemon juice works well, too. —*Mrs. Ted Measher*
Champaign, Illinois

For a carpet cleaner that I still use today, combine 1 tablespoon vinegar with 1 tablespoon cornstarch. Work it into the spot with a soft cloth and leave it for 2 days, then vacuum. You'll find this works like magic! —*Jeanette Hang*
New Berlin, Wisconsin

Seems I once spent half my laundry time picking chaff out of my husband's bib overall pockets. Then I lessened my load by stitching closed the biggest "collector"— that hard-to-empty "ruler" pocket he never used anyway!
—*Elizabeth Terrell*
Concord, New Hampshire

Here's a fast way to press napkins without ironing. As soon as your washer stops, take out the napkins and shake them hard. Place  them on a flat surface, pulling from one side to the other with your flat palm. Do this until they are perfectly flat and you see no wrinkles.

Leave overnight or until dry. You can even do six napkins, one on top of the other. When they dry, you simply fold and put away. Even without ironing, they'll look crisp.
—*Beverly Linder*
Tacoma, Washington

To rid a room of tobacco odor, put a pint of hot water in a bowl and add 3 tablespoons of ammonia. Leave the bowl in the closed room overnight. Then air out the room in the morning. —*Tom Steeples*
Millersburg, Ohio

When I'm finished ironing a blouse or shirt for someone with arthritis, I button all but one button. That way, the person can pull the piece of clothing over their head like a jersey, avoiding the difficulty of buttoning up. —*Judith Stecker*
Tacoma, Washington

Before shampooing your carpet, put plastic sandwich bags over the legs of pieces of furniture that are too big or heavy for you to move. This does two things: It keeps the legs from getting wet and it keeps them from marking the carpeting. —*Anne Cooper*
Watertown, Wisconsin

When leaving on a trip, place houseplants in the bathtub with about 2 inches of water. That way there's no need to ask someone to water them while you're gone.
—*Helen Svaren*
Arlington, South Dakota

To remove gum from leather, just put a dab of peanut butter on the gum. In a bit, the gum will peel right off. —*Marjorie McKinsey*
Miami, Florida

CHAPTER 4

FOOD & KITCHEN MONEY-SAVERS

Don't throw away that old flannel-backed tablecloth. I spread it down on my kitchen carpet when canning or making jelly, etc. Sure saves the carpet and makes for easy cleanup. —*Mrs. Eddie Fuller Flagler, Colorado*

Take your slow cooker along with you on your next trip in a camper. At bedtime, fill it with meat and vegetables and let it cook during the night. Next morning, cover the cooker with a heavy towel and at noon, lunch will be ready to eat.

This relieves the cook of some duties so she'll be free for more fun and sight-seeing. —*Ruby St. Clair McLeansboro, Illinois*

To cut a pie into five equal pieces, slice a "Y" into the pie and then divide the two large pieces in half. —*Mildred Sherrer, Bay City, Texas*

Save those oatmeal cartons. They make wonderful containers for giving your special home-canned fruit, pickles or preserves. Wrap them prettily and tie with a ribbon for an attractive and thoughtful gift. —*Adeline Roseberg, Isle, Minnesota*

Like most of you these days, I'm clipping a lot of coupons to save on grocery bills. To make sure that I can always put my finger on the coupons I need, I put them into an alphabetically arranged file box as soon as I clip them.

So, now, when I put coffee on my grocery list, for example, I just look under "C" in my coupon box and immediately pull out the coupon I need. —*Mrs. Harold Iburg Williamsburg, Iowa*

When planning the noon meal for neighbors who help with the haying, I refer to cards in the back of my recipe box that I keep for each of the neighbor men who eats an occasional meal with us. I note what foods he likes and dislikes, whether

he prefers tea, coffee or milk to drink, etc. This way I can always present the help with a pleasing meal. —*Mrs. Olin Kennedy*
Forest City, Illinois

Remove both ends of a tuna can and its label, and you have a perfect mold for poached eggs.
—*Mrs. Randy Nelson*
St. James, Minnesota

Since I don't use corn syrup very often, I had problems with it getting moldy before I could use up a bottle. Then I discovered that the mold will not form on the syrup if I store the bottle upside down in the cupboard. —*Mrs. John Beck*
McComb, Ohio

A pound of rhubarb equals 3 to 4 cups sliced or 2 cups cooked and pureed. —*Priscilla Weaver*
Hagerstown, Maryland

When sending candy, line a cardboard box or stationery box with foil. Butter the foil like you would a pan and then pour the candy into the box. Let it cool and fold the foil over the top. Put the lid on and mail the candy this way instead of cutting before you pack it. —*Dorothy Kirby*
Linnens, Missouri

"Frost" green grapes by dipping a small bunch of them into a slightly beaten egg white and then coating with granulated sugar. Dry on waxed paper. These make a pretty garnish for a special occasion.
—*Mrs. Rudolph Busacker*
Long Prairie, Minnesota

A potato helps bind soup seasonings together.
—*Ruth Earnshaw*
Winchester, Virginia

Add optional ingredients to any basic shortbread cookie recipes for fun and variety. A recipe calling for 1 cup flour might include one of the following: 1/2 cup chopped pecans, 1 teaspoon of instant coffee, 2 tablespoons baking cocoa or 1 to 2 teaspoons grated orange or lemon peel.

A fun way to decorate shortbread cookies is to dip one end into melted chocolate. —*Dianne Conway*
London, Ontario

A 1-pound loaf of bread will make up about 8 cups of loosely packed crumbs for stuffing. Allow 1 cup of stuffing for each pound of turkey. —*Edna Hoffman*
Hebron, Indiana

When going camping, put each
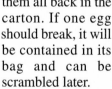
egg in a small plastic bag and then put them all back in the carton. If one egg should break, it will be contained in its bag and can be scrambled later.
—*Mrs. Pat Rodeffer*
Ferris, Illinois

A chopped turnip adds a delicious slightly sweet taste to a beef stew. —*Sharon Evans*
Rockwell, Iowa

Beef may be frozen in the grocery store packaging for up to 2 weeks. For longer storage, you should repackage it in heavy-duty foil, plastic freezer bags or freezer paper to prevent freezer burn. (Attach the package label or write the cut of meat and date on the package for easy identification.) —*Nancy Olsen Minneapolis, Minnesota*

A large round-bone pot roast can provide three different meals: Cut a piece from the round end and cube for stew, cut a slice from the flat end for Swiss steak, then use the rest for pot roast. —*Edna Hoffman Hebron, Indiana*

Roast beef and baked ham are two easy Sunday meals to prepare. Just add water and seasonings and pop in the oven to cook while you're at church. —*Esther Gilbertson Ketchum, Idaho*

For special Sunday potato dishes, I cook spuds with skins on the day before. Then I can make a quick potato salad on Sunday…or slip the skins off, put potatoes through a sieve, place in a skillet, add a little bit of water and heat through. Sometimes I peel and cube potatoes, heat through and top with cheese sauce. —*Irene Slabaugh, Lott, Texas*

A quart berry basket makes a good egg keeper—it holds about a dozen eggs and takes up little refrigerator space. —*Ethel Williams Lawrenceville, Pennsylvania*

Cook fresh rhubarb for sauce with whatever water adheres to the stalks after washing—don't add any more. Add sugar to taste. —*Anita Jean Maybury Darby, Montana*

Don't forget this fruitful formula —2 to 3 medium apples make about 1 pound. —*Florence Lorence Racine, Wisconsin*

Add diced rhubarb to apples when making applesauce to give it a tangy flavor. —*Paula Pelis Rocky Point, New York*

IT WORKED FOR GRANDPA!
Some "seasoned advice" from Grandpa Zeb:

WONDERING whether an egg is too old to use? Jut put it in a pan of cold water. If it lies on its side, the egg is fresh. If it tilts, it's at least 3 or 4 days old. If it stands upright, it probably is at least 10 days old. If it floats, don't use it...unless you don't mind eating rotten eggs!

I wear light cotton gloves while removing the skin from a chicken. The gloves don't slip on the skin, and I can easily launder and use them again. —*Irvin Felix*
North Riverside, Illinois

A pound of thinly sliced smoked sausage ring can substitute for bulk sausage in most soup recipes.
—*Billye Green*
Las Cruces, New Mexico

For a nice change of pace, turkey ham can be substituted for ham in all recipes. Have your butcher shave it for sandwiches; use it for a hearty ham and bean casserole.
—*Pat Stewart, Granger, Indiana*

For moist and colorful poultry stuffing, add 1 diced unpeeled apple to your favorite stuffing recipe.
—*Lisa Nyquist, Cokato, Minnesota*

After carving jack-o'-lanterns, add cutout pumpkin pieces to beef and vegetable stew for a fun fall flavor. —*Elsie Kolberg*
St. Joseph, Michigan

Need a fast appetizer? Combine ketchup and brown sugar to taste; add cocktail sausages or slices of hot dogs. Heat and serve in a slow cooker or fondue pot.

Spread cream cheese on a large plate. Top with cocktail sauce; sprinkle with drained canned or frozen shrimp. Serve with crackers.

Spread cream cheese combined with dill weed on party rye slices. Top each with a cucumber slice and sprinkle lightly with dill weed.

Make a pretty pizza dip by spreading cream cheese on a plate and topping with pizza sauce. Then add any or all of the following: chopped onions, peppers, tomatoes, olives, shrimp. Top with mozzarella cheese. Serve with crackers.
—*Jo Groth, Plainfield, Iowa*

Make "mini" caramel apples by dipping quartered apples on toothpicks into melted caramel.
—*Walter Van Damme*
Atkinson, Illinois

Before you store winter squash, wash it and dry well. Then keep in a single layer in a cool dry place.
—*Judy Sawyer, Attica, New York*

Ham bones hard to find? Substitute a package of maple-flavored bacon (fried and diced) and a cup of smoked ham in soup recipes.
—*Rosemary Birette*
Les Cedres, Quebec

Cut up and freeze fresh parsley and young green onion stems to enjoy next winter in soups and stews.
—*Donna Corbett, Exeter, Ontario*

Add a box of strawberry-flavored gelatin to rhubarb you're using in a recipe, then mix until it's coated and

blended in. It adds flavor, sweetens and gives the rhubarb a pretty red color. *—Joanna Matt Galloway, Ohio*

For long-term storage, wrap individual unbruised apples in tissue paper and keep them in a cold place. *—Terry Hager Oldtown, Maryland*

I freeze tomatoes for soup rather than canning them. *—Vivian Watts Russellville, Missouri*

For extra-rich tasting homemade cranberry sauce, add vanilla extract (a teaspoon or more) after cooking. *—Ruth Fenner Albuquerque, New Mexico*

Don't throw away worn tablecloths. Instead, make a variety of dish towels and napkins from them. *—Helen LaMance Modesto, California*

Add 1 cup of whole cranberries to your favorite double-crust apple pie for a rosy-red color and delightful sweet-tart taste. *—Linda Bell, Billings, Montana*

Fill a plastic milk jug with water and freeze, then place in a cooler in your vehicle while you shop to keep meat, ice cream and perishables cool during the trip home. *—Doris Hogg Rocky Mount, Missouri*

Fresh cranberries are easier to grind in a food processor or a food grinder if you freeze them first. Allow ground berries to drain well before using. *—Carol Schultze Fairmont, Minnesota*

For a delicious hamburger variation, mix equal parts ground turkey and ground beef. *—Sharon Smith Caledonia, Michigan*

Add a sweet surprise to holiday silverware. Roll up place settings in cloth or paper napkins, tuck

Apples add appeal to leftover oatmeal! Combine 4 cups water, 1 teaspoon salt and 2 tablespoons of butter in a large saucepan; bring to a full boil. Stir in 2 cups old-fashioned oats, 1 cup of chopped peeled apple, 1/2 cup raisins, 1/2 teaspoon cinnamon and 1/4 teaspoon nutmeg. Cook 5 minutes at medium heat, stirring occasionally. Cover; remove from heat. Let stand 2-3 minutes before serving. *—Martha Doyle Kalispell, Montana*

a candy cane alongside and tie together with bright-colored ribbons. Place silverware "packages" in a wicker basket on your serving table.
—*Caryn Wiggins*
Columbus, Indiana

For a delicious do-ahead dessert, layer yellow or pound cake, fresh or frozen berries, vanilla pudding and whipped cream in a large bowl and chill overnight. The next day, serve it fresh from the refrigerator! —*Jennifer Lowd*
La Tuque, Quebec

Make fruit kabobs by alternating cut-up apples with marshmallows and bananas on skewers. They are a fun snack for kids. —*Kathy Atwell*
Lebanon, Missouri

Your kitchen scale accurate? Here's a way to tell: Place nine pennies on the scale. They should weigh exactly 1 ounce.
—*Karen Ann Bland, Gove, Kansas*

To make stuffing easy, cook the giblets until done, cool and chop with celery and onion in a food processor. —*Susan Buch*
Baldwin, Illinois

Stretch maple syrup by adding 1 cup applesauce to 1 cup syrup. Heated, it makes a delicious topping for pancakes and waffles.
—*Edna Hoffman*
Hebron, Indiana

For a sugarless apple pie, thaw a 6-ounce can of frozen unsweetened apple juice concentrate. Combine it with 2 tablespoons flour and 1 teaspoon cinnamon in a container with a tight lid. Shake well. Pour into a saucepan; cook over medium heat until mixture boils and thickens. Remove from heat. Add 6 cups sliced peeled apples; stir to coat. Spoon into pie shell. Bake as usual.
—*Darlis Anderson, Badger, Iowa*

Place unripened tomatoes with other fruit, especially pears, to speed up ripening. —*Anne Schofield*
Kezar Falls, Maine

For a field lunch that's just right on a hot day, prepare a pasta salad and toss with thin strips of sauteed beef.
—*Corlene Bartels*
Gonvick, Minnesota

To make apple-mint tea, combine 4 cups apple juice with 1-1/2 cups of chopped fresh spearmint. Microwave or cook on stovetop until mixture boils. Let steep 30 minutes; strain. —*Lorraine Thompson*
Rosalind, Alberta

As an economical substitute for chopped nuts in cookie recipes, use quick-cooking oats browned in a bit of butter or margarine.
—*Mary Jane Swanner*
Decatur, Alabama

The best way to roast a turkey is in a shallow pan with a "tent" of heavy aluminum foil over it. Roast at 325° for about 15 to 20 minutes per pound. After roasting, let the turkey stand for 15-20 minutes before carving. —*Margaret Dahlgren Bird Island, Minnesota*

Get every bit of cream soup out of the can with this easy trick: Make a slight puncture in the bottom of the can, then remove the top as usual. Run a knife around the inside of the can; turn upside down. The entire contents will come out at once. —*Ada Thomas, Mt. Morris, Illinois*

Freeze rhubarb whole by rolling a half dozen or so stalks together in freezer paper or brown paper and securing with a rubber band. To thaw, dip in hot water—and peels will slip right off the stalks. —*Rose Jares Grand Island, Nebraska*

I keep three 2-pound coffee cans in the freezer—one for leftover vegetables and the water they were cooked in…one for leftover rice or pasta… and one for leftover meat, chicken and gravy or juices. When cans are full, I defrost contents and combine in a pot (if there isn't enough gravy or juice, I add stock to make mixture "soupier"). It makes a different and delicious soup! —*Dorothy Reed Fairfax, California*

Running several soda crackers through your meat grinder is all that it takes to remove any moisture and leftover scraps. —*Barrie Hiatt Hanna, Wyoming*

Right after the cranberries have "popped", I like to add fresh or frozen raspberries (without syrup). This homemade cranberry sauce is a delicious side dish for serving with turkey or chicken. —*Doris LaVerne Newport, Rhode Island*

If you're family's like mine and doesn't care for chunks of tomato in homemade soup, simply put the tomato through the blender first. —*Amelia Sinyard Texarkana, Arkansas*

Avoid last-minute rush when entertaining by setting your table(s) with plates, silverware, glasses and napkins well in advance, then covering with a clean tablecloth until party time. —*Caryn Wiggins Columbus, Indiana*

I add yogurt to soups I season with curry to reduce the "heat". —*Lois Heslop, Irricana, Alberta*

To serve fresh-from-the-oven dinner rolls on Sunday, try setting them to rise before leaving for church. When you come home, they will be ready to bake. —*Betty Cannell Reading, Pennsylvania*

For delicious acorn squash in a jiffy, use your microwave. Choose a small to medium squash and pierce in several places with a sharp knife to allow steam to escape. Place on paper towels and cook on high for about 5 minutes. Cut partially cooked squash in half (be careful—it's *hot*!) and remove seeds.

Place halves, cut side down, in a baking dish and microwave until they're tender (about 5 minutes).

—*Kimberly Schuffert*
Westville, Indiana

I rinse salty sauerkraut thoroughly in a colander before cooking so we can enjoy it even on our low-sodium diets. —*Dorothy Simonton*
Mosinee, Wisconsin

It's easiest to freeze pieces of rhubarb in the amount you're likely to use most often—in quart containers, for instance. —*Jane Nadler*
Wright City, Missouri

Make Christmas cookies tiny —they look prettier, and guests have room to try them all! —*Kathy Wells*
Brodhead, Wisconsin

When making bar cookies, line the baking pan with foil. After the cookies are cool, simply lift out the entire batch and freeze it whole right in the same foil (defrost cookies before cutting). There's no cleanup!

—*Marie Herr, Berea, Ohio*

Make a "sandwich wreath" by alternating slices of party rye and pumperknickel bread filled with deviled ham and chicken spread. (Add a bit of chopped celery and a dash of Worcestershire sauce to ham filling; chopped apple and sour cream to chicken spread.) Arrange sandwiches in a ring around the rim of a 9-in. plate. Fasten a bright red

COUNTRY TRIVIA

BLUEBERRIES, Concord grapes and cranberries are the only commercially grown fruits native to North America.

bow to upper right-hand corner of "wreath". —*Virginia Gentry*
Sutherlin, Virginia

For a tender juicy meat loaf, first mix all of the ingredients except for the beef. Then add the meat and mix lightly. When shaping the loaf, handle only as much as necessary.

—*Ethel Bregant, La Salle, Illinois*

Some measures to have handy around the kitchen are these: 4 tablespoons equal 1/4 cup; 2 tablespoons equal 1 ounce; 2 cups equal 1 pint; 2 pints equal 1 quart; 16 ounces equal 1 pound; 16 cups equal 1 gallon. —*Juanita Packard*
Oklahoma City, Oklahoma

Place a paper doily on top of unfrosted cake and sift confectioners' sugar onto the doily until all spaces are white with sugar. Lift doily carefully off cake to reveal a pretty snowflake pattern.

—*Mrs. Rudolph Busacker*
Long Prairie, Minnesota

Meatballs make a fun substitute for stew meat in beef vegetable soup. Combine 1 pound ground beef, 1 egg, 1-1/2 cups bread crumbs, salt,

pepper and nutmeg to taste. Mix well; shape into 1/2-inch meatballs. Add to soup base, along with your vegetables, and cook for 30 minutes.
—Mina Bruinsmau
Bowmanville, Ontario

Save time making nut cookies by chopping several cups of nuts at once in the food processor and storing until needed. —Jenelle Miller
Marion, South Dakota

Set out straight pretzel sticks instead of wooden picks for spearing meatball appetizers. Since the "pick" is edible, you won't have to clean up loose toothpicks after your party. —Caryn Wiggins
Columbus, Indiana

For a delicious soup, cut 3 medium zucchini and 1 medium onion into chunks and cook in 3 cups chicken broth until tender. Puree in a blender with 3 ounces of cream cheese and 1/2 teaspoon of curry powder until smooth.
—Mary Kelly, Hopland, California

After a meal of baked ham, I always slice and package the leftovers in meal-size servings in aluminum foil, then label and freeze them to use later. Small pieces of ham I put into freezer bags for casseroles...the bone I keep for my husband's favorite bean soup. —Dale Rusan
Blue Springs, Missouri

Marinating tenderizes and adds flavor to beef. For most large cuts, marinate 6-12 hours in the refrigerator. Never marinate for more than 24 hours, however. —Jane Polaski
Milwaukee, Wisconsin

To prevent burning when you reheat frozen soup, place it in a kettle. Set kettle in a frying pan containing a small amount of water. Stir occasionally while it's warming.
—Linda Enslen, Schuler, Alberta

Cut rhubarb into pieces with kitchen shears than with a knife. It's much easier. —Sharon Thompson
Elgin, Illinois

For a very tender pot roast with nice rich gravy, first brown meat on all sides over high heat in a little butter or oil. Add water or beef broth; reduce heat and simmer over low heat for 2-4 hours. (A pan without "nonstick finish" will make browner gravy.) —Mary Jane Swanner
Decatur, Alabama

When making an apple pie, add the required amount of sugar to the apples immediately after slicing. This prevents the fruit from browning before baking.
—Mildred Sherrer, Bay City, Texas

Save the last-minute rush when you're serving turkey and stuffing to a large group. Roast the turkey the day before, carve it and store the meat and stuffing—separately—in the refrigerator. To reheat, place in wire salad baskets in an improvised steamer. (Place an empty tin can in

the bottom of a large kettle and set the basket on top of can; add enough water steam. Cover; steam for 30 minutes.) —*Susan McClure*
Nimes, France

Carrots stored in fall *can* last all winter long! Cover the bottom of a 5-gallon plastic pail with damp dirt. Put in a layer of carrots; cover with dirt. Layer more carrots, then dirt, until the bucket is full. Finish with a top layer of dirt. Put cover on pail; store in a root cellar.
—*Eunice Bruckner*
Colome, South Dakota

Bread won't rise to the occasion? Set dough in a covered bowl on top of an electric heating pan turned on low. —*Pat Morin*
Middletown, Indiana

To prevent browning when working with a quantity of peeled apples, slice them into water with 1 tablespoon of fresh lemon juice added.
—*Bernetta Rokusek*
Elgin, North Dakota

Since I most often serve dinner to a crowd on Sunday, I prepare my meal as much ahead as I can. Before going to church, I peel potatoes and put them in cold water to keep from turning brown, then put the meat in the slow cooker and turn it on low. As soon as we get home, I boil and mash the potatoes and fix a quick salad.
—*Lorena Hebb*
St. George, West Virginia

Store Christmas cookies as you bake them in 3-pound coffee cans

lined with waxed paper. Layer the cookies and top each layer with a square of waxed paper. Seal cover with freezer tape and label.
—*Carol Lindberg*
Ironwood, Michigan

For a tasty variation to your favorite apple crisp recipe, try adding a handful of raisins.
—*Rebecca Henning, Paris, Ohio*

Keep fresh-picked parsley fresher by placing stems in a bowl of water in the refrigerator.
—*Desoree Thompson*
Cabazon, California

The carcass and leftover meat from a 10- to 11-pound smoked grilled turkey makes a wonderful base for a bean soup. Cover with 6 quarts water and add 2 cups chopped onion, 6 chopped celery stems (with leaves), 4 peeled and shredded carrots, 6 chopped garlic cloves, 2 tablespoons of seasoning/herb mixture and salt to taste. Simmer for 2 hours.

Remove the bones; reserve meat. Cool stock; skim fat from top. Add

Try a pinch of mild paprika for soup eaters who don't like "hot" seasonings. It adds flavor and color—without turning up the heat! —*Evelyn Funda*
Lincoln, Nebraska

about 2 pounds of soaked navy beans to stock; simmer until beans are halfway cooked. Add reserved meat; cook until the beans are tender. —*Margaret Lane*
Versailles, Kentucky

Spinach can usually be substituted for Swiss chard when you're making soup. —*Betty Saginario*
Elmira, New York

To take out any "bitter" taste in rhubarb before using it, cover it with boiling water, put lid on pan and let stand for 30-60 minutes.
—*Jeanie Castor, Decatur, Illinois*

Spread crunchy peanut butter on apple wedges for a quick and a healthy snack. —*Becky Llewellyn*
Fremont, Michigan

Steaming is a great way to cook winter or summer squash—it preserves both the nutrients and pretty color. —*Brenda Thompson*
Chicora, Pennsylvania

Add leftover apple peel or orange and lemon peel to your tea as it steeps for wonderful flavor and aroma.

Freeze clusters of grapes to float in holiday punch—they'll keep it cold while adding color.
—*Greta Wierda, Brighton, Ontario*

When guests are coming for Sunday dinner, I'll set the table as soon as the breakfast dishes are cleared...prepare and refrigerate relish trays...chill a large pitcher of water to cut down on ice use...and get out serving bowls and utensils.
—*Lila Schmidt*
Mobridge, South Dakota

For best flavor, store tomatoes at room temperature. Do not refrigerate. —*Jeanette Strobel*
Brainerd, Minnesota

Try this variation on dried apples: Peel, core and halve 2 quarts of apples. Shred the apples coarsely onto a buttered baking sheet; bake at

NIP OF NATURE
Is it true you can tell which way the wind is blowing by looking at a herd of cows?

YES, on a windy day, cows will always turn away from the wind, because they don't like wind in their face any more than you do.

So, as country-wise folks have known for years, while driving down a rural road, they always know the direction of the wind—the opposite way the cows are facing.

Blow into the face of your dog sometime and see if he likes it. For this reason, almost all animals do this.

The only exception is the buffalo. Since he has all that "bulk" up front and a tiny behind, he prefers to face into the wind.

225° until dry. Remove from cookie sheet with a pancake turner. Break into pieces; store in an airtight container. —*Carol Jean Swartz Spencerville, Ohio*

Tomatoes can be ripened and kept for weeks by wrapping individually in newspaper. —*Jeanne Naumann Tonica, Illinois*

Save vegetable cooking liquid and use instead of water for added flavor when simmering cuts of beef. —*Nancy Smith Scottsdale, Arizona*

Dice up leftover turkey or roast beef and freeze in 1-1/2-cup portions for quick casseroles or to toss in salads. —*Julie Beth Lamb Lindsay, California*

When I make clam chowder, I omit the flour and some or all of the potatoes. Then I thicken the chowder with instant mashed potatoes for a smooth base.
—*Roberta Schrock, Iowa City, Iowa*

Here's a way to make thick ham slices special. Dust with flour, dip in beaten egg and coat with bread crumbs. Brown in butter over medium heat until both sides are golden. Garnish each slice with a parsley sprig; serve with cranberry sauce on a small lettuce leaf on the side. —*Tina Principato Hampton, New Hampshire*

To remove cooked squash from its shell, use an ice cream scoop—no mess, no fuss! —*Sharon Hallack Hart, Michigan*

For an easy Sunday dinner, pour a 27-ounce can of sauerkraut into a Dutch oven. Top with a pork roast (3-4 pounds) and another can of sauerkraut. Rinse cans; pour water over the roast. Cover and cook over low heat about 3 hours or until the roast is tender. Thicken juices if desired. Serve with mashed potatoes and rye bread. —*Barb Saylor Aberdeen, South Dakota*

Store gingerbread and other soft cookies in a tin with an apple slice to keep them from becoming hard.
—*Kathy Wells, Brodhead, Wisconsin*

To keep apple pie crust from getting too brown, give the apples a "head start" so they won't have to bake as long to get tender. Put sliced apples in a pie plate the same size as the pie that you're making. Cook in microwave for 8-10 minutes. Place partially cooked apples in your prepared crust along with other filling ingredients. Put top crust on and bake. —*Shirley Miller Browns Valley, Minnesota*

For moister white meat, turn your turkey on its breast when roasting. —*Lorna Jacobsen Arrowwood, Alberta*

To add pizzazz to beef stew, stir in an 8-ounce bottle of French dressing for each pound of beef cubes. Thin gravy with water if desired.

—*Darlene Sedlar*
Manistee, Michigan

I like to freeze berries for use in future jam making. It's best, I've discovered, to freeze fruit in measured amounts and not to wash the berries until I'm ready to thaw them. Since the freezing process normally softens fruit, there's no need to mash the berries.

—*Donnie Clayton*
Raleigh, North Carolina

When making caramel apples, roll dipped apples in a mixture of chopped peanuts and chocolate chips for a special taste treat.

—*Darlis Anderson, Badger, Iowa*

"Heat" up a summer meal— with chili corn in husks! Trim ends off eight large ears of unhusked corn. Remove about half of husks. Push the remaining husks aside and remove corn silk. Replace husks and tie in place. Put ears on a rack in a large covered kettle. Add 2 cups water; cover and steam for 20 minutes or until corn is tender. Remove husks. Heat 1/2 butter and 2-3 tea-

spoons of chili powder; brush on corn just before serving.

—*Jill Kinder, Richlands, Virginia*

To make gravy in chicken-and-noodle dishes prettier, add a few drops of yellow food coloring.

—*Mary Bengston-Almquist*
Petersburg, Illinois

When stir-frying beef, slice each piece to the same thickness and stir constantly to assure even cooking.

—*Rosemary Perry*
Weatherford, Texas

A cabbage head can easily "flavor" a party. Cut your cabbage into a shell, then hollow out and fill with dip. Use as a centerpiece and place vegetables around it. Or fill a cabbage shell with your favorite salad and serve for a ladies' luncheon or brunch.   —*Paula Pelis*
Rocky Point, New York

For a quick party snack, spread paper-thin slices of ham with softened cream cheese and wrap around a green onion. Slice, arrange on a snack tray and serve.

—*Mary Roberts, Wildwood, Florida*

Winter squash can be substituted for pumpkin in most pie, bread and cookie recipes. Hubbard and banana squash work especially well.

—*Mary Carroll*
Fort Wayne, Indiana

Zucchini freezes well. Cut into 1-inch slices and blanch in boiling water for 2 minutes. Rinse in cold water; drain well and pat dry with paper towels. Spread in single layers on cookie sheets and freeze until solid. Pack in freezer bags. Will keep for 3-6 months.

—Heather Muncey
Cornwall, Prince Edward Island

When making several different types of cookies, first bake those calling for lower temperatures, then work up to the highest setting.

—Kathy Wells
Brodhead, Wisconsin

A new toothbrush is a dandy tool to have handy for cleaning small fish such as smelt. —Martha Mausling
Adrian, Oregon

Soggy crusts in fruit pies a problem? Try sprinkling the bottom crust with sugar before adding fruit fillings.

To keep custard and pumpkin pie crusts from becoming soggy, pre-bake crust for 5 minutes, then add the filling. —Susan Elliott
Bancroft, Ontario

When you are hard-cooking eggs, add a few drops of vinegar to the water…it will help keep shells from cracking. —Teresa Hinson
Mt. Pleasant, North Carolina

For a perfect meringue, keep these pointers in mind: Beat meringue mixture well, until all the sugar is dissolved. If your mixture tastes or feels grainy, beat some more.

Cool meringue pie gradually in a slightly warm place, one that's away from drafts.

To cut meringue pie neatly, dip a sharp knife into water; shake off excess drops. Cut a piece, then repeat the process. —Dolores Skrout
Summerhill, Pennsylvania

Freeze beef just until firm to make it easier to slice for stir-fries and Stroganoff. —Kim Champlin
Miami, Florida

Here is an oven method for freezing corn: Combine 9 cups corn, 2 cups water, 2 teaspoons salt and 1/4 cup sugar in a roaster. Bake at 350° for 30-45 minutes, stirring every 15 minutes. Cool, package and freeze. —Mrs. Norm Novotny
Bird Island, Minnesota

Don't overcook jams and jellies or they'll become tough and rubbery.

—Audrey Thibodeau
Mesa, Arizona

When freezing fresh cranberries for storage, first discard any unripe or bruised fruit. Wash and dry berries thoroughly, then freeze in a single layer on a jelly roll pan. When solid, pack berries in heavy freezer

bags or freezer containers. Store as long as a full year.
—*Mary Jane Swanner*
Decatur, Alabama

Even in a dark cellar, you won't lose sight of home-processed food if you color-code your jars. Use a small piece of colored stick-on tape (a different color for each year) and attach it next to the label on the jar.
—*Mrs. George Daniels*
Ellisville, Missouri

A paring knife can be safely carried on a picnic by packing it in a toothbrush holder.
—*Rose Vander Velden*
Vernon, British Columbia

As a flavorful alternative, I will sometimes substitute mint extract for vanilla in my brownies.
—*Andrea Hiebert, Dallas, Oregon*

I make orange marmalade when blood oranges—with their bright color and wonderful flavor—are in season, adding a little lemon juice for a bit of tartness.
—*Patrice Humke*
Fresno, California

Here's a simple way to separate leaves from the head when you make stuffed cabbage: Remove the

core and cover the cabbage with cold water. Let stand 10 minutes; remove leaves. —*Rosemarie Mueller*
Janesville, Wisconsin

For a little variety, try replacing ground beef with ham when making stuffed green peppers.
—*Cindy Hartley, Norfolk, Virginia*

Homemade peach-blueberry jam is a favorite of mine. Because the blueberries are in season earlier, I freeze them in 1-cup bags till the peaches are fully ripe. Then I can combine those great flavors!
—*Marcy Giles*
Okanagan Falls, British Columbia

Winter squash keeps longer after harvest when you pick it with a good stem attached.
—*Mildred Holm*
St. Charles, Michigan

I perk up breakfast by putting 1-inch cubes of ham in my waffle batter…that saves the need for serving a side dish of ham or sausage.
—*Susan Schroeder*
Ferndale, Washington

Don't use overripe fruit for making jams and jellies—the natural pectin decreases, yielding a very soft spread. —*Linda Ordorff*
Waverly, Minnesota

Freezer jams are generally softer than regular jams and preserves—and make excellent toppings for waffles, French toast, pancakes and ice cream. —*Debbie Keslar*
Seward, Nebraska

This tea mix will spice up the holidays: Combine 1 cup of instant tea, one 26-ounce jar of powdered orange drink, one 5-ounce package presweetened lemonade, 1/2 teaspoon allspice, 3/4 teaspoon ground cloves, 1 teaspoon cinnamon and one 10-ounce package of red-hot candies.

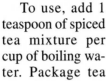

To use, add 1 teaspoon of spiced tea mixture per cup of boiling water. Package tea mix in small jars. Use a colored ribbon to tie a cinnamon stick (for stirring tea) to top of jar, along with instructions for using the mix.

—*Donna Bescheinen*
Loveland, Colorado

Here's a quick casserole you can make from holiday leftovers: Layer turkey in bottom of casserole dish. Add gravy, then leftover mashed potatoes. Add layer of cranberries, then more mashed potatoes. Dot with butter. Top with chopped onion and shredded cheese. Sprinkle with paprika. Bake until heated through.

—*Esther Hall*
New Westminster, British Columbia

For a decorative dessert, cut your brownies into pie wedges and top with whipped cream.

—*Beverly Shelton*
Jefferson City, Missouri

When packing for a picnic, put cellophane tape over salt and pepper shaker holes to prevent spilling.

For a safe easy-to-carry picnic "fire starter", saturate some rope or

COUNTRY TRIVIA

ABOUT 14 gallons of ice cream are produced for each person in the U.S. per year.

string with melted paraffin. Cut off as much as you need at a time.

—*Mrs. Harry Howell*
Flemington, New Jersey

Since cabbage is always priced so reasonably, I buy the largest head that I can. Then I chop it all and freeze it in dinner-size portions for future use. —*Susan Adcock*
Petrolia, Ontario

Turn leftover pie pastry into a special treat: Roll it out, spread some butter over it, then sprinkle with cinnamon-sugar. If desired, add chopped nuts, shredded apple or raisins. Roll up jelly-roll fashion and curve into a crescent shape. Place on a pie plate and bake at 350° for 20-25 minutes or until golden brown. Cut into 1-inch slices to serve.

—*Bernadette Colvin*
Houston, Texas

I make a ham salad that wins me raves by chopping leftover ham, then adding pimiento cheese, Colby cheese, chopped sweet and dill pickles, salad dressing and onion.

For parties, I mound the salad in the middle of a large dish, put crack-

ers around it and serve it as a dip. Or it can be grilled as a sandwich—just spoon salad between two slices of buttered bread and brown in a skillet.
—*Kay Harrison*
Ft. Pierce, Florida

Make Christmas "bells" by placing a maraschino cherry at the base of a pear half.
—*Mrs. Rudolph Busacker*
Long Prairie, Minnesota

For a quick stir-fry, combine all the leftover meat in your refrigerator (steak, chicken, ground beef, etc.). Heat 1 tablespoon of oil in a skillet. Stir-fry meat for 2 minutes. Add all leftover vegetables you have on hand (or a bag of frozen mixed vegetables).

Stir-fry 3 more minutes. Add 1 cup instant rice, 4 tablespoons soy sauce and 1 cup water. Simmer, uncovered, until most of the liquid in the pan has evaporated.
—*Cathy Barbee*
Colorado Springs, Colorado

Freeze small amounts of leftover pasta in freezer bags. To use, put bags in boiling water long enough to thaw and heat up.
—*Mina Dyck*
Boissevain, Manitoba

This speedy no-fail peanut butter fudge is one of our favorite Christmas giveaways: Melt 1 cup butter-flavored shortening. Remove from heat. Add 1 cup of either smooth or crunchy peanut butter, 2-1/2 teaspoons vanilla and 4 cups confectioners' sugar. Mix well. Pour into an ungreased 8-inch square baking pan. Let cool. Cut into squares. Wrap in cellophane.
—*Marilee Spung, Zanesville, Ohio*

I buy small picnic hams whenever they're on sale. I bake them in the microwave, then cool, slice and package them for the freezer. The

NIP OF NATURE
Why do wasps and bees sting?

MOSTLY for protection. They sting mostly when they feel threatened.

Mice and other bees sometimes raid beehives and steal honey, so bees use their stinging power to ward off these raiders.

While most wasps use their stings to attack enemies, one kind of wasp actually uses its stinger to provide food for its young. The female of this species injects her stinger into a caterpillar to paralyze it. She then lays eggs on the creature, and the baby wasps hatch and feed on the caterpillar until they are big enough to be on their own.

nice slices I save for sandwiches, and I use the meat around the bone for dicing into soups, omelets, etc.

—Donna Valen
Stonewall, Manitoba

For a deliciously different flavor when you're barbecuing, serve peppery hot corn. Mix 3 tablespoons of snipped chives or green onions, 1/4 teaspoon each of pepper, chili powder and cayenne pepper and 1/2 cup of softened butter. Chill for at least 1 hour or overnight. Serve at room temperature with fresh corn on the cob.

—Sylvia Petker
Port Rowan, Ontario

To freeze corn, blanch ears, then cool them. Place ear of corn on the cone of an angel food cake pan and cut off the kernels with an electric knife. The cake pan will catch the kernels without making a mess of your kitchen counter.

—Sue Beiswanger
Wolcottville, Indiana

Add ground ham to your favorite cheese dip, ball or spread for a change of pace. —Kathy Weisbrod
Regina, Saskatchewan

For further flavor when canning sauerkraut, add some bay leaves to the crock as you layer your cabbage and canning salt. Remove before filling the jars for processing.

—Nancy Tassaua
Ironwood, Michigan

I send Thanksgiving guests home with meals of leftovers in disposable pie tins. They can pop them

in the oven right from the fridge… and no one has to return containers.

—Kathleen Phelps
Minneapolis, Minnesota

Corn can be baked right in the husk. Peel back husks but don't remove them. Remove and discard corn silk. Spread each ear with 1/2 teaspoon softened butter or margarine and sprinkle lightly with salt and pepper. Fold husks back over corn. Wrap each in foil. Bake at 375° for 30-35 minutes. —Marsha Baker
Pioneer, Ohio

Rub a small amount of butter or margarine on the lip of your creamer and you'll have no more drips on your fine tablecloth.

—Betha Mueller
Cuba City, Wisconsin

Individual ham loaves are a handy thing to make ahead and freeze for family gatherings. Sometimes I'll send them in plastic bags with my children when they go back to college—they can pop them in the oven later.

—Denae Blair
Shawnee Mission, Kansas

If cream-style corn is a favorite with your family, treat yourself to this quick-and-easy freezer version: Combine 8 to 10 cups corn cut from cobs, 1 pound butter or margarine and 1 pint of cream in a roaster. Bake at 350° for 1 hour, stir-

ring every 15 minutes. Ladle into containers and freeze.
—*Jayette Robb, Basin, Wyoming*

I spice up chicken by adding taco seasoning or a blend of herbs to a cornmeal coating.
—*Carole Anne Smith*
Surrey, British Columbia

A little salt added to flour before mixing with water or milk will keep the flour from being lumpy.
—*Danny Cunningham*
Chandler, Arizona

If a recipe calls for buttermilk but you discover you don't have any on hand, add 2 teaspoons vinegar or lemon juice to each 1/2 cup of milk.
—*Aline Filliol*
Cornwall, Ontario

For a smoother easier-spreading jam or preserve, try using a hand-held blender to puree the mixture before canning.
—*Marjorie Franklin*
Hawkeye, Iowa

This substitution works for unsweetened chocolate squares: 3 tablespoons of baking cocoa plus 1 tablespoon of shortening or oil equals 1 square.
—*Virginia Malone*
Stratton, Colorado

We like herb butter to spread on corn on the cob. Combine 2 sticks softened butter with 1 teaspoon of chopped fresh basil or 1/2 teaspoon dried basil. Makes enough for 12 ears. This is especially tasty with corn on the grill.
—*Ellen Bower*
Taneytown, Maryland

If a recipe calls for a double boiler and you don't have one, put a metal bowl on top of a saucepan instead. (Be sure to use a pot holder when holding on to the bowl!)
—*Nancy Stansell*
Gaylord, Michigan

Use a turkey baster to fill muffin cups all the same size—and to make no-drip hotcakes! —*Teresa Graham*
Dawsonville, Georgia

If you want fancier-looking pumpkin pies, decorate the tops. Just roll out leftover pastry, then use a knife or cookie cutter to cut out shapes such as hearts or maple leaves. Brush shapes with beaten egg or milk. Sprinkle with cinnamon-sugar. Bake the shapes on a cookie sheet until golden brown; transfer to a wire rack to cool. Put shapes on pies as soon as they come out of the oven.
—*Jeanne Smith*
St. Stephen, New Brunswick

Keep mineral rings off the outside of canning jars by adding 2 tablespoons vinegar to the water in which the jars sit in the canner.
—*Anita Heistand, Galena, Kansas*

Pour leftover juice from canned fruit into a container and freeze. Thaw later for punch.
—*Julie Beth Lamb*
Lindsay, California

My upper kitchen cabinet drawers were always cluttered—until I hung a clean shoe bag inside a lower cabinet door. Now, I put all the extra gadgets I don't use often in the pockets of the bag.

—*Bonnie Baumgardner*
Sylva, North Carolina

In a jam when making jelly? Try this trick! Just before you remove jelly from the heat, drop in a tablespoon of butter or margarine. As it melts, it will make the jelly very clear—and skimming unnecessary.

—*Naomi Crowley*
Parker, Colorado

At Thanksgiving, I often buy a turkey plus a turkey breast so there will be plenty of white meat for everyone.

—*Lisa Tucker*
Streator, Illinois

In summer, I freeze most of my fruit and juices—then turn them into jams and jellies in the fall and winter when I'm not so busy.

—*Jo Raines*
Sandyville, West Virginia

If you're short on juice from the fruit you're using when making a jelly, make up the difference with apple juice. —*Norma Nichols*
Galesville, Wisconsin

When making raspberry jam, use only ripe berries. Mash some of them to a puree and leave the rest chunkier for texture. For a lovely

COUNTRY TRIVIA

THE "potato state", Idaho, is also well-known for its barley crop. Idaho became the No. 1 producer of barley in 1988.

burgundy-colored jam, substitute 1 cup of blueberries for a cup of the raspberries. —*Arlene Oliver*
Bothell, Washington

Take along a box of thumbtacks on your next picnic. When the wind blows, they're handy for tacking down a tablecloth, paper plates and other items.

—*Mrs. Harry Howell*
Flemington, New Jersey

Make "mock" scalloped potatoes by slicing leftover boiled potatoes into a casserole dish. Add white sauce and bake uncovered at 350° until heated through.
—*Mina Dyck, Boissevain, Manitoba*

Substitute brown sugar for granulated sugar for a rich caramel flavor in brownies.
—*Marcy Wright, Turlock, California*

This tradition dates to my great-grandmother. It makes the turkey very moist while adding subtle flavor!

Rinse, pat dry and stuff bird as usual. Then turn it into a "porcupine". Cut breakfast sausage links (several packages) in half. Skewer links with tooth-picks (plain wooden ones, not colored ones) and stick them in the turkey all over. Add 1 inch of water to bottom of roaster, cover bird with foil and place in oven. Roast as usual. About 1-1/2 hours before the meal, remove sausages and place on platter. Serve as appetizers. Continue roasting bird uncovered, adding water as necessary, till it turns a golden brown and tests done.

—Wendy Lee Paffenroth
Pine Island, New York

Need a *large* container for storing flour? Turn an old-fashioned milk can into a canister! Paint it in your kitchen colors and put in a convenient corner. *—Norma Nichols*
Galesville, Wisconsin

To "dress up" a ham dinner, make dressing as you would for chicken or turkey—but *without* seasoning. Bake with your ham, letting the juices flavor the dressing.

Green beans make a nice complement to baked ham. For a pleasingly different flavor, add them to the ham about an hour before you eat and bake them right with it.

—Laura Ann Nelson
Kenyon, Minnesota

Since cabbage likes cold weather, plan to plant early in the spring. Water around the sides of the plant rather than directly over heads to keep them from splitting.
—Edith Wilson, Raymond, Montana

Add a glossy look to your iced brownies by frosting them while they're still warm.

—Juanita Thompson
Grand Rapids, Michigan

When making homemade sauerkraut, choose large compact heads of fall-harvest cabbage. Earlier varieties are lower in sugar and less desirable for kraut. Wilt heads in a cool dry place for 1 week for a whiter color.

You can also ferment whole heads for making cabbage rolls out of sour leaves. Select small firm heads. Core and arrange heads in alternate layers with the shredded cabbage when making regular sauerkraut. Proceed with the standard fermentation and packing procedure.
—Roseanne Martyniuk
Red Deer, Alberta

To get Thanksgiving dinner started quicker, I put the giblets in the slow cooker the night before, with enough water to cover, and simmer them overnight. Next morning, they're ready to be chopped up, then added to the dressing mixture, as is the hot broth.
—Terri Faas, Lompoc, California

Here's a tip for perfect hard-cooked eggs every time, with no dark rings around the yolk:

Place eggs in saucepan and cover with cold water. Turn burner on and allow water to come to a full rolling boil. Turn off heat and place lid on pan.

Let stand, covered, 10 minutes for small and medium eggs and 20 minutes for large or extra-large eggs. Then pour off the hot water and run cold tap water over the eggs.

Crack and shell as usual. Your eggs will be perfect! —*Terri Reeves*
Mishawaka, Indiana

To give the coleslaw I'm making extra zest, I add a teaspoon of horseradish. —*Ruth Maershbecker*
Tappen, North Dakota

In a jam wondering how you can remove paraffin from homemade preserves? Take a corkscrew and gently screw down through the center of the paraffin. Then lift it out of the jar! —*Sherry Raser*
Milford, Pennsylvania

To grill fresh ears of corn, pull back husks and remove corn silk. Replace husks and tie in place. Soak corn in salted water for 5 minutes; drain. Roast on grill over hot coals for 10-12 minutes, turning often. Remove husks and serve corn with butter and salt. —*Jill Kinder*
Richlands, Virginia

I have a number of cookbooks and it used to take me a while to find my favorite recipes. So I got a recipe box and filing cards and now write the name of the recipe, which cookbook it's in and the page number. Now when I need a recipe, I just check the box. It sure saves time! —*Ruth Anna Miller*
Mount Joy, Pennsylvania

To make the most of citrus, grate as much as possible from an orange or lemon rind, even if the recipe calls for a smaller amount. Put the extra—in teaspoon or tablespoon portions—in small plastic bags, label and freeze for later use. —*Mina Dyck*
Boissevain, Manitoba

Use the tip of your potato peeler to remove strawberry hulls. —*Desoree Thompson*
Cabazon, California

Try leftover mashed or baked potatoes this way: Combine potatoes in a bowl with 1-2 tablespoons butter, 1/4 cup milk, 1/4 cup sour cream, 1 cup of various shredded cheeses (mozzarella, cheddar, Parmesan, etc.) and salt and pepper to taste. Beat till smooth. Place in a casserole dish. Sprinkle additional cheese on top. Bake at 350° for 30 minutes. —*Cathy Barbee*
Colorado Springs, Colorado

To cut down on back-and-forth trips to the kitchen during a backyard picnic, use a six-cup muffin tin to hold mustard, ketchup and such. —*Elsie Kolberg*
St. Joseph, Michigan

I like to "dress up" my brownies for birthdays and special occasions by garnishing them with whole strawberries, chocolate curls, etc.
—*Gertrude Sawatzky*
MacGregor, Manitoba

To microwave fresh corn, put two to four ears, with the husks still on, on wet paper towel. Microwave on high for 4 minutes. Take out and let cool. Husk, holding ear with the paper towel.

—*Marilyn McDonell*
San Andreas, California

It's easy to get a single coffee filter out of the stack if you turn the stack inside out.

—*Beverly Zimmerman*
Harrison, Michigan

Try this twist on grilled cheese sandwiches. Rather than buttering the outside of the bread, use mayonnaise (not salad dressing). It gives the sandwich a different texture and makes it less greasy.

—*Fay Meredith*
Clark Fork, North Dakota

You can beat the summer heat—and cut baking time for fruit pies in half—by combining microwave and conventional cooking. Here's how: Prepare a double-crust 9-inch or 10-inch fruit pie in a *glass* pie plate according to your favorite recipe.

Preheat conventional oven to 450°. In the microwave, cook the pie, uncovered, on high for 7-9 minutes, turning every 2 minutes. (Juices will start bubbling through slits on top of pie.)

Carefully transfer pie to preheated oven and bake for 15 minutes or until golden brown.

—*Mrs. G. Hiebert*
Winnipeg, Manitoba

Our family doesn't eat a whole chicken at one meal, and each family member prefers certain pieces. To eliminate wasted meat, cut up a whole fryer and freeze the individual pieces on a cookie sheet.

When the pieces are frozen, place them in a freezer bag. This way, you can take out only what you need. I use the bony pieces for dumplings, etc. With this method, each piece gets used and there's no waste.

—*Jan Campbell*
Purvis, Mississippi

To ripen green tomatoes when the end of the season arrives, wrap

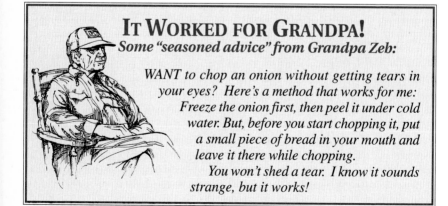

IT WORKED FOR GRANDPA!
Some "seasoned advice" from Grandpa Zeb:

WANT to chop an onion without getting tears in your eyes? Here's a method that works for me: Freeze the onion first, then peel it under cold water. But, before you start chopping it, put a small piece of bread in your mouth and leave it there while chopping.
You won't shed a tear. I know it sounds strange, but it works!

each in newspaper and place in a cool place or on the basement floor. Many of them should be ready to use in 30-45 days. —*Linda Holmes Apopka, Florida*

Want snow-white cauliflower every time? Just add about a tablespoon of lemon juice to the water you use to rinse the cauliflower. It never fails. —*Mrs. E. Baumgartner Avenel, New Jersey*

To make ground ham sandwiches special for a ladies' luncheon, shape them into hearts with a cookie cutter. —*Shana Koehn Sedan, New Mexico*

You can "recycle" meat drippings into soup bases. After browning meat in a nonstick pan with no oil, cool drippings in the refrigerator and skim off fat. Place in zip-type bags, along with any leftover meat pieces, and label them "chicken juice", "beef juice", etc.

Freeze till ready to use. If you don't have enough of one kind of "juice" to make soup, mix several for a flavorful combination.

—*Barb Holland, Tipton, Michigan*

For breakfast variety, try a combination of two or more dry cereals. Experiment with a sweet cereal and a sugarless one, or a high fiber with a bran flake, or different grains. The variety is limited only by your imagination and taste buds. Save room in your cupboard by combining small amounts of several cereals in one box. —*Margaret Storch Davenport, Iowa*

Use only ripe fruit when making peach jam. And, to remove the peels easily, dip the peaches in boiling water for 30 seconds, then in ice-cold water. The skins will slide right off. —*Tracy Supcoe Centreville, Maryland*

When green peppers are ripe in the garden, prepare them for quick winter meals. Wash, core, remove seeds and dice the peppers. Then pack them in small jars and freeze. One jar is the right amount for most family-size casseroles, soups and stews.

—*Karen Ann Bland Gove, Kansas*

You can strain fat out of meat broth by pouring it through a paper coffee filter. Works every time.

—*Ruthie Heath Carlisle, Pennsylvania*

To make pretty "bows" for holiday bowls of fruit juice and punch, try this: Peel the rind from a large orange in one long strip. Scrape off remaining white membrane on back. Cut orange strip 1/4 inch wide and tie into a bow. Float in beverages.

—*Liz Nebergall Chattaroy, Washington*

Do you love natural peanut butter but have a hard time getting the right consistency (too oily or too dry at the bottom)? Then try this:

Take the peanut butter out of the

jar and beat it in a mixing bowl for a couple of minutes. When you put it back in the jar, it will stay blended.

—*Barbara Legacy*
Holden, Maine

Use a grapefruit spoon to clean seeds from squash before cooking. They come out very easily.

—*Betty Hemminger*
Riverside, California

Here is a new use for brown grocery sacks. Soak the entire bag in water. Then put your hard  bread or rolls in the wet sack. Turn on the oven to warm, put the bag in and watch carefully for the bag to dry out. It takes only minutes. Then turn the oven off and remove the warm bag. The rolls or bread will be as soft as fresh.

—*Carla Haskell*
San Antonio, Texas

To ensure great moisture and texture in a chocolate cake, add a can of sauerkraut (well drained) to your mix.

—*Cindi Warren*
Algona, Washington

A bay leaf placed in your flour canister will keep bugs out of the flour.

—*Glena Royse, Franklin, Tennessee*

I enjoy baking pies, but I would rather not clean up the mess after each individual pie crust. To get around this, I make up a large batch of pie crusts at one time.

I roll out the crusts to the size of my pie plates. Then I roll each crust onto my rolling pin and transfer it to a piece of waxed paper that is 2 inches longer than the crust. I gently roll up each one, starting where the paper is a bit longer, so the end result looks like a candle.

Once they're all done, I place them in a bread bag and store them on a flat surface in the freezer. (Remove as much air from the bag as possible before closing.)

This way, when you want to make a pie, you just pull out one or two crusts, and in no time they soften enough to flip into your pie plate.

—*Mrs. Al Blavat*
De Pere, Wisconsin

To quickly remove silk from corn, rub ear with a dry piece of nylon net.

—*Martha Snyder*
Media, Pennsylvania

Here's a no-fuss way to cook winter squash: Wash the outside and, without cutting, pop into a hot oven. Set the temperature at the level needed for whatever you're cooking for the rest of the meal and bake until fork-tender.

When you remove the squash, cut it open and scoop out the seeds. It's never watery and retains all of its nutritional value.

—*Carol Battle*
Heathsville, Virginia

To guarantee even baking of all sorts, I have found shiny baking pans and cookie sheets are best. Dark pans absorb more heat and can cause overbrowning.

—*Eleanor Klovetter*
Plainview, Minnesota

To easily remove cabbage leaves, place head in a plastic bag and freeze overnight. Thaw the next day; leaves will be pliable and will pull off without breaking.
—*Audrey Thibodeau, Mesa, Arizona*

For quick and easy cleanup of cups used to measure shortening, rinse the measuring cup with cold water, leave wet and then measure the shortening. It will come out more easily, and with a lot less mess left in the cup.
—*Marva Lou Thiemes*
Van Orin, Illinois

I love squash but always hated to peel it. I even tried cutting it with a hatchet and dropping it onto cement to get it into ready-to-peel pieces, but it was so messy! One day I was preparing tomatoes for canning and wondered if the same method would work for squash. It did!

Fill a kettle half full with hot water. When the water is coming to a boil, wash squash and place it in the kettle. Twirl it around for a couple of minutes, then turn it to expose the other half to the water. Lift squash out and it'll peel just like a potato.
—*Tina Kelleher*
South Paris, Maine

Many casseroles call for butter after you have layered the ingredients. I have found that butter is more evenly distributed if I take a cold stick of butter and use a cheese grater to grate it over the dish. I have also found that grated butter is prettier to serve at the table than tubs of soft butter, and it's also more economical.
—*Susie Deavours*
Spicewood, Texas

I keep several different sizes of Styrofoam trays that come in meat packages and I use them in the refrigerator under leaky items or foods I'm thawing out. Just wash the trays and they can be reused several times.
—*Yvonne Castle*
Columbia Cross Roads, Pennsylvania

To keep brownies moister on top, cover the pan with aluminum foil as soon as you take it out of the oven.
—*Eddra Ritta*
Central City, Nebraska

I use baby food jars when I make jelly. To seal them, I use paraffin wax. First, I scrape wax chips into the bottom of an empty jar. The jelly melts the wax, which rises to

To separate juice from the pulp when making grape jelly if you don't have a jelly bag, use a colander with small holes (so seeds can't go through). Let juice drip through without pressure, and it'll end up very clear.
—*Virginia Dean*
Bonaire, Georgia

the top and makes a perfect seal. There is less mess than when you first melt the wax in a pan and try to pour it into the almost-filled jars of jelly.
—*Linda Jester*
Hot Springs, Arkansas

We like dilled green beans on

our salads. When we finish a jar of dill pickles, I open a can of green beans and let them mar-

inate in the remaining dill juice.
—*Elizabeth Beasley*
Lakehead, California

I often baked bundt cakes but found the cakes always stuck when I used shortening and flour on the pan. Then one day I greased my pan with shortening and sprinkled it with sugar. I've never had a cake stick since!

Just let the cake cool 10 minutes, and it'll pop right out of the pan. With the sugar, most of the time the cakes don't even need a glaze!
—*Melinda Widner*
Waxahachie, Texas

Keep your just-baked home-made cookies soft by placing a slice of white bread on top of them. The cookies will taste oven-fresh for hours.
—*Lois Hoopes*
Dillsburg, Pennsylvania

To keep a pie shell (for a cream, lemon or any type of non-baked pie) nice and flat while baking the shell, place it in the pie pan, cover it with

a layer of dry navy beans, then bake as usual. When the shell is cool, carefully remove the dry beans with a spoon.

Put the beans in a glass jar to use over and over. The shell will be perfect without any bumps.
—*Elsie Back, Madison, Wisconsin*

To make a funnel for filling salt and pepper shakers, just use a clean envelope and cut off a small corner of it.
—*Della Whitesell*
El Dorado Springs, Missouri

I store both my brown sugar and marshmallows in the freezer. They never get hard or stale!
—*Thelma Riggs, Billings, Montana*

Need a little thickening for gravy? I keep a container of instant potato flakes handy, adding a small amount to obtain the right consistency. They're great, too, for thickening chowders, soups and stews.
—*Fay Meredith*
Clark Fork, Idaho

If you slice an onion before peeling, the peel will come right off.
—*Ann Sample*
Royal Oak, Michigan

Often, it's difficult to scoop sugar out of a storage container into sugar bowls without spilling some. So I use an empty, clean, dry gallon milk jug for storing and pouring sugar. The jug holds a 5-pound bag of sugar, and all it takes is a funnel to get the sugar into the jug.

If the sugar lumps, just stick an end of a spoon or a chopstick into

the jug to break up the lumps. But usually it flows freely because the container is airtight. —*Taffy Hill*
Louisville, Kentucky

It's cheaper to make your own whipped butter. Soften a stick of butter and beat with electric mixer until creamy. Slowly add 1/2 cup vegetable oil or 2 tablespoons milk, beating until light and fluffy. Store, covered, in refrigerator.
—*Gloria Mackes*
Walnutport, Pennsylvania

Sometimes when you use an electric skillet or griddle, it sets uneven and all the oil goes to one side, making frying difficult. When this happens, I put mason jar lids underneath the "low" leg to get perfect balance. —*Terry Bray*
Haines City, Florida

I use a candy thermometer to get the correct water temperature for all recipes using yeast. No more failures! —*Betty Helm*
El Paso, Texas

My utensil drawer always seems to be cluttered, and during "corn on the cob" season, I've found it's so much easier to keep all my corn holders stuck into a large cork. They're easier to find at a glance, and it's a much safer way to store them!
—*Margie Dodd*
Oklahoma City, Oklahoma

Still waiting for thick ketchup to come out? Try putting a straw in the bottle. The straw gives it an air hole, and it pours right out.
—*Shirley Woessner*
Bowling Green, Ohio

I've always cut rolls of paper towels in half, slicing almost to the cardboard core. You rarely need a whole towel; half will dry your hands or wipe up a spill, and you end up saving paper and money.
—*Sheila Berg*
Lucas Valley, California

To bake potatoes quickly, boil them in salted water for 10 minutes, then put into oven. The boiling water will heat them through more rapidly than if they were placed cold into the oven.
—*Maxine Martin*
Hillsville, Virginia

Need bread crumbs fast? Put two slices of bread in the toaster, transfer into a sandwich bag, then crush with a soup can or rolling pin.
—*Dawn Leedy*
Franklin, Ohio

To easily peel hard-cooked eggs, pour off all of the water from the container in which the eggs were boiled. Cover the container and knock the eggs around in it to loosen the shells. Add cold water, and the shells will fall off.
—*Felice Anspacher*
Agoura Hills, California

I use up any marshmallows that have become hardened by putting

then in hot applesauce or stewed rhubarb. They add a different and delicious taste to either dish.
—*Mrs. Richard Miller, Lima, Ohio*

To get all the shortening out of your measuring cups when making cakes or cookies, crack an egg in the cup first.

Tilt the cup to coat all sides with the egg, then pour out. Now fill the cup with shortening—it will plop right out, all in one piece. Cleanup is easier, too! —*Jennifer Baugh Star City, Arkansas*

A pepper mill works great for grinding cardamom and other seeds and spices for recipes.
—*Joann Opsal Alamo, North Dakota*

To get cakes to pop out of the pan easily, melt about 2 tablespoons of butter or margarine and pour it into the pan. Then turn the pan around and around until it's coated evenly on the bottom and sides.

Put the pan in the freezer, and the butter or margarine hardens in a few minutes. Pour the batter into the pan and bake, and the cake never sticks to the pan. —*Noalene Shows Inverness, Mississippi*

To keep cheese from molding, I spread the cut side with butter or margarine and then refrigerate in a sealed plastic bag. —*Nancy Smith Scottsdale, Arizona*

When freezing fruit for pies, mix in all the ingredients called for in the recipe. Then line a pie pan with plastic wrap and freeze the filling in the pie pan.

When the filling is completely frozen, remove it to a plastic bag. This way, the filling is ready to drop into a pie shell and bake at a moment's notice. —*Susan Smith Pinehurst, North Carolina*

To keep your hands clean while greasing a baking pan, place your hand inside a plastic sandwich bag before dipping it into the can of shortening. The pliable bag greases the surface more easily than a piece of waxed paper, too.
—*Karen Merrick Marietta, Georgia*

Adding a few teaspoons of lemon juice to the water when boiling potatoes will keep them nice and white. —*Evelyn McKenna Salix, Iowa*

Using a pastry blender to chop hard-cooked eggs saves a great deal of time and does a thoroughly neat job. —*Julia Kanpinos Norwich, Connecticut*

A neat trick for removing excess fat from soup or gravy is to skim the surface with ice wrapped in a cheesecloth. The fat congeals and clings right to the cloth.
—*Linda Hoadley Paradise, California*

For perfect bacon, soak the strips in cold water for a few minutes before frying. This lessons shrinkage and curling. Then place in a cold skillet and begin heating. Turn and drain grease often, and you'll wind up with delicious and delicious-looking bacon. —*Ruth McCalvin Donalsonville, Georgia*

Use spring-type clothespins to seal plastic bags. They're quicker and more convenient than twist-ties or rubber bands, and are especially time-saving for freezer bags or bread bags that you open for just a little something and then close up again.
—*June Blair, Columbia, Missouri*

To use every last bit of shortening, heat your almost-empty can of shortening in the oven. When the shortening has melted, pour it into a newly opened can. You'll usually save at least 1/4 cup of shortening with this method. —*Laura Meulman Houston, Texas*

Inexpensive canned biscuits can be used for a variety of things. Cut a hole in the middle and deep-fry them in fat for doughnuts. Or, flatten them for mini-pizza crusts. Stretch and wrap them around wieners and bake for pigs-in-a-blanket.

For tea biscuits, flatten them, spread with butter, and sprinkle with sugar and cinnamon. You can make cheesy snack crackers by adding 1/2 cup shredded cheddar cheese to one can of biscuits, rolling the dough thin, cutting it into small squares and baking until crisp.
—*Dale Kelley, Durango, Colorado*

COUNTRY TRIVIA

GEORGIA produces more pecans than any other state, with about 130 million pounds harvested annually.

To quickly clean a food grinder after chopping nuts, raisins, etc., run half a peeled apple or half a cup of dry cereal through the grinder to pick up the remaining bits. Consider adding this to your cake or cookie batter; I do.

After grinding meats, run a few crackers through the grinder. This, too, can be added to other dishes, such as meat loaf or meatballs.
—*Denise Kohlberg Atlanta, Georgia*

To freshen biscuits, bread or doughnuts, place them in a wide-mouthed jar and cover with a dampened paper towel. Close the jar tightly and leave in place overnight. You'll wake up in the morning to fresh bread! —*Cindy Weisbrod Lancaster, Pennsylvania*

Here's an idea for finishing up those odds and ends in cereal boxes:

Melt 1/2 cup butter or margarine, 1/4 cup peanut butter and 35 to 45 regular-size marshmallows in the top of a double boiler. When melted, pour over approximately 6 cups of any dry cereal combination.

Stir until blended and press into a 13-inch x 9-inch x 2-inch pan. Cut

while warm. This makes a fast and nourishing after-school snack.
—*Mary Daniels, Wildwood, Florida*

To keep bananas for a week or 2, put them in a white (not clear) plastic bag. Store them in the crisper of your refrigerator. The skins will darken a little, but the bananas will stay white and solid.
—*Dorothy Lisfield*
New Windsor, New York

For lighter, creamier mashed potatoes, add a teaspoon of baking powder before vigorously mashing.
—*Barbara Gracy*
Spring City, Tennessee

To keep potato chips, popcorn and other munchies fresh, keep them in the freezer until you're ready to eat. This is especially useful in summer.
—*Mrs. J.C. Parker*
Durham, Connecticut

Next time you need a little more work space for canning, preparing large meals, etc., set up your ironing board in the kitchen. It makes a handy extra "table". Protect the board by covering it with newspaper and a tablecloth.
—*Kathy Nelson*
Sacramento, California

Tomatoes sliced vertically, rather than horizontally, will stay firmer in your salad and help keep the salad dressing from getting watery.
—*Ruby Willliams*
Bogalusa, Louisiana

When you find cellophane stuck to the frosting on packaged cup-

cakes, hold the package under cold running water for a moment before unwrapping it. The cellophane will come off cleanly.
—*Diane Hixon*
Niceville, Florida

To keep strawberries fresh for several days, put fresh unwashed berries in a container and top with a folded napkin. Cover the container, turn it upside down and store in the refrigerator.
—*Mrs. LeeRoy Van Voorhis*
Caledonia, Ohio

To soften cookies that have gotten too crisp for your liking, put them in a plastic bag with a piece of bread. The next morning you'll have nice soft cookies again!
—*Patrice Melcher*
Fort Wayne, Indiana

A cake frosting bag and tip work great for filling deviled eggs —it's decorative and fast.
—*Dawn Lofthus, Olney, Maryland*

To measure less than a cup of solid shortening, fill the measuring cup with the amount of water that equals 1 cup. For example, if I need 1/3 cup shortening, I pour 2/3 cup of water into the measuring cup and then add shortening until the water reaches the 1-cup level. Then I just pour off the water and use.
—*V.C. Brendecke*
Seattle, Washington

To quickly cut butterhorn rolls, I use a pizza cutter wheel. Roll out dough in a circle, then use a pizza cutter to cut it into pie-shaped pieces. It's very easy this way, and the dough doesn't stick to the cutter.

—*Mrs. James Kelley*
Hastings, Iowa

When a cake or cookie recipe calls for corn syrup or molasses, first use nonstick cooking spray on your utensils and measuring cups. You'll be surprised at how easily everything comes off later.

—*Nancy Goss, Pocahontas, Illinois*

Coffee filters are difficult to separate because they're packed tightly. I cut a slit about 1/2 inch long through the corrugated sides of all the filters at once. It takes a sharp pair of scissors, but the slit helps me peel the filters apart.

—*Martin Wurth*
Paducah, Kentucky

To see if baking powder or soda is still working, put a teaspoonful in hot water. If the water fizzles, it's still good.   —*Martha Beckman*
Granada Hills, California

Mustard and ketchup squeeze bottles, emptied and thoroughly washed, are great for decorating cakes and cookies. Fill them with frosting and you can write or make designs with no mess!

—*Edith Lundquist*
Wollaston, Massachusetts

When cooking cabbage, place a small cup or can half-filled with vinegar on the stove. It will absorb all the odor from the cabbage.

—*Mrs. Larry Kerns*
West Mansfield, Ohio

Do you like pickled eggs? Next time you buy pickles at the store, save the brine and boil eight or so eggs in it. Cool and peel them, then return to the brine along with 1/4 teaspoon salt and 1 teaspoon vinegar. Refrigerate for about 2 days…then enjoy!

—*Joseph Schmidt*
Center, North Dakota

When baking a double pie crust, here's a way to keep the outer edge of the crust from getting too brown:

Cut out the center of a foil pie tin and place it over the pie. The center crust will get brown, but the outer edges won't burn. It's a lot easier than piecing tinfoil around the edges.   —*Dorothy Krec*
Lac du Flambeau, Wisconsin

Before frying bacon—especially "fatty" pieces—coat the strips in flour. The flour absorbs the fat and makes for crisp bacon.

—*Dorothy Boorse, Casper, Wyoming*

When a recipe calls for both dry mustard and salt, mix them together first before adding. The mustard will not float this way.

—*Mrs. Wendell Davis*
Albuquerque, New Mexico

When food sticks to pans after cooking, the best way to ensure an easier washup later is to remove the food from the pot or pan, then put the lid back on right away. When it comes time for washing, the clean-up will be much easier.
—*Gladys Bednark, Pierz, Minnesota*

Before peeling new potatoes, soak them in salted cold water for half an hour. Not only do the skins come off easily…your hands don't get stained. —*Ruby Shelton King, North Carolina*

When I buy bacon, I lay all the pieces on a large cookie sheet so none of the pieces are overlapping. Then I place the cookie sheet in the freezer until the bacon is frozen.

Once it is all frozen, I put the pieces in a large freezer bag and return the bacon to the freezer. When I need a strip or more, I can take them out and they're not all stuck together. —*Joyce King Ridgeland, South Carolina*

Adding a tablespoon of vinegar to your homemade pie crust while mixing it will help prevent sogginess. —*Emma Miller Conewango Valley, New York*

When making chocolate cake, use cocoa instead of flour to coat your cake pan. This will keep the cake from having that white-flour

"dust" on it when you remove it from the pan. —*Lois Hill Lexington, North Carolina*

A deep-fryer basket comes in handy when hard-cooking eggs or boiling small vegetables—it makes it easy to lift foods out of boiling water for cooling without risking being burned by the hot water.
—*Hazel Steele, Camden, Ohio*

When you buy a package of bacon, cook it all, drain it and freeze. When you want one or more slices, they're ready to heat up in the microwave. This is especially handy for people living alone.
—*Ruth Johnson Avon Park, Florida*

To save time cutting fresh rhubarb, run it through the thick slicing blade of your food processor.
—*Sue Whitefield Peterborough, Ontario*

A spatula comes in handy for separating stubborn or still-frozen strips of bacon. —*Irene Halgren Great Falls, Montana*

When you want to be assured your cauliflower is "snow-white", cook or steam it with a wedge of lemon and about 1/4 cup of milk. It works even when the cauliflower is not real fresh. It will improve its looks and taste.
—*Mrs. Robert Davidson Buellton, California*

Add "zip" to your popcorn by sprinkling dry salad dressing mix on

it after it's made. (Don't use too much—a little goes a long way.) Or, if you have a sweet tooth, use powdered fruit-flavored gelatin. Sugar-free works just as well as regular.
—*Nancy Omvig*
Eagle Grove, Iowa

When I bring chicken home
from the grocery store, I wash it, put it in a freezer bag, pour marinade on it and freeze the entire package. It saves so much time. When it is thawed, I just throw it on the grill.
—*Linda Grathan*
Roswell, Georgia

Don't discard vita-
min-rich liquid when draining canned vegetables. Store it in a tightly covered container in your freezer and use it as a base when you make vegetable soup.
—*Karen Ann Bland*
Gove, Kansas

When you're frying bacon, does
it sometimes sizzle and pop all over you and your stovetop? Throw a few celery leaves in the pan along with the bacon. Believe it or not, the celery leaves will stop the bacon grease from splattering.
—*Betty DeOrnellas*
Millington, Michigan

To make perfectly round hamburger patties, use the hollow
ring from a large-mouth canning jar. Press the meat into the circle and push out onto paper. This results in attractive perfect patties for freezing or using immediately. No one will complain about the size, either!
—*Shirley Flatau*
St. Paul, Minnesota

Don't throw away potatoes that
have become soft and wrinkled. Peel them, place in a bowl, cover with cold water and refrigerate for a few hours or overnight. They will become firm again.
—*Mrs. Ben Hansen*
Cottonwood, Arizona

When you grate an onion, don't
cut off the root end. Just pull off the peelings, wash and dry the onion, then grate it. The root will hold the onion together until you've grated all but the outside layer.
—*Mrs. Glenn Talbott*
Veneta, Oregon

After squeezing an orange,
lemon or grapefruit, turn the rind inside out and rub the pulp over the sink. Then put it in the disposal. This cleans the sink and creates a nice fresh smell. —*Mildred Everett*
Pine Bluff, Arkansas

Don't throw out those bread
crusts you don't use! Put them in a plastic bag and freeze them. The next time you bake, get some old

crusts out of the freezer and put one or two in the top of a jar of fresh cookies.

The crusts will keep the cookies fresh longer. After the crusts get hard, replace them with new ones. If you're like me and bake a lot around Christmas, you'll use a lot of old crusts.   —*Janne Atkinson*
Sheffield Lake, Ohio

Before using your cheese grater, spray it with nonstick cooking spray. That makes cleanup a breeze! The cheese washes right off without any scrubbing.   —*Leslie Hampel*
Palmer, Texas

When recipes call for a small measurement of an item, you sometimes have no choice but to open a large package. That's often the case with tomato paste. So, to have 1 or 2 tablespoons readily available, I measure tablespoon-size dollops onto a plate, put the whole plate inside a zip-top bag and then keep the plate in the freezer.   —*Verle Darby*
Modesto, California

Don't throw away sweet pickle juice, especially if it is from chunk pickles mixed with spices. Instead,

 pour the juice into a kettle and add a can of drained small whole beets.

Bring to a boil, then simmer for about 5 minutes. Pour into a serving dish and refrigerate. Now you've

got some quickly made pickled beets.   —*Louisa Schell*
Beaverton, Michigan

Whenever I'm making a big batch of cookies or other goodies, I double the work space in my small kitchen by fully opening all the drawers and laying cookie sheets across the sides.

This way, the table remains clear for rolling, cutting and shaping dough. You can have cookie sheets ready to pop into the oven as soon as the previous ones are ready to come out.   —*Lillian Sykora*
Bolingbrook, Illinois

When making hamburgers, put the patties in a cold skillet. They won't stick so much when you try to flip them. This also works for sausage patties.   —*Verna Cross*
Harrisonburg, Virginia

Don't throw away shriveled lemons. If you soak them in water overnight, they will be fresh and usable in the morning.
—*Mary Stager*
Silver Bay, Minnesota

A slice of stale bread placed on top of cabbage while it is cooking absorbs the odor. Of course, I always discard the bread when cooking is finished.   —*Florence Bush*
Brazil, Indiana

I do a lot of bread baking. One of my favorite recipes calls for milk to be scalded, then cooled and added to the yeast. I am an impatient person and so have tried to find

To keep your pie crust nice and flat (for cream pies), place another pie pan of equal size on top of the crust and press down. Leave it there until crust is baked.
—*Avis Reese, Hallock, Minnesota*

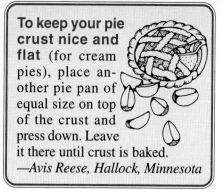

Here's a way to recycle the foil from sticks of margarine and cook potatoes that taste better.

I save the foil from margarine sticks and then wrap one or more of the pieces around a potato when I'm going to bake it. Place the butter side of the foil against the potato. It adds flavor and keeps the potato soft.
—*Christine Stutzman*
Goshen, Indiana

ways to shorten the time it takes to cool the milk.

I put four to five ice cubes in a tight-sealing plastic freezer bag and swish the bag around in the milk. Use a candy thermometer to check the temperature because cooling is rapid. —*Karen Van Keuren*
U.S. Army, Germany

To make bread crumbs, put stale bread in a paper bag and twist the top to close it. Once the bread has dried, grate it or put it through a blender. It will not mold if dried this way. —*Dorothy Labart*
Alva, Florida

Both a potato masher and pastry blender work great for smoothly and evenly mixing up the ingredients for a sandwich spread like chicken or ham salad.
—*Olga Holten, Houston, Texas*

When you have to slice, dice, mince or chop onions, always cut off the top and leave the root end alone. As long as the root end isn't cut, it will never make you cry. Try it! —*Helen Lobitz*
Cincinnati, Ohio

Easily shell lima beans by taking a vegetable peeler and cutting over the outside seam of the pod two or three times. Open the cut side of the pod and remove the beans— this saves lots of sore fingers.
—*Maurine Hoffman*
Bellville, Ohio

For tasty flavorings in cakes and frostings, save the peels from oranges, lemons, limes and grapefruit, cut them into long thin strips and mince in a blender at high speed. Store in an airtight container until needed. —*Lorraine Vohen*
Beaver Dam, Wisconsin

I like to use the plastic top from an empty shortening can to clean up messes and spills on the kitchen counter. Just cut the top in half... you can even scoop up a broken egg with it. —*Fay Meredith*
Clark Fork, Idaho

I have been putting a pinch of dry mustard in my coffee for more than 50 years. The mustard takes away the slight bitterness of the coffee. —*Thelma Litchard*
Jasport, New York

For the lightest pancakes or waffles you ever tasted, use club soda instead of the usual milk. But you must use all of the batter as soon as it's made because it can't be stored. —*Jean Tuten Easley, South Carolina*

If brown sugar has hardened, use a grater to "shave" it.
—*Teresa Daniels Huntington, Indiana*

Freeze extra tomatoes in the summer by cutting them in quarters and packing in half-gallon freezer bags. When you need tomatoes for stews or soups, remove what you need and run them under cool water—the skins slip right off.
—*Martha Williams, Jerome, Idaho*

I find that dipping beaters in hot water before mixing keeps shortening from clinging, especially if the shortening is cold. —*Mary Yode Montezuma, Georgia*

Does your pasta stick together when you refrigerate it? Add a little vegetable oil first.
—*Elizabeth Altstaetter Bellefontaine, Ohio*

I buy large bags of onions on sale, peel them, chop them in my food processor and freeze them in plastic bags in desired amounts. This is great for later use in soups and casseroles. —*Millie Kozlak St. Paul, Minnesota*

Here's a way to freeze a casserole without having to leave the dish you cooked it in in the freezer very long. Before making the casserole, line the dish with several layers of foil. After the casserole has been cooked and frozen, pull it out of the dish with the foil.

Then wrap the foil completely around the frozen casserole and return it to the freezer *without* the dish.
—*Becky Hade Devore, California*

Keep your flour sifter in a plastic storage bag so you don't have to wash it after each use.

To keep brown sugar from caking up after you open the box, put a piece of lettuce in with it. Change the lettuce whenever it dries out.
—*Dorothy Lehman Hamilton, New York*

Put a layer of marshmallows in the bottom of pumpkin pie, then add the filling. It will make a nice topping as the marshmallows will come to the top as it bakes.
—*Mrs. Edwin Hill Santa Barbara, California*

Here is a quick way to make creamy whipped honey. Soften 1/2 cup butter or margarine and beat with a fork until creamy. Slowly add

3/4 cup honey, beating until smooth. Store in the refrigerator. It's delicious! —*Christa Hebbel Eldridge, Iowa*

I keep a lazy Susan in my refrigerator for storing leftovers. Small containers don't get pushed to the back, and one "spin" lets you know what you need to use up.
—*Theone Neel, Bastian, Virginia*

Looking for an easier way to slice cinnamon roll dough? Slide a length of waxed dental floss under the roll, bring the two ends straight up, cross them and pull. This will give you nice round slices and the floss won't stick to the dough.
—*Penny McNutt Winner, South Dakota*

I pour snacks like pretzels into a colander dish before serving to get rid of some of the extra salt.
—*Y.M. Bassett Laurel Springs, New Jersey*

Store onions in an old piece of hosiery with a knot tied between each one. This enables you to remove one that sprouts without harming the others.
—*Esther Brown, Oakville, Iowa*

Don't have sour cream on hand? You can make sour cream by using 1 cup of sweet cream and adding 4 teaspoons of lemon juice or vinegar. Similarly, you can substitute whole milk for sour milk by adding the same.
—*Juanita Packard Oklahoma City, Oklahoma*

If you're in a hurry while making biscuits, roll out the dough and cut it into squares. This way, you won't have scraps that you must roll out and cut again. —*Jean Tuten Easley, South Carolina*

Freeze leftover peach or pear juice from canned fruit and use it in your next batch of applesauce. You won't need to add any sugar.
—*Mabel Embler Guilderland, New York*

I like to save beef, chicken or pork broth in a jar, but I don't like to skim the fat off the top. To avoid this, I simply store the jar upside down in the refrigerator. Then, when I turn it right side up to use, the fat is on the bottom. —*Karen Miller Gallipolis, Ohio*

If you burn biscuits on the bottom, don't throw them away. Instead, rub them gently over a cheese/vegetable grater to remove the burned layer. —*Felice Anspacher Agoura Hills, California*

Save the round cardboard pieces used under frozen pizzas and cover them with aluminum foil. They make great platforms for decorating cakes! —*Debbie Hall Goreville, Illinois*

If a recipe calls for softened butter and yours is hard, just shave

it into small pieces with a grater. It makes the butter much easier to stir in. —*Lori Crum*
Grand Lake, Colorado

If muffins stick to the pan after baking, place the hot pan on a wet towel and they will slide right out. —*Marie Esch, Monee, Illinois*

Popcorn frozen in a plastic sandwich bag makes a super emergency ice pack. —*Helen Backus*
Barberton, Ohio

If you frequently use grated or shredded cheese, process several pounds at a time, then divide it up in reusable margarine containers. Put the containers in the freezer, then thaw as needed. —*Chris Hausted*
Lincoln, Nebraska

Since I'm too busy picking fruit during the summer to make jam, I pulp the fruit and freeze it in amounts needed for jam recipes. Then, during the year, I can make jam whenever I want.
—*Shirley Sybesma*
Ontario, California

In a pinch, an 8-ounce yogurt cup doubles as a 1-cup measuring device. —*Violet Watkins*
Pasco, Washington

Instead of baking a whole recipe of cookies at one time, arrange some of them unbaked on a cookie sheet and freeze them overnight. The next morning you can put them in a plastic bag and keep them in the refrigerator. Then, anytime you want fresh-baked cookies, put them on a cookie sheet, let thaw for an hour or so and bake.
—*Alice Pfingsten, Sibley, Iowa*

Make your own "slice and bake" cookies to bake at a moment's notice: Place cookie dough on waxed paper and roll up, tape the ends of the paper and refrigerate or freeze. Then all you need to do is slice the roll, place slices on cookie sheets and bake.
—*Kathryn Simmons*
Point Pleasant, West Virginia

If you're having trouble getting cookies off a cookie sheet, slide a strand of unwaxed dental floss under them. They'll slip right off.
—*Lillian Staab*
Dover, Delaware

If your brown sugar gets hard, put it in a plastic container, place two pieces of bread on top and seal tightly. The bread soaks up the moisture, and in 2 or 3 weeks, the brown sugar will be soft again.
—*Mrs. Peter Schwartz*
Seymour, Missouri

Spray paper cupcake liners with nonstick cooking spray before filling them with batter. They won't stick to the cupcakes.
—*Helen O'Key*
Litchfield, Connecticut

To "chop" nuts quickly and without any mess, put the nuts into a plastic bag and give it a couple quick hits with a rolling pin.
—*Flo Burtnett, Gage, Oklahoma*

Instead of buying waxed paper, use the linings from cereal boxes. They work great! —*Norma Unruh Copeland, Kansas*

To always have crumbs on hand for casseroles, breading meats and other cooking needs, I spread left-over toast, garlic bread or stale bread on a cookie sheet and dry it on low heat in the oven. Then I put the bread in a plastic bag and crush with a rolling pin. I also crush potato chips and cereal crumbs. I keep the bags in the freezer, ready to use at a moment's notice.
—*Audrey Thibodeau, Mesa, Arizona*

Instead of cheesecloth, I use a metal tea ball to hold pickling spices when I am canning. Less fuss that way. —*Helen Glass Mickleton, New Jersey*

To distribute herbs and season-ings evenly throughout a meat loaf, first combine the beaten egg and liq-uid (if the recipe calls for them), then add the herbs and seasonings before the meat. —*Dorothy Boron Belleville, Illinois*

Line your freezer shelves with plastic-coated freezer paper, putting the plastic side down. Frost will col-lect on the paper instead of freezing on the shelves. When the frost gets thick enough, the paper can be lift-ed out with very little mess.
—*Geneva Block Virginia, Minnesota*

If it's cool in your house and you want to raise bread or doughnut dough, take a heating pad and place a tea towel on it. Then place the pan of dough on that and cover with an-other tea towel. Wrap the bowl with a third towel to keep it warm. Your dough will rise beautifully!
—*GeorgeAnn Frisdkorn Wellsville, Ohio*

If your cookie cutters aren't handy (or if, like me, you can't lo-cate them!), just go to your cup-board for a small can of corn or an-other vegetable. The can's just the right size and makes perfect round cookies. —*Dorothy Blessing South Sioux City, Nebraska*

Pour the crumbs from cereal boxes in a jar and use them when a muffin recipe calls for cereal. The assorted grains blend nicely and provide a wonderful flavor.
—*Dorothy Mills Hendersonville, North Carolina*

To crack black walnuts more easily, first freeze them overnight.
—*Hope Huggins Santa Cruz, California*

If you keep flour on hand all the time, place the flour in the freezer for a few days every few months. That will keep the bugs out of it.
—*Hazel Williams Gillette, Wyoming*

Instead of using a hand sifter to sift dry ingredients for baking recipes, I blend them with a wire whisk. It works much faster than sifting and there's less to clean up.
—*Jane Neave, Zion, Illinois*

If you need to move heavy appliances in the kitchen, first rub a small amount of vegetable oil on the linoleum. The appliance will slide easier and won't scratch the floor.
—*Kimberly Novotny*
Carson City, Nevada

To cook corn on the cob in a microwave, wrap each ear separately with plastic wrap after cleaning; twist the wrap at each end. Microwave on high for 2 minutes. It comes out juicy and crunchy!
—*Donna Church*
Duluth, Minnesota

Vegetable oil is wonderful for cleaning auto grease and dirt off hands. It leaves them soft, too!
—*Hilda Parker*
Colorado Springs, Colorado

I use carrot tops instead of parsley. They are cheaper, tastier and more nutritious. Dry the carrot tops by hanging them on the clothesline in summer, or leaving them in a pie tin for about 5 days in winter. When the leaves crumble, crunch them with your fingers and store in a sealed jar.
—*Marty Lehr, Torrance, California*

Instead of discarding orange peels, cut them into small pieces and place in water in a teakettle or covered pan. Simmer over low heat, adding more water as it cooks away. Your house will have the delightful aroma of a citrus grove.
—*Marie Kupecz*
Yucaipa, California

Here's an idea for holding recipe cards while you're cooking. Place a card between the tongs of a fork and put the fork upside down in an empty glass. This holds the card at the right angle to read and also keeps it off the counter and out of the way.
—*Barbara Gottlin*
Trenton, Michigan

If you use cooking spray on your outdoor grill, not only will food come off easier, the grill will be easier to clean. But *don't* use the spray when the grill is hot…only when cold.
—*Donna Brockett*
Kingfisher, Oklahoma

To easily remove pumpkin peels, cut a hole on top and remove the seeds and pulp. Then set the pumpkin in a pan of water and bake at 300° for about an hour. The rind will peel right off without wasting any meat. It works for me!
—*Edna Sutherland*
Clintonville, Wisconsin

To have plenty on hand for salads or sandwiches, I fry one to two packages of bacon at a time, drain the slices well on paper towels and then store in freezer bags.

—*Mary Weeks*
Central, South Carolina

A brand-new wok made of carbon steel should be "seasoned" once before use. Wash it with hot soapy water, dry well, rub about 2 teaspoons cooking oil evenly over the inside with a soft cloth, then heat empty wok over medium for a few minutes. —*Barbara Ivanic*
Cleveland, Ohio

To keep okra from "roping" while cooking, add a spoonful of lemon juice. —*Rubie Gantt*
Andalusia, Alabama

Recycle plastic milk jugs and store reusable plastic bags at the same time—cut a 3-inch-diameter hole in the side of the jug and stuff plastic bags inside. Bags can be dispensed one at a time through the hole. —*Janet Varan*
Trenton, New Jersey

To keep bananas from spoiling, place them in a paper bag along with a hard-cooked egg and close the bag. Store at room temperature in the pantry or on your kitchen counter. —*Erma Fridenpacker*
Kamloops, British Columbia

For a delicious quick lunch, layer hot cooked asparagus and sliced hard-cooked eggs on toast. Top with a cheese or white sauce.

For an outstanding appetizer, dip asparagus spears in a light batter and deep-fry about 2 minutes. Serve

COUNTRY TRIVIA

PENNSYLVANIA is the No. 1 mushroom state, accounting for 47% of all U.S. mushroom production.

warm with hollandaise sauce or your favorite dip.
—*Teresa Lilycrop, Puslinch, Ontario*

A slow cooker is perfect for preparing beans—but first precook them for 10 minutes in boiling water. Then drain and add beans and 6 cups water per pound of beans to the slow cooker. Cover and cook on low for 12 hours. Season to taste.
—*Pam Anderson*
Minneapolis, Minnesota

To keep brown sugar from lumping, empty it out of the box or bag and store it in a tightly sealed glass jar. —*Marjorie Ware*
Louisville, Kentucky

Use nonstick cooking spray on scissors to prevent sticking when cutting dried fruit. It also helps prevent pasta water from bubbling over if you spray the inside of the pot first.
—*Elizabeth Gaylord*
Eden, New York

Chocolate-covered pretzels are easy to make. Simply melt white or

dark chocolate in the microwave and dip your favorite pretzel shapes. Allow to harden on waxed paper.
—*Edna Hoffman*
Hebron, Indiana

To make whipped cream last longer on refrigerated desserts, sweeten it with several tablespoons of corn syrup instead of sugar.
—*Mrs. R.L. Davidson*
Buellton, California

For a refreshing, nutritious raspberry drink, crush ripe berries in a blender on low speed, strain puree through a medium sieve, pour into ice cube trays and freeze solid. To serve, combine cubes, sugar and cold milk to taste and blend at high speed.
—*Mildred Sherrer*
Bay City, Texas

When making muffins or cupcakes, use an ice cream scoop to put the batter in the baking cups. I use a trigger-type ice cream scoop, but the other kind works well, too.
—*Darline Broten, Viking, Minnesota*

To prevent the mercury in your candy thermometer from separating, hang it or store it upright in a cup when not in use.
—*Pearl Cochenour*
Williamsport, Ohio

Try using a drinking straw to hull strawberries. It works well and is easy to do.
—*Teresa Daniels*
Huntington, Indiana

To easily crack black walnuts, use a vice in your husband's workshop.
—*Lois Monk*
Maryville, Missouri

Before frosting a cake, put strips of waxed paper under the bottom layer. After frosting, carefully remove the waxed paper—you'll have a clean plate.
—*Joy Lepak*
St. Albert, Alberta

When making muffins that require sticky ingredients such as honey or molasses, first measure the required amount of oil. Then use the same cup to measure the honey or molasses; it'll slide right out.
—*Marlene Winch*
Littleton, Colorado

To tell a cooked egg from a raw one, place it on a flat surface and spin it. The cooked egg will spin; the uncooked egg will not.
—*Tom DeMaria*
Jacksonville, Florida

To tenderize meat with little mess, place a piece of plastic wrap over the meat before pounding. This will keep the juice from splattering.
—*Sherry Klein*
Edwards, Mississippi

When removing labels from cans or coupons from boxes, use a seam ripper to save time and aggravation.
—*Harold Morse*
Flint, Michigan

To remove fat from gravy, remove the meat and add a small piece of ice. The fat will harden and ad-

here to the ice. Also, to remove fat from hot broth to be used for soup, pour it through a piece of cheesecloth that's been rinsed in cold water. —Leona Prusha
Belle Plaine, Iowa

When rewrapping meat for freezing, I tape the supermarket label on the freezer package. That way I always know the date of purchase and the exact weight. Also, if there's a problem of any kind, I know where to return it and I have the proof of purchase. —Tina Calitri
Seekonk, Massachusetts

To take cool water on a picnic, fill a jug half full and place it in the freezer. Once frozen, fill the remainder of the jug with water. People will wonder how you got such a big ice cube in the jug!
—John Blatchford
Port Orange, Florida

When serving tuna, egg, potato or macaroni salads, use cake or gelatin molds for an attractive twist. Line the mold with clear plastic wrap, with about 3 inches extra around the edge. Pack the mold with the filling, flip it over onto a serving plate and refrigerate until serving time. I like to use a chicken mold for egg salad and a fish mold for tuna salad! —Lily Zandel
Culver City, California

To find the edge of cellophane kitchen wrap, place the box in the refrigerator. When it's cool, the wrap is easier to handle.

Another way to find the edge of the wrap is to use a piece of tape, touching the roll lightly until the edge adheres to the tape and comes up.
—Danny Lou Cunningham
Chandler, Arizona

If you're in a hurry for more ice cubes, leave three or four cubes in the tray when you refill it. The "old" cubes will chill the water faster and you'll have new cubes ready quicker.
—A.C. Schultz
Corona, California

When you boil sweet potatoes with the skins on, put a teaspoon of shortening in the water. It eliminates the hard-to-clean ring that usually forms on the side of the pot at water level.
—Pauline Powers
Siler City,
North Carolina

Cooked beans may be kept in the refrigerator for 5 days and in the freezer for up to 6 months.
—Kathy Smith, Bar Harbor, Maine

To remove silk from corn on the cob, wrap a clean dry washcloth around the ear of corn and rub gently. Wash the corn before cooking.
—Loretta Couch, Dumas, Texas

When your house is too cool to make bread dough rise quickly, grease the inside of an electric slow cooker. Turn the heat on low and allow it to warm up. Then turn it off and put the dough in and cover the pot. —Mrs. G.F. Anderson
North Canton, Ohio

Whenever I cook cabbage, I put a piece of celery in the kettle to kill the cooking odor. No cabbage smells in this house!—*Mrs. E.T. Bangert*
Waco, Texas

Before opening a canned ham, run hot tap water over the container for a few minutes—the ham will slip out easily. —*Patsy Steenbock*
Shoshoni, Wyoming

Wrap a rubber band around the handle of your mixing spoon if you have trouble with it falling into the gravy or whatever you're cooking. The rubber band will keep the spoon from sliding into the pan.
—*Lillian Mahr*
Minneapolis, Minnesota

When browning ground beef, add water to the pan. Instead of the grease frying into the meat, it comes out into the water and can be poured out. —*Donna Taylor*
Aguilar, Colorado

To keep rolls warm longer, place a sheet of tinfoil under the napkin in the bun basket.
—*Hannah Sagehorn*
Long Beach, California

When pouring paraffin onto the top of your jelly, try putting a string in the paraffin. Leave one end of the string loose. When you're ready to take the paraffin off, just pull on the string. —*Valdean Schulz*
Fergus Falls, Minnesota

When stuffing a turkey, I never tie it shut. Instead, I take the end piece of a loaf of bread and the piece next to it and use them to block the opening, with the crust side of the end piece facing out.
—*Beatrice Goguen*
Leominster, Massachusetts

To keep water from leaving a lime deposit at the bottom of a double boiler or steamer, add about 1 teaspoon of vinegar to the water.
—*Edna Frye, Tawas City, Michigan*

When I buy brown sugar, I divide the entire package into 1/2-cup servings and wrap in plastic wrap. These premeasured packs are real handy for baking. I do the same thing with chopped nuts.
—*Virginia McBride*
Edwardsville, Illinois

Before squeezing citrus fruit for juice, roll it on a countertop, pressing down firmly with the palm of your hand. The fruit will be easier to squeeze and produce more juice. —*Clara Nenstiel*
Pampa, Texas

When I make fresh coffee, I don't make it to drink...I make it to freeze. I use four or five times the amount of grounds you would normally use.

When this very strong coffee is finished brewing, I pour it into one or more ice cube trays and place in the freezer. Then, when I want a cup of coffee, I put two cubes of frozen coffee in a cup and fill the cup with hot water.

If more heat is needed, I use the microwave. With this method, I can have several weeks' supply of coffee in the freezer, thus saving lots of time and effort. —*John Novicki Salina, Kansas*

When I mix ground meat with other ingredients, I put the meat and ingredients in a plastic bag and zip it shut. Then I knead the mixture in the bag. This way, I don't have to wash either a bowl or my hands afterward. I can also freeze whatever I don't use right in the bag.

—*Helen O'Key Litchfield, Connecticut*

Dip fresh strawberries into sour cream or yogurt and roll in strawberry-flavored gelatin granules for a tasty treat. —*Anna Krawczyk North Providence, Rhode Island*

For a refreshing snack, combine 1-1/2 cups orange juice, a peeled banana and a tray of ice cubes in a blender. Blend on high speed until smooth and creamy.
—*Kim Young, Chico, California*

Eggs won't roll off the countertop while waiting to be used if you set them in plastic milk jug rings.
—*Carole Billig North Branch, Michigan*

When I am beating or whipping something with my hand mixer, I cover the bowl with a plastic lid from a large coffee can. I punch a hole in the lid and stick the beater through it. There's no splatter!
—*P.J. Remenecz, Burt, Michigan*

When celery loses its crispness, place it in a pan of cold water along with a sliced raw potato. Let it stand for a while and the celery will again be crunchy. —*Linda White Akron, Ohio*

An electric salad slicer/shredder works beautifully for grating chocolate garnish directly onto cakes or cookies.
—*Brenda Aileen Sommers Amery, Wisconsin*

When freezing corn on the cob, I remove only the tassels and the first layer of husk. To cook, remove from the freezer and microwave for approximately 6 to 8 minutes per ear. It comes out just like fresh-picked corn. Do not remove the husks before cooking.
—*Eunice Membrere Bainbridge Island, Washington*

Citrus peel can be a flavor enhancer in many recipes, eliminating the need for additional salt.
—*Cindy Black, Billings, Montana*

Here's a favorite fast cheese appetizer: Cut six 6-inch corn tortillas into six wedges and arrange them on a baking sheet coated with nonstick cooking spray. Top each wedge with 2 teaspoons shredded mozzarella cheese and 1/2 teaspoon chopped green chilies. Bake at 350° for 8-10 minutes or until cheese is melted and tortillas are crisp. Serve with salsa for dipping.

—Bonnie Gilbertson
Merrillan, Wisconsin

Freeze smashed or crumbly berries in heavy plastic bags for winter jam-making. You'll have more time then…and you'll appreciate the extra heat and humidity in the kitchen! *—Donna Murphy*
Tecumseh, Michigan

Out of pancake syrup? Make your own! Mix 1-1/2 cups of brown sugar and 1 cup of water in a small saucepan; boil 1 minute. Add 1 tablespoon butter, 1/4 teaspoon vanilla extract and 1/4 teaspoon maple flavoring. *—Edna Hoffman*
Hebron, Indiana

I began canning meat 60 years ago, but I just recently discovered this "trick" that other subscribers might want to try. To get rid of a stubborn brown stain in a jar, crumple up a paper towel and put it in right after removing the jar's contents. Then—since hands are usually too large to fit— swirl the paper towel around with a rubber or wooden utensil. The towel should soften but not tear as it removes the stain.

—Esther Hoffman
Redmond, Oregon

For foolproof scalloped potatoes, layer sliced potatoes, sliced onions, ham pieces, flour, milk and a can of cream of celery soup. Top with bread crumbs and Parmesan cheese; bake at 350° until sauce is bubbly and potatoes are tender.

—Susan Morris
Cazenovia, New York

If a chocolate cake is difficult to remove from the pan, return it to a warm oven for 30-60 seconds. Then invert it onto your plate or cooling rack. *—Marilyn Gift, Clive, Iowa*

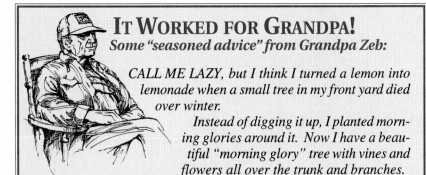

IT WORKED FOR GRANDPA!
Some "seasoned advice" from Grandpa Zeb:

CALL ME LAZY, but I think I turned a lemon into lemonade when a small tree in my front yard died over winter.

Instead of digging it up, I planted morning glories around it. Now I have a beautiful "morning glory" tree with vines and flowers all over the trunk and branches.

At Christmastime, I string lights on the tree. You might try something like this next time you're "stumped" by a dead tree.

For quick baked potatoes, first cook 3 minutes in the microwave, then 20 minutes at 375° in a conventional oven to crisp the skins. (Remember to pierce the skins before microwaving!)
—*Betty Maschke*
Young America, Minnesota

When preparing peeled apples for drying, drop them in pineapple juice, which will keep them from discoloring. Then drain and put apples in dryer. —*Leslie Meierding*
Missoula, Montana

For fresh-tasting frozen raspberries, thaw 1 pint of frozen berries in a syrup solution of 2 cups water to 1/2 cup granulated sugar. Drain and use immediately.
—*Ruth Dyck, Forest, Ontario*

Freeze whole strawberries on a cookie sheet until firm; transfer to heavy plastic bags or 5-quart plastic ice cream pails for storing.
—*Elnora Plaster*
Cushing, Wisconsin

If you use a double boiler to melt chocolate, be careful not to get water in the chocolate—it will stiffen. If you don't have a double boiler, use a small saucepan inside a larger saucepan filled with water and heat on low.
—*Linda Dragomir, Dayton, Ohio*

If syrup's too sweet to suit you, make a fruit topping for pancakes, waffles or French toast. Place 2 cups fresh or frozen blueberries in small saucepan; mix together 1 tablespoon cornstarch and 1/3 cup water and pour over berries. Cook over medium heat until thick and clear. Sweeten to taste, using artificial sweetener if desired. —*Jude Page*
Edenville, Michigan

Forever fishing for food buried at the bottom of your freezer chest? Pick up some stackable plastic crates with handles. Fill foods of one type (beef, vegetables, etc.) into crates of the same color to keep them separate.

I like to keep a pad and pencil nearby also to jot down each item and the date frozen, then cross it off when I use it. —*Elinor Fink*
Thornton, Colorado

Tie serving-size bunches of asparagus stalks together with kitchen twine and cook, covered, in boiling water for 8-15 minutes. Each bunch can be easily lifted from the water—then just snip the twine and serve.
—*Linda Spadoni*
Bethlehem, Pennsylvania

Fresh asparagus stores longer if kept standing, cut side down, in an inch of water in the refrigerator. Use a tall pitcher or large beverage container and replace water as needed.
—*Sheryl Sue Keefer*
Papillion, Nebraska

Grated citrus peelings can be made easily in a food processor. Remove peels with a vegetable peeler;

cut into 1-inch pieces. Place in processor bowl along with 1/4 to 1/2 cup sugar and process until peel is finely minced.   —Anneke Jakes
Pittsboro, North Carolina

Here's a quick potato appetizer: Boil very small new potatoes until tender, leaving the peels on. Drain and cool; wrap each potato with a half slice of uncooked bacon and fasten with a toothpick. Heat 1/4 cup oil in a skillet and cook potatoes until bacon is crisp. Drain on paper towels. Serve immediately.
—Dee Simpson, Jefferson, Texas

Hollowed-out orange or grapefruit halves make ideal "bowls" for relishes, fruit salads and summer desserts.   —Rose Berman
Norwich, Connecticut

If a bean recipe calls for tomato, lemon juice or vinegar, add it *after* the beans are tender. Otherwise, acid in those ingredients will delay softening of the beans.
—Georgia Hennings
Alliance, Nebraska

Many cheeses can be frozen. For best results, cut cheese into pieces that weigh less than 1 pound and are no more than 1 inch thick; wrap in moisture-proof freezer paper. Thaw in refrigerator. Varieties that can be frozen are cheddar, Edam, Gouda, Muenster, Swiss, provolone, mozzarella, Camembert and Brie. Do not freeze cottage cheese or Neufchatel.
—Pat Stephens, Lamesa, Texas

For more volume in beaten egg whites, let stand to room temperature before beating. Use a glass or metal bowl (not plastic) with a tapered bottom and a wide top. (Egg whites expand six times when beaten, so be sure bowl is large enough.)
—Claire Liska, Maplewood, Ohio

When mashing potatoes, use hot milk. If you have been in the habit of using cold milk, you'll be surprised at the difference in lightness of the potatoes.
—Sarah Dickinson, Sagle, Idaho

Lemon juice may be substituted for vinegar in many salad and vegetable recipes. Just a squeeze makes most vegetables taste livelier also!
—Patty Reed, Conyers, Georgia

Here's how to keep corn on the cob garden-fresh for up to a week: Immediately husk the corn and remove silk. Then place cobs in zip-top plastic bags in between layers of paper towels you've soaked in cold water. Refrigerate. When ready to cook, remove as many cobs as you need.
—Mildred Flory, Elkhart, Indiana

If you're making a cream-style soup, add a cubed potato to the mixture as it cooks. When you puree the mixture, you'll love the extra body it gives the soup.
—Joey Ann Mostowy
Bruin, Pennsylvania

Make super-fine sugar by whirling granulated sugar in a blender or food processor until powdery.
—*Barbara Wood, Glenview, Illinois*

Pancakes will brown just beautifully if you add 1 tablespoon of molasses to your batter.
—*LaFlorya Gauthier*
St. Didace, Quebec

Making chocolate-dipped candies? First prepare two or three small wooden boards by drilling rows of tiny holes (large enough for round toothpicks). Then insert a toothpick in each candy, dip, stick the toothpick in the board and chill until chocolate sets. As an alternative, use Styrofoam squares to hold toothpicks after dipping candies.
—*Diane Adkins*
Council Bluffs, Iowa

Making pie crust is easier if you mix the flour, salt and shortening ahead and store in the refrigerator

Use a wet knife to slice sticky, moist cakes and cheesecakes. (Keep a tall glass of water handy and dip the knife before cutting. Wipe with a paper towel after each cut.)

Unfrosted cake layers can be frozen on a cookie sheet until firm, wrapped separately with plastic wrap and kept in the freezer. When they're ready for use, just thaw, frost and serve.
—*Susan Holtz*
Ripon, Wisconsin

until time to prepare your pie. Then just add water to make dough.
—*Michelle Cochrane*
Wyandotte, Michigan

Melt chocolate squares for recipes right in their wrappers in the microwave oven. (Be sure the wrappers are *paper, not foil*.) Then just scrape the melted chocolate into the mixing bowl. —*Norma Mauser*
Klingerstown, Pennsylvania

Place your grater/slicer on top of the slow cooker so vegetables drop directly into it. —*Berdene Hofer*
Bridgewater, South Dakota

Nothing gets me hotter than boil-overs on my stove burners! So here's how I keep my composure when cooking rice or macaroni: I grease the top 2 inches of the inside of the pan, and the water stays just where it should. —*Joyce Sitz*
Wichita, Kansas

Save and freeze tangerine or tangelo peels to use in recipes when the fruit is out of season. You'll love the flavor in nut breads, cookies, cakes and icings. —*Nancy Smith*
Scottsdale, Arizona

Peanut oil is an ideal choice for cooking with a wok, I've found, since it doesn't smoke at high temperatures.

You can prevent spatters by adding 1/2 teaspoon of salt to the oil before frying. Then just omit salt from the recipe.

If fresh gingerroot is available only occasionally in your area,

mince it and freeze in measured portions to fit your recipes. Wrap well to avoid freezer burn.
—*Phyllis Erickson, Killam, Alberta*

Pie dough will keep for several days in the refrigerator, and for months in the freezer. Let stand to room temperature before rolling.

Making a lattice crust? Use a pizza cutter to trim crust into strips.
—*Shirley Roberts, Brea, California*

Out of hot dog relish and don't have time to run to the store? Drain the juice from a jar of pickles... place pickles in food processor... and presto—instant relish! Store leftover relish in empty pickle jar in the refrigerator.
—*Sharon Stoltzfus*
Gap, Pennsylvania

Potato salad is much simpler to prepare if you peel and dice the potatoes *before* cooking. No more waiting for the potatoes to cool or burning your fingers on hot potatoes!
—*Bonnie Viebrock*
Calhoun, Missouri

Simmer beans gently to prevent skins from splitting. Add a tablespoon of oil to beans while simmering to prevent foaming. To avoid overcooking, check on beans 15 minutes or so before the recommended cooking time is reached.
—*Marie Srolic, Bonnyville, Alberta*

To speed preparation, measure all cake ingredients before you begin mixing your recipe.

When baking a cake, don't open the oven door until it is almost done.

Let cakes cool completely before icing or frosting (unless directions specify otherwise).
—*Cindy North, Ontario, New York*

Toasting nuts brings out their flavor and aroma. Spread whole or chopped nuts on a cookie sheet in a single layer and bake at 350° until lightly browned, about 5 minutes. Watch carefully.
—*Mary Gross*
Bar Harbor, Maine

To keep fruit pies from bubbling over, cut small vents in top crust and place a macaroni piece upright in each vent. The juice will boil up inside the macaroni and *won't* boil over in your oven!
—*Mrs. Arthur White*
Lawrence, Kansas

Preserving dill pickles can be a messy business! To keep the hot vinegar solution from spilling over on your counters, use a porcelain teapot to heat and pour "pickle juice".
—*Ruby Neese*
Liberty, North Carolina

To easily remove the tough scales from the lower portion of asparagus stalks, use a vegetable peeler.
—*Nancy Clark*
Auburn, New Jersey

Most cheeses taste better at room temperature. So remember to remove cheese from the refrigerator about 20 minutes before serving.

Low temperatures are best for recipes that have cheese in them; high heat tends to "toughen" cheese. When adding cheese to a hot mixture, do it last and remove saucepan from heat immediately.

—*Carol Shaffer*
Edinburg, Virginia

To make a quick soup, chop and cook asparagus spears until tender. Drain the liquid and add a can of ready-to-serve cream of mushroom or chicken soup. Garnish with fried crumbled bacon.　　—*Lucy Euvrard*
Okeana, Ohio

Put orange peels in a plastic bag and store in the freezer. Then, when a recipe calls for grated orange peel, simply grate it frozen.

—*Sherry Mann, Ossian, Indiana*

Raspberry butter is delicious on muffins, toast or pancakes. To make it, blend 1 cup butter (room temperature), 2 cups confectioners' sugar and one 10-ounce package of frozen raspberries (thawed). Refrigerate.

—*Cindy Kuhl, Sayre, Oklahoma*

Recycle plastic gallon milk jugs into new uses. Cut the bottom off—then use the top as a funnel to fill baby calf bottles with powdered or mixed milk. You can also turn the top into a feed scoop by simply putting on the lid.　　—*Jana Lyle*
Haverhill, Iowa

Refrigerate fresh strawberries in shallow containers as soon as you pick them, and wash berries in cold water only when you are ready to use them. Do not allow berries to soak.　　—*Laura Iverson*
Flanagan, Illinois

To keep sugar crystals from sticking to the sides of your pan during cooking, butter the sides first, bring candy mixture to a boil and cover the pan for 2-3 minutes until enough steam forms to force sugar crystals from the sides. Then uncover and cook as usual.

—*Mary Ellen Wells*
Alliance, Nebraska

Stir homemade strawberry jams and jellies occasionally while they cool to prevent berries from floating to the top.　　—*Ida Wester*
Shelbina, Missouri

This is my method for perfect hash browns: Parboil potatoes until just tender when tested with a fork, then refrigerate them whole overnight. Next morning, peel and shred potatoes. Heat oil in a skillet on high and cook the potatoes until golden brown on both sides.

—*Jan Noonan, Bath, Maine*

Strawberry ice cubes are pretty in punch or in a glass of lemonade. Place a whole unhulled strawberry in each square of an ice cube tray,

97

then fill with mineral water, punch or lemonade and freeze.
—Sally Hoffman
Castorland, New York

Swimming goggles may seem like an unusual kitchen helper. Wear them when you peel onions, however, and even the most pungent one won't prompt a tear! —Lois Brown
Sioux Falls, South Dakota

To add a great taste and extra nourishment to tomato soup, stir in three or four slices of American cheese until melted, then serve.

For richer, creamier mashed potatoes, substitute cream cheese for butter and milk. Whip as usual.
—Leanna Boynton
Ophiem, Illinois

One medium orange contains 1/3 to 1/2 cup juice, and one medium lemon will yield 1/4 to 1/3 cup juice.   —Barbara Wood
Cleveland, Ohio

To blanch almonds, cover with boiling water and let stand 1 minute. Drain and slip the skins off. To ensure they'll stay fresh for later use, store leftover nuts—whether whole or chopped—in the freezer.
—Ceal Langer
Milwaukee, Wisconsin

The seeds from grapefruits or lemons can be planted and will grow into pretty green plants that are nice for the kitchen windowsill.
—Rosalie Jane Perfler
Ione, California

When stir-frying, I make additional sauce in a separate pan to serve at the table. It's great over rice.
—Marlene Miller
Hillsdale, Michigan

Slicing raw meat into thin strips for stir-frying is easier if you freeze it first for about 1 hour.

For even cooking, cut all vegetables into uniform sizes.

Measure all ingredients before beginning to cook. Once you start to stir-fry, there won't be time!
—Katie Koziolek
Hartland, Minnesota

To make an easy fruit syrup, combine 1/2 cup water, 2 tablespoons sugar and 1/2 teaspoon lemon juice; heat until sugar dissolves. Cool. Add 1/2 cup jam or fruit preserves. Add more lemon juice to taste if desired.   —Kristi Carroll
Grafton, North Dakota

Strawberries will form their own natural juice if you slice them, sprinkle lightly with confectioners' sugar and let stand overnight in the refrigerator.   —Darlene Russell
Rock Hill, South Carolina

When you broil pork (or any similar meat), put water in the bottom of the pan to keep grease from splattering or smoking.
—Pat Gossi, Oxbow, Oregon

To quick-soak beans, put 1 pound of dry beans in a kettle and cover with 6 to 8 cups hot water. Bring to a boil and cook for 2 minutes; cover and remove from heat. Allow to stand for 1 hour. Drain, rinse and cook beans in fresh water.

If you want to soak beans overnight, add 6 cups of cold water to 1 pound of beans. Let stand at room temperature at least  6 to 8 hours. Drain in morning; rinse and cook beans in fresh water.

Whichever method of soaking you use, simmer the beans afterward for about 2 hours or until tender, adding more water if necessary.
—Cheryl Miller
Ft. Collins, Colorado

When "very ripe" bananas are on sale, buy a bunch. Peel, bag and freeze them. Then, when you make banana muffins or bread, remove as many bananas as the recipe calls for, thaw, mash and use as usual.

—Trudy Croco, Lebanon, Oregon

Vary the flavor of French toast by using raisin/cinnamon bread instead of plain white bread.
—Darlene Rosten
St. Joseph, Minnesota

To wash raspberries, place in a colander and submerge twice in a sinkful of cold water. Drain well.

To freeze, coat a cookie sheet with a fine layer of nonstick cooking spray; spread berries in single layer on sheet and freeze solid. Transfer frozen berries to plastic bags.
—Candace Kreiter
Heaton, North Dakota

To prepare perfect whipped cream, chill cream, bowl and beaters before whipping.
—Edna Hoffman, Hebron, Indiana

Substitute onion salt for regular salt to add flavor to your meat pie pastry.
—Katie Dowler
Birch Tree, Missouri

To remove sand from fresh asparagus, boil 2 to 3 minutes, then drain and discard cooking liquid. Add fresh water and continue cooking to desired doneness.
—Michelle Cochrane
Wyandotte, Michigan

Don't say "nuts" to nut bread that's failed. Put it in the freezer. Later, thinly slice frozen bread and "zwieback" it in the oven (at 250°, until bread dries out). Serve as a crunchy nut-and-fruit treat!
—Nancy Smith, Scottsdale, Arizona

To keep frozen asparagus from sticking together, freeze whole spears or cut pieces in a single layer on a cookie sheet, then place in heavy-duty freezer bags.
—Marcie Keckhaver
Burlington, Wisconsin

Need to make a quick turnover crust? Thaw some frozen bread dough and use that.
—Laura Iverson, Flanagan, Illinois

CHAPTER 5

GARDENING SHORTCUTS & SUGGESTIONS

Add a few drops of castor oil to the dirt around plants to make their leaves a little greener.
—*Mrs. Arnold Paperfuss*
Dakota, Minnesota

If you must be gone from home for several days and have no one to care for your houseplants, cover them with lightweight plastic bags to retain the moisture.
—*Mrs. L.E. Ford, Portland, Oregon*

After saving seeds for next year's use, put them in your freezer. This will keep bugs and rodents out of them, and the seeds are sure to come up the next year.
—*Mrs. Tommy Barnett*
Auburn, Kentucky

Flowerpots around the railing on the porch are easily blown off by strong winds. If you drive a nail about 3 inches long into the top of the railing and slip the hole in the bottom of the pot over the nail, you will have no more trouble with a pot falling off.
—*Wilma Shauers*
Beeler, Kansas

To keep rabbits out of your garden, place dried sulfur around the edge of your garden. You can get sulfur at just about any farm or garden supply store.
—*Crystall Deri*
Chicago, Illinois

Pour 1 quart of oil over dry sand in a metal container. When through with your garden tools, work them up and down in the sand to clean and oil them.
—*Mrs. W.C. Jerris*
Somerville, Massachusetts

Use ice cubes to water indoor plants. They melt slowly and don't spill over.
—*Mrs. Eddie Nordstrom*
Winner, South Dakota

Instead of investing so much money in hotkaps, I use the plastic ditch liner my husband uses in his ditches. I anchor it at one end and keep it rolled up at the end of my row. When bad weather is brewing, all I have to do is go out, unroll the plastic to the other end of my row and anchor it. —*Mrs. Marvin Kuper Dalhart, Texas*

To start poinsettias, cut off a slip about 6 inches long and place it in wet sand in a can in July. Make holes in the can for drainage. Turn a glass over it and leave it there.

Keep the sand moist, but not too wet. It takes a while to root, so be patient. By fall, it will be ready to pot. And it will bloom by Christmas. —*Nadine Adaiar Townsend, Montana*

If you cut the bottoms out of gallon-sized plastic milk jugs, they make excellent covers for small garden plants. Just remove the caps to let in fresh air. They are transparent enough to admit sunlight.
—*Mrs. Tom Claflin Sheldon, Missouri*

Your plants will double in size and beauty with this once-a-month treatment. To 1 gallon tepid water, add 1 teaspoon baking powder, 1 teaspoon Epsom salts, 1 teaspoon saltpeter and 1/2 teaspoon household ammonia. —*Mrs. Tillman Charlie Ville Platte, Louisiana*

Fill a string mesh bag with suet and scraps of leftover food and

hang from a tree limb for those cheery winter birds.
—*Mrs. Otto Stank Pound, Wisconsin*

A geranium cutting can be started easily by boring a hole in a potato, placing the cut end of stem in the potato and planting the potato in soil. —*Ethel Bullock Waynesburg, Kentucky*

Mix pinecones with wood chips and place on top of landscaping fabric to inexpensively keep weeds out and hold moisture in.
—*Elaine Green Dodge Center, Minnesota*

A neighbor told me that when you start seeds indoors in pots, it's best to plant them in a small amount of dirt at first. Gradually add more dirt as the plant grows.

Do this and your plants will be much stronger and will do better after you set them outside.
—*Mrs. J.S. Millhouse, Piqua, Ohio*

Don't throw away the pole lamp that you're no longer using. Instead, pull out the wires, take out the bulbs, turn the light fixtures up and tighten the screws so the fixtures will stay upturned. Then place some potted plants on the upturned fixtures and you have a lovely planter for displaying your favorite plants.
—*Willeta Peterson Fremont, Nebraska*

During spring gardening, I put one of my small boys in his wagon and pull him up and down the garden so the wheels can mark the rows for planting. It's a fun way for me and my boys to get straight rows that are a good distance apart.

—Lois Noby
Great Falls, Montana

If you have a large garden, but not a lot of time to weed, put two layers of newspaper between your rows. This keeps the weeds down, which saves you a lot of time!

—Wendy Schoonover
Stroudsburg, Pennsylvania

Plant pole beans next to sunflowers. The beans will climb the lower part of the sunflowers and you won't need to use any poles.

—Della Whitesell
El Dorado Springs, Missouri

Keep woodchucks at bay by putting some glass gallon jugs around the edge of your garden and filling them with water. Apparently when the woodchuck sees its reflection in the jug, it thinks it's another animal and runs away.

Sounded silly to us, too, but it seems to work.

—Lessie Rissen
Woodward,
Oklahoma

To save overwatered terrarium plants from ruin, roll a paper towel very tightly and place it in the pot so that one end of it is just touching the soil. The towel will soak up the water in no time. Repeat if necessary.

Use this method to save any overwatered plant that is potted in a container that doesn't have drainage holes. —Alma Tallman
Atlantic, Iowa

If you want to keep tomato plants "standing tall" in strong winds, brace tomato cages with an old broom or mop handle.

—Margaret Shauers
Great Bend, Kansas

If you're the "pickup" person at harvest, wear a wristwatch and

IT WORKED FOR GRANDPA!
Some "seasoned advice" from Grandpa Zeb:

AFTER you use a flower vase for some time, it sometimes looks kind of foggy. Want to make it look like new again?

Just drop two denture cleaner tablets into the vase and add water. In minutes, you'll have a cleaner and newer-looking vase.

Now, if you're such a young pup you don't have any denture cleaner tablets around, don't call me. Call one of your more "seasoned" friends and test out your tact by "bridging" the subject!

time how long it takes the driver to combine the first hopper load of grain. You'll know about when to return to the field for the next load. (But remember time may vary from field to field…and combines may have different-sized hoppers, of course—so do take care with this timely tip!) —*Lynda Fretheim Shelby, Montana*

Place rubber crutch tips, or wrap strips of moleskin, around the handles of your garden tools. This will protect you from blisters and callouses and helps you get a "firm grip" on your garden chores.
—*Mrs. W.E. Jervis Somerville, Massachusetts*

In late summer or in fall, collect seeds from your flower and vegetable gardens. Let dry thoroughly in the sun. Place in plastic bags, label, seal and put in the freezer. In spring, you'll be all set for planting!
—*Elsie Kolberg St. Joseph, Michigan*

Don't throw away your leftover coffee in the morning. Pour it around your geraniums to promote blooming. —*Ethel Bullock Waynesburg, Kentucky*

Your African violets will bloom longer, prettier and more abundantly if you stick a few rusty nails in the soil alongside them.
—*Julie Klee, Streator, Illinois*

Don't forget that rhubarb *leaves* are poisonous. Eat only the stems. Pick stalks when they are as thick as your thumb by twisting (not cutting) them off near the base of the plant. For easy harvesting, gather the outer stems first.
—*Priscilla Weaver Hagerstown, Maryland*

At harvesttime, we put a heavy coat of floor wax on the bottom of each corn wagon. The cobs all slide out *fast* into the elevator!
—*Viola McCabe, Mt. Pleasant, Iowa*

Be sure you remove the flower stalks from rhubarb as soon as they form so all the plant's energy is directed toward the edible stalks.
—*Naomi Gardner Baldonnel, British Columbia*

Do you get splinters while raking and pruning raspberry bushes— even through gardening gloves? Put on oven mitts over those gloves for added protection.
—*Avis Nelson, Red Wing, Minnesota*

For a neater-looking garden row, measure as you go! Paint marks on hoe and rake handles at 18-, 24- and 36-inch intervals. Mark your trowel for proper bulb planting depth, too!
—*Lucille Pitkin, Forest City, Iowa*

Green peppers fresh from the garden just don't last long in the refrigerator. A good way to get them to last as long as possible is to wash them and hollow out their

insides. Then cut them into whatever sizes you want.

Dry them before putting them into a plastic bag, then freeze them. When you need green peppers next, in whatever amount, you'll have them right there—and still fresh!

—*Marilyn Nobles*
Ft. Ogden, Florida

To keep mint, lemon verbena, etc. from taking over in your herb garden, pull out the amount you need by the roots. Enough root will remain for the plants to continue growing. —*Micki Robideau*
Flint, Michigan

Instead of using gravel, line the bottom of a flowerpot by cutting a sponge to size. It will absorb water better and keep dirt from sifting out. This is also a good way to recycle old sponges. —*Teresa Hinson*
Mt. Pleasant, North Carolina

Save large salt shakers to use as handy dispensers when it's time for planting your garden. Fill them with seeds, then shake out in neat rows. —*Desoree Thompson*
Cabazon, California

To remove dead leaves from perennial flower beds in spring

without damage to plants, use a child's rake to get in among them.

—*Alma Hansen*
New Denmark, New Brunswick

We use four fireplaces to heat our house—so we carry out lots of ashes! I spread them on my vegetable garden plot for the next year, and over rosebushes and lilacs, as a good fertilizer base.

—*Joan Regenaur*
Nicholasville, Kentucky

You can treat tomato transplants to a little light reading! Dig hole just a bit bigger than needed and line with newspaper. It will absorb and hold more water for the plant's roots and will add nutrients as it decomposes. —*Mildred Sherrer*
Bay City, Texas

For slow and thorough watering of garden plants (such as tomatoes), punch three or four holes in the bottom of an empty

1-gallon plastic milk jug. Bury jug in the soil next to the plant and fill with water. As water seeps out, the plant's roots will absorb it. To add nutrients, put a dropperful of concentrated plant food into the water every other time.

—*Betty Splittgerber*
Sandy Valley, Nevada

When ants or cutworms are causing a problem in your garden, don't throw away your old coffee grounds. Sprinkle them around the infested area and the ants and cutworms will take a "coffee break" from your garden!

To discourage root maggots from attacking your cabbage, beets and onions, spread a mixture of lime and wood ashes around the plants. If you're just transplanting any of these, dunk the roots of the transplants in the mixture before setting them in the soil. If you don't have lime, wood ashes alone may do the trick. —*Ann Stovall*
Flint, Michigan

To avoid getting water on the leaves of your African violets, water them with a meat baster.
—*Violet Sticka, Bridger, Montana*

A teaspoon of mild detergent will revive a vase of wilted flowers.
—*Violet Powell*
Cowpen, South Carolina

If you don't have a pair of rubber gloves to wear when gathering okra, slip bread wrappers on your hands to keep them from itching.
—*Virginia Kiser*
Piedmont, Missouri

Sweet corn ears are ripe and ready for harvest when the top of the cob is rounded, not pointed.
—*Jeanette Strobel*
Brainerd, Minnesota

When cultivating cauliflower, try covering the heads with old nylon hose—it will keep them from burning in the sun and protect them from bugs. The nylon will stretch as the cauliflower grows.
—*Geri Yohler, Gypsum, Colorado*

Spend a lot of time on your hands and knees in your garden? Fill an old hot water bottle with sand, sawdust or Styrofoam packing beads and use as a kneeling pad.
—*Wanda Maness*
Reagan, Tennessee

Always water your lawn, garden and houseplants thoroughly. Frequent light sprinklings do more harm than good.
—*Mrs. W.D. Wondercheck Jr.*
Newman Grove, Nebraska

If your rhubarb patch is surrounded by quack grass, put square bales of straw all around the plants. They'll keep the quack grass under control, plus catch extra moisture and snow cover during the winter.
—*Eula Page, Didsbury, Alberta*

To save space in my garden, I put out cabbage plants and sprinkle radish seeds around them. By the time the cabbages leaf out, the radishes are all harvested.
Similarly, I'll plant onion bulbs around the tomato plants…the onions are all eaten by the time the tomatoes spread out.
—*Mrs. Victor Wittrock*
Halbur, Iowa

When digging up dahlias or gladiola bulbs in fall, separate them by color and store in nylons or in knee-high stockings. Use a same-color ribbon or rubber band to tie ends shut *and* remind you which colors you're planting next year!

—Mrs. Charles Musser
Selinsgrove, Pennsylvania

Save the water you've boiled potatoes or eggs in. It's nutrient-rich and, when cool, is ideal for watering houseplants.

—Martha Beckman
Granada Hills, California

Plants looking a bit sickly? Give them some first aid! Try feeding them a small amount of Geritol regularly for about 3 months.

To help cut flowers last longer, apply hair spray. *—Nelly Smees*
Hopewell, Nova Scotia

Don't discard shells after cracking nuts. They work nicely in the bottom of flowerpots for drainage.
—Elva Pate
Williamston, North Carolina

Keep dogs and cats out of your flower beds with mothballs. Use masking tape to reseal the open end of small, empty vegetable cans and fill about half with mothballs. In the closed end of the cans, punch a few small holes, then place the cans in your gardens. The mothballs will last longer and the odor will keep animals away.
—Sibyl Northcutt
Yoakum, Texas

After steaming vegetables, use the leftover water for houseplants. It's full of vitamins that make plants flourish. *—Lisa Becker*
Vulcan, Michigan

Do crows get in your garden and eat things? Tie strips of black, red or orange cloth to posts in the garden. When the wind blows, you won't have a crow within miles!
—Gayle Harrison
Frankfort, Kansas

For tender rhubarb stalks, be sure to water plants well for a day or two before picking.
—Sherry Maxwell, Seward, Alaska

My right "green thumb" pokes through garden gloves faster than my left. To avoid this, turn the gloves inside out after a washing. Then wear, wash and reverse again, repeating until the gloves wear evenly. *—Helen Backus*
Barberton, Ohio

To "silk" ears of corn, I use a wet terry towel washcloth. It does a great job of removing the silk and doesn't do any damage to the kernels. *—Eva Nell Glenn*
Bessemer City, North Carolina

Pudding, yogurt and cream cheese cups are perfect for starting seeds

in the spring. You don't need to bother with buying seed trays.
—*Sandra McKenzie*
Braham, Minnesota

Sprinkle powdered detergent or ground cayenne pepper in the dirt around your sweet corn and it will keep the raccoons away.
—*Ruth Schoeff*
Huntington, Indiana

Keep your fingernails clean while working in the garden by scraping them over a bar of soap before starting. This fills the underside of your nails with soap so dirt can't get in. When you're finished, just wash thoroughly and brush out the soap.
—*Beverly Jo Hamman*
Stratford, Oklahoma

For homegrown gardening gloves with "give", look for old cotton dress gloves (usually 25¢ or less at rummage sales). They come in larger sizes than most gardening gloves and won't wear out as quickly. When you're done gardening, wash them and hang to dry— they'll be ready for next time!
—*Neva Decker*
Dorchester, Wisconsin

Your ferns will love it if you add eggshells to the water and let them soak for a short while before using it to water them. Whenever I use an egg, I drop the shell in a container of water with a lid on it and save it until it's time to water the ferns.

In less than a year, my fern outgrew its pot, then was planted into a larger pot. I had to transplant it

COUNTRY TRIVIA

THE NUMBER of tractors surpassed the number of mules and horses on U.S. farms for the first time in 1954.

again later! I thank my mother-in-law for sharing her "eggshell water tip" with me! —*Rhoda Zimmerman*
East Earl, Pennsylvania

Put the "plastic peanuts" used for shipping packing in the bottom of your flowerpots. They're lightweight but still allow for drainage.
—*Sally Griffith, Gadsden, Alabama*

Dandelions will do a disappearing act if you spray pure white vinegar where the roots were after pulling. Don't worry about the grass— it will grow back fast.
—*Verda Baerg*
Fort Vermilion, Alberta

If you have trouble holding a cactus while repotting or transplanting, use a kitchen tongs to hold the plant in place while putting dirt around its roots.
—*Hazel Lutz, Wichita, Kansas*

Use a sturdy old dinner fork for weeding the flower bed...the tines get under weed roots better than most tools. Also, use a grapefruit knife to cut dandelions from your lawn. —*Martha Goessling*
Red Bud, Illinois

Wait until morning dew has disappeared before picking raspberries—dry fruit is less perishable than wet.

Store berries in small, shallow containers so that the weight of the top berries doesn't crush those underneath. —*Nathalee VanderLugt Edgerton, Minnesota*

Raspberries are ripe when they slip off the stem into your hand without resistance.
—*Frieda Nitsch, Boelus, Nebraska*

When you repot a houseplant, place a paper coffee filter in the bottom of the pot. This prevents soil from falling through the drainage holes. —*Jeanne Robinson Cinnaminson, New Jersey*

To kill grass in cracks of the sidewalk, pour full-strength vinegar on the cracks. Within 2 days, the grass will be dead.
—*Melody Haney, Barberton, Ohio*

Water hard-to-reach hanging houseplants by placing ice cubes on the soil around the outer edge of the flowerpot. As ice melts, plants "sip" slowly—and you suffer no more spills!

Kneeling got you feeling sore when you're weeding the garden? Try sewing knee patches to your jeans, leaving the seam open at the top. Then cut a kitchen sponge to fit each opening. Your knees will be glad you did.

Don't throw out those sprouting onions. Plant in flowerpots and place on a windowsill. With a little care, new sprouts will soon appear, and you can snip them off to use in salads, soups, etc. I do the same with garlic buds. —*Alma Hansen New Denmark, New Brunswick*

Old small round curtain rods make great plant supports. Place the rod in the flowerpot, then tie the plant or vine to it. Extend the rod to keep up with the plant's height as it grows. —*Rebecca King Bluff City, Tennessee*

I take an old mailbox to my garden in summer for storing gloves and small tools. It keeps them handy...and out of the weather! You can also easily carry the box along as you work.

—*Frances Hooper Normangee, Texas*

Ordinary eggshells can give your plants a nice early start indoors. Break several so the halves are intact, place them in an empty egg carton, fill the shells with good soil and plant your seeds.

When the weather's warmed and the plants have grown enough to be transplanted, all you have to do is crack the shells around the roots and plant them—shell and all. The shells act as a very effective natural fertilizer! —*Glenna Roberts Parkersburg, West Virginia*

I plant butternut squash around the perimeter of my garden to keep out raccoons. I'm told they don't like to scratch their bellies on the prickly squash vines and won't cross into the area. It worked amazingly well for us. —*Mrs. Delmar Miller Whiting, New Jersey*

When using hard water to water your plants, put a tablespoon of powdered ammonia in a gallon of water. It's better for the plants. —*Nadine Adair, Townsend, Montana*

To quickly remove the kernels from an ear of corn, scrape it with a shoe horn. —*Joan Albertson Tulsa, Oklahoma*

I tried about everything to keep raccoons away from my sweet corn. I was advised to put mothballs by the stalks. That worked till

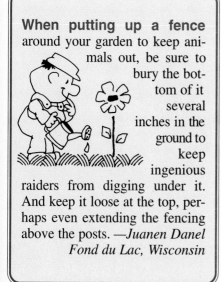

When putting up a fence around your garden to keep animals out, be sure to bury the bottom of it several inches in the ground to keep ingenious raiders from digging under it. And keep it loose at the top, perhaps even extending the fencing above the posts. —*Juanen Danel Fond du Lac, Wisconsin*

it rained and washed away the smell. I was told to spread human hair from the barbershop or dog hair along the edge of the patch. Again, that worked until it rained.

Then I was advised to put a radio out in the garden, and protect it by covering it with plastic. That *works* …if the garden isn't outside your bedroom window and you don't have nearby neighbors. For what it's worth, I found the raccoons particularly disliked polka music.
—*Roy Reiman Greendale, Wisconsin*

We have fresh dill all year long. After picking the dill, we cut the flowers off, then clean and freeze the rest in a plastic bag. Take out only what you need when you're ready to use it. —*Madeline Knapp Chicago, Illinois*

To keep fresh parsley from spoiling, wash, pat dry and freeze in plastic freezer bags. When needed, chop the amount required while it's still frozen. —*Norma Lee Volkman Westminster, Maryland*

I catch rainwater in gallon buckets, then fill empty milk jugs with the water and store them in the basement. My houseplants thrive on the fresh rainwater…and I conserve water. —*Sandra McKenzie Braham, Minnesota*

When your garden is producing abundant supplies of green peppers, take time to prepare them for quick meals next winter. Wash, core, remove seeds and dice the peppers;

then lightly pack the peppers into clean glass baby food jars, gently shake down the contents, and freeze. One jarful is the right amount for most family-size casseroles, soups and stews. —*Karen Ann Bland Gove, Kansas*

Coffee grounds placed on top of soil in potted plants greatly benefits them. This is especially true for ferns. —*Gibby Mikina St. Clairsville, Ohio*

Use your car mats as gardening knee pads. They never get wet and they save wear and tear on your knees and pants.—*Mildred Toomey Moorhead, Minnesota*

If deer are snacking on the branches of your trees, hang some strongly scented soap on the branch-es to discourage them. Also, try spreading human hair (the local barber will gladly let you take it off his hands) around your garden crops to scare off deer. —*Lenora Tennison Arthur, Illinois*

To get rid of moles, dip an ear of corn in roofing tar and place it in the animals' tunnel. They don't like the smell of tar one bit. You can get the tar at a roofing supply store. —*John Fulco Waretown, New Jersey*

When you bring in cut flowers from the garden to make a bouquet in the house, always cut the stems on a slant or angle instead of straight across. This apparently exposes more surface and increases the water intake, keeping the flowers fresher. I've also found that adding part

NIP OF NATURE
What's the "meaning of flowers"?

WHETHER fact or fiction, a noted flower authority some time ago compiled this list of what well-known flowers are noted for:

Geranium...Gentility; Goldenrod...Encouragement; Heather... Loneliness; White Heather...Good Fortune; Hollyhock...Ambition; Honeysuckle...Friendship; Hyacinth...Sorrow.

Ivy...Trustfulness, Wedded Love; Laurel...Fame; Lilac...Fastidi-ousness; White Lily...Purity; Marigold...Contempt; Myrtle...Beau-ty's Crown, Wedded Bliss; Narcissus...Vanity; Oak Leaf...Patriotism, Hospitality; Palm Leaf...Victory; Pansy...Thoughts; Peony...Indig-nation.

White Poppy...Oblivion; Primrose...Early Youth; Rose...Love; Rosemary...Remembrance; Shamrock...Loyalty; Sweet William... Gallantry; Yellow Tulip...Hopeless Love; Violet...Modesty; Water Lily...Purity of Heart; Yellow Rose...Jealousy.

of a can of white or lemon-lime soda to the water improves the appearance of the flowers.
—*Hazel Mallory, Vallejo, California*

Instead of throwing away 2- or 3-liter plastic soda bottles, cut the top and bottom off, leaving a 6-inch or so cylinder open at both ends. This makes a great planting sleeve for cabbage, broccoli and tomato plants. It helps prevent cutworm damage and creates a nice reservoir for water, too.   —*Paula Barnhart Olive Hill, Tennessee*

Slugs like a slug of beer! So if you have slugs in your garden, fill some flat shallow pans with beer and position around your garden with the rims flush with the ground. The slugs will be attracted to the beer, and when they get in the pan, they'll drown.   —*Charlene Miler Keokuk, Iowa*

Raccoons seem to know just when each ear of sweet corn is ripe, and will only then nibble on it. This method isn't easy, but worth the effort: Using a small paintbrush, paint vegetable oil on the leaves covering each ear, then sprinkle on some red pepper. It works!
—*Marcel Ausbarn, Hesston, Kansas*

During hot weather, pick raspberries *every day* or they'll become overripe.   —*Mary Lou Barnharst New Lisbon, Wisconsin*

If you grow lots of cucumbers, this idea will save you a lot of time in cleaning them. Just put them in your washer filled with cold water and some ice. Put it on "gentle" and, of course, no "spin dry". It does the job well, fast and easily.
—*Shirley Hamlin Edmonds, Washington*

During fall planting of tulips or other bulbs, put two or three mothballs around the tulips. This will keep gophers from eating the bulbs.
—*Martha Goessling Red Bud, Illinois*

A remedy for removing slivers (such as those from raspberry bushes that are difficult to remove with a needle) that still works today is to make a poultice from heated bread and milk. Apply this directly over the sliver and then wrap with a clean bandage. After a few hours, this concoction will "draw" out the sliver.
—*Phyllis Bunqart Jackson, Michigan*

111

CHAPTER 6

DEALING WITH STAINS & ODORS

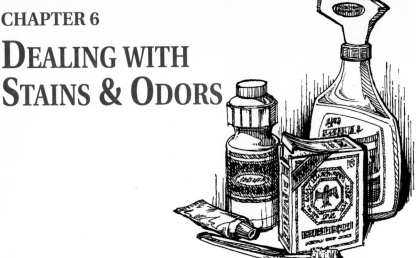

To remove lipstick stains from linen, treat the stain with petroleum jelly, then wash the item in hot water.
—*Marcia Stranberg*
Weymouth, Massachusetts

Not wanting to empty my freezer when chopped onions left an odor, I placed about 1/2 cup fresh ground coffee in a dish and set it inside the freezer to get rid of the onion smell. This method also freshened a china closet that had a peculiar odor even after being washed repeatedly.
—*Mary Jecklin*
Polo, Illinois

Place a peeled raw potato in your refrigerator for a couple of days to eliminate odors.
—*Ann Nelson, Minneapolis, Kansas*

A farm bathtub can really take a beating and end up with a dreadful ring. I invested in a child-sized broom that works beautifully for scrubbing out the ring without stooping or kneeling. Wet the inside of the tub, sprinkle with cleanser and sweep. The stiff bristles clean the tub in record time, and a quick showering will leave it shining.
—*Lacy Simpson*
Las Cruces, New Mexico

Household ammonia will remove stubborn scorch stains.
—*Mrs. John McSloy*
Havre, Montana

If your kids put pens in the pockets of their school clothes, you can remove ink stains easily by spraying ordinary hair spray on the garments. For old stains, you may have to apply the spray several times. Wash as usual.
—*Mrs. Ernie Straw*
Madison, South Dakota

Grass stains can be removed from clothing by using wood alcohol or ammonia. If material is colored, sponge it with denatured alcohol. Sometimes, if the stain isn't

too severe, rubbing it with butter-milk or sour milk will remove the stain. Commercial rust removers will also work on certain fabrics.
—*Mrs. Charles Goesls*
Two Rivers, Wisconsin

To avoid odor when frying fish, put a small spoonful of peanut butter in the pan.   —*Hollis Mattson*
Brush Prairie, Washington

A paste of baking soda and water removes perspiration stains and odor when rubbed on a garment before you throw it into your machine. Works great on hard-to-clean polyester knits, too!
—*Mrs. Lavern Wolf, Otoe, Nebraska*

Hands stained from vegetables can be easily cleaned by rubbing them with a slice of wet potato.
—*Myrna Sinner*
Delta, Colorado

To remove a soil or grease spot from a nylon or wool rug, just apply cornstarch to the soiled area, rub with a nylon vegetable brush and sweep up with a vacuum.
—*Mrs. Edward Kauffman*
Haven, Kansas

Salt is great for removing fruit and wine stains from your tablecloth or towels and napkins. Cover the stain immediately with salt; let stand a short time. Wash in cool water.
—*Mrs. C.J. Adams, Arlington, Iowa*

To remove gum from fingers or skin, simply rub peanut butter into the gum. The gum will rub right off.

—*Mrs. V. Walston*
Bedford, Iowa

I keep a squeeze bottle filled with bleach on my sink to squirt into my dish water. Those few drops are especially good at making short work of food odors.
—*Mrs. Byrle Cosner*
Woodhue, Illinois

To remove grass stains from jeans, pour a little rubbing alcohol on the stains. Wait a few minutes, then put in the wash with the rest of the laundry. Stains come out every time!
—*Julie Strefling*
New Carlisle, Indiana

You can remove stains from the inside of your dishwasher inexpensively and without scrubbing if you use this hint. Just fill the soap dispenser with dry orange-flavored breakfast drink mix (Tang) and run the empty dishwasher through a cycle. The dishwasher will sparkle!
—*Mrs. Glenn Kirk*
Rockton, Pennsylvania

An egg white will remove chewing gum from anything, including hair, without a trace.
—*Mrs. Ralph Stellick*
Stoddard, Wisconsin

An uncorked bottle of lemon juice is an effective bathroom deodorizer. The lemon juice doesn't give off any odor of its own, and is a pleasant alternative to sweet-smelling commercial air fresheners.

—Mrs. Charles Enocksen
Cedar Lake, Indiana

To remove gum from your carpet, put cheesecloth around an ice cube and rub the gum vigorously. This will make it hard. Then cut it away with a utility knife.

—Colleen Tarno
Royal Oak, Michigan

Hot vinegar will take paint spots off windows. And a good way to clean hardened paintbrushes is to soak them first in vinegar and then in hot soapy water.

—Mrs. John McSloy
Havre, Montana

One of the oldest ideas for removing rust stains—and one that still works best for me—is to moisten the stain with lemon juice, cover it with salt and dry in the sun. Then wash as usual.   *—Mrs. John Lewis*
Thayer, Kansas

To get out rings from shirt collars, rub hair shampoo into the collars. Wash as usual.

—Mrs. Chester Powell
Potomac, Illinois

Spray fabric protector onto clean garments under the arms, and you'll have no more perspiration rings! It's also good for men's ties, because it repels food drips.

—Mildred Sherrer, Bay City, Texas

To remove tar from a vinyl floor, carefully scrape off the excess, then rub vigorously with margarine or butter. Scrape again, then wipe dry with a cloth.

—Dorothy Kelly
Larkspur, California

If your thermos jug or other tightly closed bottle or jar picks up a musty smell when not in use, clean it thoroughly with ammonia water and rinse well.

To prevent this musty odor from appearing again, drop a clove or two

IT WORKED FOR GRANDPA!
Some "seasoned advice" from Grandpa Zeb:

I'VE LEARNED that if you slice an onion before peeling, the peel will come right off. But after you chop it, you'll still have to deal with onion odor on your hands. No problem: Just put a little mayonnaise on your hands, rub them together, then use soap and water. End of onion odor.

Also, if you find it hard to remove "fishy" smells from your hands, try washing them with toothpaste. This works so well my wife and I carry a tube of toothpaste in our tackle box.

into each container before putting away.
—*Maureen Beaver*
Sparta, Wisconsin

Rub a raw potato or vinegar-soaked cloth over your winter boots to remove salt stains.
—*Mrs. Henry Josephs*
Gardenville, Pennsylvania

To remove rust and tea stains from fabric, soak in lemon juice, then hang in the sunshine.
—*Kenneth Bates, Licking, Missouri*

Here's a way to remove chewing gum from fabric. Just put the garment (even a shoe, sometimes) in a plastic bag and pop it into your freezer. The plastic bag keeps the moisture away from the gum. When it's frozen, the gum will come right off.
—*Eileen Lawsin*
Giles County, Tennessee

Salt spots can easily be removed from leather boots with a mixture of vinegar and water.
—*Mrs. Albert Rehak*
Denmark, Wisconsin

Those stains on your nonstick cookware should be removed to prolong the life of your pots and pans.

Minerals in the water often leave a white spotty film that can be removed by rubbing the pan with a soft cloth soaked in lemon juice or vinegar. Before using the pan again, wash and dry it; then wipe the inside surface with cooking oil.

Stains left by grease and burned foods can be removed with this home remedy: Mix 1 cup water with 1/2 cup liquid household bleach and 2 tablespoons baking soda. Simmer the mixture in the stained pan for 5 minutes or until the stain is gone. Again, wash the pan and rub it with cooking oil before using it.

You can prevent stains by using a plastic pad to remove bits of food, preventing grease buildup and avoiding high cooking temperatures.
—*Agriculture Information Office*
University of South Dakota

To get onion aroma off your hands, simply wet them and gently rub in salt. Then rinse and wash with your usual soap—the smell will be gone.
—*Kathy Firmin*
Baton Rouge, Louisiana

To eliminate household odors, mix a teaspoon of vanilla extract with a half-pint of water in a spray bottle and spritz around the room. For stronger odors, use a little more vanilla.
—*Barbara Stonecipher*
Haines, Alaska

To clean ballpoint ink from most clothing, apply rubbing alcohol before washing.
—*Alice Neily*
Clarksburg,
West Virginia

"Dew" you know how to get grass stains out of blue jeans? Hang jeans on the clothesline overnight. The dew will make the stains disappear!
—*Margie Ward, Pasadena, Texas*

Tarnished silverware can be cleaned by placing it in potato water and letting it stand for an hour. Then remove it, wash it and it will look like new. —*Rosalee Zipp Grand Junction, Colorado*

If frozen food packages leave an inky mark on your Formica countertop, clean it off with window cleaner. There's no abrasive in it, and it leaves a nice shine.

—*Mrs. Wallace Tvedt Argusville, North Dakota*

To remove the odor of bleach from your hands, put a little mouthwash in your palm, rub hands together and wash off with soap and water. This is good for removing fish odors, too. —*Mrs. R.B. Gelver Bonnots Mill, Missouri*

Use a regular pencil eraser to remove stubborn black marks from no-wax vinyl floors. It's quick and you don't have to worry about scratching a shiny surface.

—*Betty Galvin Juneau County, Wisconsin*

Placing a slice of stale bread or toast on top of cauliflower as it cooks will keep the house odor-free. This really works! —*Suzan Wiener Spring Hill, Florida*

If you have a water ring on a painted ceiling from a water leak, you can fix it. When repainting, cover the area first with a spray lacquer. Paint after lacquer dries. The ring will not bleed through the paint.

—*Mrs. James Sleaford Mineral, Illinois*

To remove scorch without rewashing the entire garment, sponge the scorched area with a mixture containing equal parts of hydrogen peroxide and water. Rinse well, let it dry and try ironing again—only this time, be careful!

—*Mrs. John Lewis, Thayer, Kansas*

Chewing gum on the car seat came off when I put a piece of adhesive tape over it and pulled it up.

—*Mrs. Gary Wilson Odin, Minnesota*

Gritting your teeth over grease, grime and grass stains? Relax! Rub first with a waterless hand cleaner, then with a good liquid laundry soap and wash as usual. (This works well for winter coat collars and cuffs, too.)

—*Barb Juhasz Edon, Ohio*

To take flower stains out of my hands, I lather them well and rub with a piece of plastic foam. It does a good job.

—*Ann Zawistowsi Coon Rapids, Minnesota*

To remove rust spots from a garment, boil it in a solution of 2 tablespoons cream of tartar to 1 quart of water for about 10 minutes. Rinse well.
—*Francis Markham*
Dunn County, Wisconsin

Shortening can make short work of removing oil or tar from work clothes—just rub some into the spot and wash as usual. —*Rhoda King*
Cochranville, Pennsylvania

To keep your hands from smelling when you're working with fish, chill the fish thoroughly before you begin to prepare it.
—*Teresa Daniels*
Huntington, Indiana

During the winter when we have the central heat on, I slip a static cling-free dryer sheet in the vents, weaving it in and out of the little louver bars. It not only gives the house a spring-day smell, it just about eliminates static electricity on those dry days.
—*Dolly-Marie McClure*
Orangevale, California

To remove fish odor from your hands, hold a stainless steel spoon under the cold water faucet and rinse your hands with the water that cascades off the spoon.
—*Scharlotte Klein*
Boonville, Missouri

Here's a good ecological way to recycle excess cooking fat: Just pour it in an empty metal coffee can and put the lid on. When you have about a cup, remelt it slowly on your stove, add about 1/2 cup of birdseed and stir.

Fill empty yogurt containers or paper cups with the mixture and refrigerate. When hardened, dip into hot water to remove, tie a string around each and hang in the trees for the birds to enjoy. —*Linda Steiger*
Forestville, New York

To remove the sticky price tags from new merchandise, rub gently with lighter fluid. It won't leave oily stains and is almost odorless. Of course, keep away from any fire or flame. —*Sue Kappen*
Cass City, Michigan

If your hog farmer's chore clothes are unpleasantly "aromatic", add 1/4 cup vinegar to the rinse cycle when washing them. Vinegar can eliminate hog odor from your hands also! —*Monica Penner*
Elma, Manitoba

To remove water marks from wood finishes, rub in some mayonnaise. Let it stand an hour or two, then wipe with a soft cloth.
—*Carrie Schumacher*
Fall Creek, Wisconsin

To eliminate odors while cooking broccoli, cabbage or cauliflower, toss a rib or two of celery in the pot. —*L. Larson*
Homestead, Florida

Room air fresheners aren't very efficient. I find a better method is to place a scented dryer sheet under the doily that I have on top of the toilet tank, or in the bottom of the wastebasket.
—*Betty Graham*
Valley View, Texas

To get rid of musty or damp odors in your basement, put a layer of barbecue charcoal in the bottom of a flat cardboard box (like the ones soda cans are shipped in). Sprinkle the charcoal with about 1/2 gallon of Epsom salts. This should be effective for several months.
—*Ruth Wilson, Newark, Delaware*

Eliminating cooking odors is easy with this tip. Just boil a tablespoon of vinegar mixed with a cup of water. That's it! —*Shirley Sykes*
Dover, Tennessee

Hydrogen peroxide works to remove blood stains from clothing and other washable items. Pour some on the stain and let it sit awhile before washing. Unlike bleach or other harsh substances, hydrogen peroxide won't hurt the material.
—*Mrs. Don Greetan*
Carlsbad, New Mexico

I save the waxed paper that comes inside cereal boxes, then place a strip of it across my chopping block whenever I'm cutting maraschino cherries or other red foods. This keeps the chopping block from getting stained.
—*Dorothy Peterson*
Tucson, Arizona

Get rid of odors in plastic food containers by stuffing newspaper in them, then sealing and leaving them for 2 days.—*Mrs. Allen Zimmerman*
Fairbury, Illinois

Here's a tip for removing coffee or other stains from white items—linen, cotton, lace or denim. Dissolve two tablets of denture cleaner in 1/2 cup of warm water. Lay the item to be cleaned on a flat surface and dampen the spot with warm water. Slowly pour still-fizzing denture cleaner over the stain. Let stand for half an hour or so, then wash as usual. *Do not* try this on colored items.
—*Eloice Markham*
Whitewater, Wisconsin

Potpourri blends add a pleasant aroma to your home, but their fragrance is generally short-lived... unless you expose them to heat. With that in mind, I stuff old nylons with my favorite blends and dangle them in front of the heater vents.
—*Tricia McKinney*
Eagle, Idaho

When babies or pets have an accident on the rug or mattress, wash with a vinegar-and-water solution to take away the stain. Then fill a saucer with vinegar and set it in the room to get rid of the odor.
—*Lee Nelson, Waco, Texas*

Prevent musty smells when packing away seasonal clothes by placing fabric softener sheets on the bottom of the storage box, and also between alternating layers of clothing. It works with woolens, too. What a nice surprise when you unpack! Try sheets in your purse or luggage as well. —*Betty Fields Hendersonville, North Carolina*

To remove coffee stains from cups or mugs, drop a denture cleaning tablet into it and fill with warm water. Let sit overnight. Do the same with glasses, bowls and basins stained by well water deposits. (Large items may need more tablets.) —*Catherine Chinske Havre, Montana*

When cooking strong-smelling vegetables, fried fish, etc., place a small amount of vinegar in a cup and place next to the stove. The vinegar absorbs all unpleasant cooking odors. —*Irene Moore, Cabool, Missouri*

To minimize foot odor in winter boots, insert a sheet of fabric softener in each one. —*Bonnie Gelle Grand Rapids, Minnesota*

Instead of using sachets to make the clothes in drawers smell nice, use a small scented candle. It's cheaper, makes your clothes smell wonderful and provides you with

COUNTRY TRIVIA

NEW JERSEY has some of the most productive fishing ports on the East Coast. Over 2,500 residents are involved in harvesting shellfish and finfish.

lots of readily accessible candles if the electricity ever goes out! —*Beverly Phillips Ellsworth AFB, South Dakota*

To get stains out of a carpet, rub foam shaving cream on the spot and let it sit until the cream dissolves. Wipe up any remaining cream with a damp sponge or rag. —*Amy Pech, Nekoosa, Wisconsin*

To remove scuffs from kitchen floors, squeeze a bit of toothpaste on the area and work in with a nail brush. Then just wipe it off with a cloth. —*Lynn Sled Coldwater, Ontario*

Has a missed crayon in a pocket accidentally "colored" clothes in your washer or dryer? Rewash the load in water as hot as the clothes can safely take along with baking soda (a half to a full box, depending on size of load). —*Deb Riness Traverse City, Michigan*

I use cream of tartar rather than abrasive silver polish to clean coffee or tea stains from cups. It's also good for cleaning stainless steel sinks. —*Margaret Borrecco Centralia, Washington*

If you like soft fresh-smelling clothes, try using vinegar in the rinse cycle of your washing machine. A half cup works with a large load. —*Martha Harrell Mulberry, Florida*

Make your own mothballs for closets by mixing oil of cloves and oil of cinnamon, then soaking cotton balls in this mixture. Place the cotton balls in muslin bags.
—*Mrs. T. Peterson Knife River, Minnesota*

Use baking soda to remove grease spots from carpeting. Brush soda on generously, leave overnight and vacuum clean in the morning.
—*Mrs. Walter Peterson Catawba, Wisconsin*

Summer's heat can sometimes cause garbage cans to give off an unpleasant odor. If you grow mint and it begins to overtake your garden like mine does, you'll have plenty to cut a fresh sprig and place in the garbage can each day. It keeps it smelling fresh all season long.
—*Michael Sienkowski Norwich, Connecticut*

To remove coffee or tea stains from cups and mugs without using an abrasive cleanser, place some silver polish on a damp cloth or paper towel and rub over the stains. Wash afterward with your regular dish detergent.
—*Sandra Burn Red Bank, New Jersey*

To get socks really white, add a slice of lemon to a pot of boiling water, then add the socks and let them soak for about an hour.

For perspiration stains, soak the garment in warm vinegar water.

To remove mildew, dry clothes in the sun after covering with lemon juice and salt. Then wash with detergent. —*Marcia Mooney Bend, Oregon*

Pretreating stains is easier than ever if you fill an empty roll-on deodorant bottle with liquid laundry detergent or prewash liquid. Just roll it on. —*Priscilla Connor Winthrop, Maine*

Put a few potpourri pearls in your vacuum cleaner bag. This will give your house a pleasant aroma whenever you vacuum.
—*Doris Mills, Bellefontaine, Ohio*

To make your own "prewash" solution for your laundry, mix 1/3 cup household ammonia, 1/3 cup liquid dishwashing detergent and 1/3 cup water in a spray bottle. Spray on collars or other soiled areas and wash immediately. It works great! —*Mildred Stubbs Hamlet, North Carolina*

Spills can "roll" right out of your carpet! Use your rolling pin to press down the towels that you're wiping up with—it covers a larger area faster than hands or feet, and it seems to make the towels absorb the liquid quicker.

—*Mrs. Joseph Faivre*
DeKalb, Illinois

Treat sneakers with spray starch to keep them clean longer.

—*Jo Weston, Tucson, Arizona*

To remove yellow stains left on porcelain basins by dripping water, moisten pulverized chalk with ammonia and apply with a stiff brush.

—*Renee Johnson, Pierpont, Ohio*

Remove tree pitch or sap from fabric by pouring boiling water on the affected spot and adding a small amount of soap. Rub the material together. Add more boiling water as needed. —*Marge Schloesser*
Hibbing, Minnesota

Do your pickle jars retain their odor even after you've washed them in soapy water? Add a teaspoon of baking soda and hot water to each jar, then let soak 15 minutes. They'll soon be sweet-smelling!

—*Janis Plourde*
Smooth Rock Falls, Ontario

Don't dispose of baking soda after it's "done time" in your freezer or refrigerator. Instead, moisten with water and use to rub off stains on dishes—especially coffee cups —in just seconds! —*Stella Blawat*
Viking, Minnesota

When I buy bars of soap, I put them in my bedrooms first. With wrappers removed, they "perfume" clothes in dresser drawers and closets. Later, after the bars have lost their scent, I bring them into the bathrooms—since time's hardened them, they last longer than newly unwrapped bars! —*Lorraine Vohen*
Beaver Dam, Wisconsin

To remove stains from plastic containers after storing chili, spaghetti or any tomato dish, wash the container and place in the sun for several hours. The stain will disappear like magic, and the sun will not damage the container.

—*Mrs. Clark Bloom*
Jacksonville, Florida

When the weather is hot and humid, dishcloths and bath washcloths often get a musty smell. To avoid that unpleasant smell, rinse them in cold, cold water after you are done using them. They won't get a sour or musty smell no matter how long they hang before you use them again. —*Margaret Anderson*
Hector, Minnesota

If you spill food on your clothes, wet the spot with cold water, rub it with table salt and wash. This works in removing spaghetti sauce, coffee or tea stains, etc.

—*Margaret Fauci*
Dumont, New Jersey

Cut raw potatoes are handy as onion-odor "eaters". Rub your hands with them after cutting up an onion, and the smell will disappear.
—*Betty Maschke*
Young America, Minnesota

To clean sheep-lined jackets, dust well with talcum powder. Leave overnight. Next morning, shake well outside and then brush out the powder. This leaves the lining clean and fragrant.
—*Nadine Adair*
Townsend, Montana

Fingernail polish can be removed from most fabrics such as linen (but not cotton or polyester fabrics) the same way you remove it from your nails. Just sponge on some fingernail polish remover and then rinse it with water. —*Ruth Johnson*
Rome, Georgia

To freshen up your hubby's favorite cap, spray it with a foam carpet or upholstery cleaner, then rub gently with a damp cloth. This won't ruin the "bill" the way washing will. —*Evelyn Siewert*
Cameron, Wisconsin

To remove grease from clothes, spread vegetable shortening over the stain. Let it stand for 15 minutes, then rub vigorously. It works!
—*Arah Mae Sheppard*
Bridgeton, New Jersey

Hog chores leave your hands with a not-so-sweet scent? I scrub mine with mouthwash, then follow up with liquid dish soap.
—*Helen Vroman, Milroy, Minnesota*

To freshen a room, boil some cloves and orange peel in a pan and set the hot pan of liquid in the room for a while. It'll do wonders!
—*Mrs. B.W. Register*
St. Petersburg, Florida

Remove dried fruit stains from linen by rubbing the spot on each side of the fabric with a bar of soap.

NIP OF NATURE
Where do insects go in the winter?

IT VARIES with the insect. Ladybugs who settle in northern areas, as well as orange and black monarch butterflies, migrate to warmer country.

Crickets scurry to underground nests, where they sleep or hibernate all winter long. Ants lock themselves in their homes most of the time and only come out on warm sunny days.

But most adult insects die at the end of summer. Problem is, they leave large numbers of eggs behind, which hatch in spring and start the whole process over again.

Then apply a thick mixture of cornstarch and cold water. Rub this mixture in well, then expose the linen to the sun and air until the stain disappears.

If it isn't gone in a couple of days, do this one more time. This trick always works for me!
—*Zelma Crossland*
Chatfield, Minnesota

Even badly soiled canvas shoes can turn white again when sprayed with foam upholstery cleaner and scrubbed with a brush. Let shoes dry and brush again for best results. —*Elsie Kolberg*
St. Joseph, Michigan

To clean a burned pan, fill it with boiling water and add a few tablespoons of white vinegar. Let it set for a while and then you'll be surprised how clean it rinses.
—*Rosie Atkinson*
Port Orchard, Washington

To remove a water spot from a silk dress, let the spot dry thoroughly, then rub it with tissue paper. Surprisingly, that seems to work.
—*Gibby Mikina, St. Clairsville, Ohio*

To remove tea stains from porcelain teacups, put a small amount of toothpaste on a damp cloth and rub it on the stain. Rinse the cup well and dry thoroughly. Presto, they're gone! —*Nancy Kline*
Larksville, Pennsylvania

To remove white spots or water rings from furniture, spread a generous amount of petroleum jelly on spots and leave them for a few hours or overnight. I left it on one bad spot for days. Wipe clean—it might take a bit of wiping. Then polish as usual.

I have used this treatment for 42 years and I've only been disappointed once. —*Mrs. McDonald Miller*
Morrisville, Vermont

Here's an all-purpose cleaner I've used for years: Mix 1/2 cup household ammonia, 1/2 cup white vinegar, 1/4 cup baking soda, 1/2 gallon of water. Combine in a glass or plastic bottle with a secure cap. It works for all general household cleaning. —*Jennie Harris*
Feasterville, Pennsylvania

CHAPTER 7
PAINTING & DECORATING AIDS

If you're doing some outdoor painting and find insects sticking to your just-brushed-on coat, try this. Add a tablespoon of citronella per gallon of paint and mix well. Bugs will be on the fly till the paint's dry! —*Mary Filion*
Swift Current, Saskatchewan

When hanging a picture, heat the nail with a flame before driving it into the wall. You won't crack or chip the plaster.
—*Mrs. Clarence Gisick*
Timken, Kansas

To make decorative place mats, arrange snapshots, greeting cards, pictures that your kids have drawn, etc. on both sides of poster board and cover with clear Con-Tact paper. —*Mrs. William Calhoun*
Walker, Iowa

Before starting a painting job, I always thoroughly rub my hands, face and a little way up my arms with petroleum jelly. This keeps the paint from absorbing into and drying on the skin. When I'm finished painting, a good washing with soap and water gets me clean in a few minutes—and softer, too.
—*Mrs. Dale Fisher*
Halliday, North Dakota

Add 2 tablespoons of vanilla to 1/2 gallon of paint to cut down on paint odor. —*Mrs. Edwin Olson*
Dallas, Wisconsin

Don't let the mess discourage you from painting. I line my roller pan with aluminum foil. When I finish painting, I simply throw away the mess. —*Bernice Dietrich*
Valley City, North Dakota

You can keep your screened porch or other room private if you paint the screens with aluminum paint. You can see out, but no one can see in! —*Mrs. R. Longnecker*
West Plains, Missouri

If you spatter paint and hate cleaning up with turpentine, try a little baby oil on a rag. It wipes up paint spots just as well.
—*Mrs. Roger Hesse, Denver, Iowa*

Dip a sponge into hot vinegar water and rub over wallpaper you want to remove. Before you know it, the wallpaper will peel right off.
—*Mrs. Fred Cluck*
Highland, Kansas

My kitchen had a built-in ironing board cupboard that I never used. So I lined the cupboard with inexpensive 1/4-inch paneling, added 1/2- x 3/4-inch cleats and 1/2-inch pine board shelves and made it into a roomy spice cabinet. It's now so easy to put my finger on just the spice I need, and it only cost about $5 to make!   —*Mrs. Rubert Kerl*
Dane County, Wisconsin

When painting a window or picture frame, rub soap around the edges of the glass next to the frame. Any paint that splatters onto the glass is easily removed when the paint is dry.
—*Mrs. Greg Pape*
Elgin, Nebraska

No matter how economical it might seem, never use leftover exterior paints for inside projects, unless the label reads "for exterior AND interior use". Some exterior paints contain poisonous chemicals such as mildew inhibitors that give

off fumes that are dangerous to inhale.
—*Mrs. Harvey Muller*
Danboro, Pennsylvania

To keep insects off the exterior of your freshly painted house, add a little insect repellent to the paint before you begin.
—*Mrs. L. Friesen*
Bowsman, Manitoba

After using patch plaster to fill in nail holes or other wall cracks, use a soft damp cloth to smooth the surface before repainting. This will save you from the messy dust that's left behind after smoothing plaster with sandpaper.
—*Mrs. Marvin Ulmer*
Bucyrus, Ohio

To preserve a small amount of paint for future touch-up jobs, pour it into baby food jars and seal with melted paraffin. It will keep for years without drying up.
—*Mrs. Harvey Rush*
Westcliffe, Colorado

Pop Con-Tact paper in the freezer about an hour before you use it and it will handle much easier.
—*Mrs. Ronald Schomberg*
Lone Tree, Iowa

When painting stairs, paint every other step. When those steps dry, you can use them to paint all the remaining stairs.   —*Hazel Hillegas*
Friedens, Pennsylvania

Many times I must quit painting to prepare a meal or such. Instead of cleaning my paintbrush each time, I just wrap the brush in plastic wrap. When I'm ready to paint, the brush is, too. —*Mrs. Phillip Hillery Cottage Grove, Wisconsin*

To patch cracked walls, make a paste with flour and your paint. Let it dry, and paint right over the crack.
—*Mrs. David Guhde Auburn, Nebraska*

Here's an easy way to shed some "spooky" Halloween light—paint an old vegetable grater black and place it over a votive candle.
—*Mrs. Edmund Hager Rugby, North Dakota*

To soften hardened paintbrushes, I soak them in hot vinegar and wash them in warm soapy water.
—*Teresa Hinson Mt. Pleasant, North Carolina*

Before painting screens, wash them down with a mild solution of ammonia. The paint will not stop up the tiny screen holes.
—*Mrs. R. Longnecker West Plains, Missouri*

Make quilting pattern blocks out of linoleum instead of cardboard. Linoleum is more durable and keeps its shape longer to give you more uniform quilt pieces.
—*Florence Gruenbacher Andale, Kansas*

For an attractive natural table centerpiece for fall, arrange Golden Delicious or Honey Gold apples in bowl with bright-colored leaves. For the Christmas holidays, select the

IT WORKED FOR GRANDPA!
Some "seasoned advice" from Grandpa Zeb:

NEXT TIME you wash windows, try my never-fail method of getting them squeaky clean and making them stay that way for a long while.

Mix 2 rounded tablespoons of cornstarch in a quart of water. Soak your roughest washcloth in this solution, then squeeze out most of the water and wash the window with the cloth.

Rinse the cloth, wipe the window once more, then polish the glass with an old soft cloth.

After windows have been washed two or three times with this method, you'll only need to polish them occasionally with a clean dry cloth because nothing—even water spots—will stick to them. You'll never "wash" windows again!

reddest apples available, then wash and polish them until they shine. Pile on a wooden tray with sprigs of evergreen. —*Margaret Hertzler Milton, Pennsylvania*

Apply a thin coat of wax to your wooden picture frames. It improves their appearance and makes them easier to clean. —*Helen LaMance Modesto, California*

When making bows, make the loop out of the strand on the bottom, and wrap the other strand over the top. Your bows will always come out straight this way.

—*Mrs. Bernie Starkey Berthoud, Colorado*

Save time when painting. Rather than cleaning the brush every time you stop for lunch or another chore, just wrap it in plastic wrap and then in aluminum foil. Put the brush in the refrigerator and the bristles will stay soft for several days.

—*Wilma Masolo Townsend, Montana*

I use bright paper tablecloths for wrapping large presents. It's economical and saves having to tape sheets of wrapping paper together.

—*Avis Reese Hallock, Minnesota*

When you're painting and can't finish the job until later, whether you're using latex or oil-based paint, just submerge the "working part" of brushes, rollers or edging pads completely under water. When restarting the job, roll or brush the wa-ter out on cardboard or old wood, and start painting again.

When I worked in a factory, we would paint for 3 months straight using this method, and I've been doing it for years since. It saves time and brush cleaner. —*Greg Mueller Dalton, Wisconsin*

Oven cleaner gets out oil paint stains beautifully and won't harm fabric. —*Mary Potts Groveport, Ohio*

Lay large groups of pictures on your floor to create the best arrangement before hanging them on the wall. It saves lots of frustrating rearranging and rehanging—not to mention those extra holes in the wall. Also,  take a photo of large picture groupings before removing them for wall painting. This makes it easy to put the pictures back up in the right order. —*Margie Dodd Choctaw, Oklahoma*

When you close paint cans, place a piece of plastic wrap between the lid and the paint can edge. It prevents that tough scummy layer from forming on the paint.

—*Mrs. Otis Howard Cedar Lake, Indiana*

Look for other uses for everyday decorations instead of packing them away at Christmastime. Last year I hung one of my favorite decorating items—an antique rug beater—on the back of the bathroom door with

a loop hook and used it as a towel holder.
—*Kathleen Grahek*
Wauwatosa, Wisconsin

Make an inexpensive bulletin board

that matches your kitchen or bedroom decor by cutting a ceiling tile in half and wrapping it in coordinating wallpaper. Insert two small eye-loop screws with glue and it's ready to hang. —*Lois Manning*
Holden, Massachusetts

When I'm invited to a bridal shower,

I wrap the gift in a dish towel and use a dishcloth as a "bow". Instead of just throwing away gift wrap, the bride receives something useful. —*Theone Neel*
Bastian, Virginia

Save old egg cartons

for storing your small Christmas lights. Put the bulbs inside the carton and wrap the cord around the outside—bulbs won't break, and the cord won't get tangled. —*Claire Spencer*
Fawn Grove, Pennsylvania

Instead of using masking tape

to prevent splatters when painting or varnishing windows, cut narrow strips of paper (I use newspaper), dip them in water and stick them to the glass. When the job's done, just gently peel them off—they leave no residue. —*Joyce Beito*
Strathcona, Minnesota

Dry colorful fall leaves

between the pages of a telephone book. When Thanksgiving arrives, I remove the leaves and use them for place cards by writing names on them with a felt pen. —*Ann Devendorf*
Paso Robles, California

I painted my bedroom

all white first. Then, using a natural ocean sponge, I applied pink paint over the white. The result was an interesting textured look. —*Carol Ostberg*
Fairfield, Montana

Ever decide to paint a ceiling

but were worried you would leave an uneven line of color along the top of the wall? Just hold a dustpan where you want the even line to be. This gives you a nice edge and keeps paint from dripping. —*P. Spindler*
Garden Grove, California

When painting cabinets,

be sure to leave the frames and doors for last. That way, you won't get paint all over your arms trying to reach inside. —*Melinda Neal*
Muncie, Indiana

Don't cry over spilled paint!

By simply attaching a pie tin to the top of your stepladder—as a "holder"—you can discourage tipping…and the resulting frustrating mess. It's also handy for nails and screws.
—*Germaine Stank*
Pound, Wisconsin

You don't see the top

and bottom edges of a door, so it's easy to forget

to paint them. Yet those edges are the ones most exposed to moisture, especially on exterior doors. So you should always be sure to paint those edges; otherwise moisture will seep into the unfinished surface and the door will swell.

If you don't know whether the bottom of a door has been painted, here's a way to check without taking it off its hinges: Just slide a mirror under the door. —*Don Kraning*
Battle Creek, Michigan

Constantly cutting too much or too little wrapping paper? Loop string around the gift, then stretch the string out on the wrapping paper to calculate exactly how much paper you need. —*Mary Ellen Martin*
Lincoln, Illinois

When working with latex paint, instead of washing the brush after each use, wrap it in foil and place in freezer. Thaw an hour before using again.

We painted the entire inside of our house and only had to wash brushes and rollers once—at the end of the job! —*Sandra Funke*
Earlysville, Virginia

To prevent paint from peeling off of cement milking parlor floors, "paint" them first with white vinegar, let dry—then apply a real coat of paint. —*B. Geck*
New York, New York

Having a hard time keeping paintbrushes soft? Wash after each use, then rinse in water containing a capful of fabric softener.

Country Trivia

AT 4-1/2 miles long and over 1 mile wide, Emmons Glacier in Mount Rainier National Park, Washington is the largest glacier in the "lower 48".

Place brush in crease of several paper towels folded in half and roll around gently. This will also keep the brush from bristling.
—*Vera Laubscher*
Lock Haven, Pennsylvania

When painting indoors, wear an old pair of socks over your shoes. It will save your shoes from dripping paint and you can quickly wipe up splattered floors by rubbing your feet over any spots.
—*Maureen Beaver*
Sparta, Wisconsin

Need a quick candlestick? Just core an apple, orange or grapefruit—then put a candle in the middle. (This makes a pretty last-minute centerpiece, too.)

When using an oil-based paint, keep a little bit of nail polish remover handy. Dabbed on a cotton ball, it will wipe away splatters with ease. —*Elsie Kolberg*
St. Joseph, Michigan

CHAPTER 8

MORE FOOD & KITCHEN MONEY-SAVERS

A muffin tin is a handy holder for carrying hot baked potatoes.
—*Joan Dirkman, Ahmeek, Michigan*

If homegrown carrots aren't as sweet as they should be, soak them peeled and sliced in a solution of 1 quart water and 1/2 teaspoon granulated sugar. Let stand for several hours. —*Mrs. Earl Squire Burlington, Wisconsin*

Do not tap the beaters on the edge of the bowl when beating egg whites. This jars the bowl and will cause the whites to lose a lot of their body. Hold the beaters over the bowl and tap them with your hand instead. —*Mildred Sherrer Bay City, Texas*

For crisp lettuce salad with mayonnaise dressing, minus the last-minute rush, mix the dressing in the bottom of the salad bowl. Top with broken lettuce, and place it unstirred on the table. With just a quick stir when the hot food is put out, your salad will be ready.
—*Mrs. Paul Olson Williams, Minnesota*

Crush broken pieces of potato chips left in the bottom of the bag. Collect these in a tightly covered jar and store in the freezer to use for toppings on casseroles.
—*Mrs. Orlin Petersen Utica, South Dakota*

I keep a quart freezer container handy for leftover vegetables. I add them layer upon layer and store in the freezer until I'm ready to make homemade vegetable soup. These "useless" bits add up quickly to make a delicious soup.
—*Mrs. Harry Ahlers, Minier, Illinois*

To make leftover mashed potatoes special, re-whip cold potatoes, adding a bit of milk, a couple of tablespoons butter or margarine, salt, pepper and, if you like, some minced onion. Pile them into a greased baking dish; sprinkle with shredded American cheese. Bake until they're piping hot and the cheese has melted. —*Mary Feese Lake Ozark, Missouri*

I save potato chip cans for freezing cookies. Each can holds about 14 cookies, which is just enough for small picnics, camping trips and Sunday afternoon drives.

I find that if I put a can in the freezer, I always have a nice variety and supply on hand.
—*Mrs. Carl Beeler, Sutter, Illinois*

Add a little mashed sweet potato to your sweet roll dough and you'll be adding delicious flavor and a lovely color. —*Opal Griebel Milburn, Nebraska*

If you put sugar cubes in your cheese containers, the cheese will stay mold-free. —*Alice Costello Fond du Lac County, Wisconsin*

Sprinkle your French toast with sesame seeds before frying. You will love the crunchy taste.
—*Mrs. T.F. Mitchell Portland, Oregon*

When a recipe calls for sharp cheddar cheese, and you haven't any on hand, a dash of pepper, dry mustard and Worcestershire sauce added to a mild cheese will give it a sharp flavor. —*Ann Zawistowski Coon Rapids, Minnesota*

Cut pieces of aluminum foil the same size as your cookie sheets. While the first batches of cookies are baking, drop dough onto foil. When baked cookies are removed from a hot cookie sheet, just place one of the sheets of foil onto the pan.
—*Mrs. Hiram Katterheinrich New Knoxville, Ohio*

An easy way to fix beets is to wash them thoroughly and boil them in their skins. When boiled, drain and plunge them into a basin of cold water. A little pressure will easily remove the skins, leaving the beets unmarred and ready to serve.
—*Mrs. Einar Haaland Woodbury, Connecticut*

Try adding 1 cup cooked rice to your meat loaf. It will be moist, slice firmly and taste new.
—*Mrs. Amos Hoover Denver, Pennsylvania*

A slice of fresh bread fastened with toothpicks to the cut edge of a cake will keep the cake from drying out and getting stale.
—*Ella Murray, Burlington, Iowa*

When lemons get dry and hard, place them in a hot oven for a few minutes. It will freshen them.
—*Helen Svaren Arlington, South Dakota*

You'll use fewer pots if you cook your vegetables in the bottom of a double boiler while you make a sauce for them in the top pan. And at

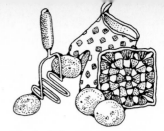

breakfast, boil eggs in the bottom of the double boiler while you cook cereal in the top. —*Cecelia Raiser Jefferson County, Wisconsin*

I save bits of cookies and crumbs of all kinds in a plastic bag in the refrigerator or freezer. Before long, there are enough to make a pie crust. Sometimes I add nut meats, too.
—*Mrs. Henry Sandahl Essex, Iowa*

When freezing corn, peas, strawberries or raspberries, I use pint-sized plastic bags inside my empty butter and margarine boxes. They stay fresh and pack better in the freezer. —*Mrs. Harold Jensen Villard, Minnesota*

Try thickening your home-made gravy with pureed vegetables instead of flour.
—*Mildred Sherrer, Bay City, Texas*

Here's a quick frosting idea. Place a solid chocolate-mint wafer on top of each cupcake after removing a batch from the oven. After it has softened, spread the wafer over the top or leave as it is.
—*Mrs. Andrew Peifer Stonesville, Pennsylvania*

For extra crispy French toast, pop your bread in the toaster first, then dip it in batter and fry.
—*ClaRae Strand Seattle, Washington*

Many years ago, my dad came up with a foolproof method to prevent onions from sprouting during winter storage. We just burn the root hairs

off by holding them over a low flame on the stove. In all these years, not a single onion has sprouted.
—*Mrs. Edwin Volk Battle Creek, Nebraska*

Use crushed potato chips instead of bread crumbs for meat loaf filler. The flavor of the chips makes an excellent addition.
—*Mrs. Clarence Huss Hartington, Nebraska*

For French fries to pull from the freezer at a moment's notice, peel potatoes, cut them into thin strips and fry in hot fat until the potatoes are a very light, golden brown. Drain on paper towels. When cool, package, label and freeze immediately. They are ready to broil or pan-fry in only 8 to 10 minutes.
—*Josephine Nelson St. Paul, Minnesota*

Pull a wire clothes hanger so that it forms a hook with a long handle. This hook is handy to have around the kitchen to reach high objects or to arrange pans in the oven.
—*Mrs. Clyde Ketcherside DeSoto, Missouri*

A small funnel is handy for separating egg whites from yolks. Crack the egg over the funnel. The whites will run through, and the yolk will remain. —*Joan Dirkman Ahmeek, Michigan*

The next time you need divider trays for your kitchen utensils, try the tops of egg cartons. They work much better for me, plus they're free! —*Sue Ratliff, Dumas, Texas*

When frying breaded meat, roll the meat in flour before dipping it into the egg and crumbs. You'll find the flour keeps the coating on the meat, not in the pan.
—*Beatrice Boyd, Humeston, Iowa*

To keep pickles from turning soft, add a grape leaf to each jar. A small bit of alum or turmeric will also do the trick, but too much will change the flavor. —*Mrs. Amos Hoover Denver, Pennsylvania*

When baking a layer cake, I take a double sheet of waxed paper, set the cake pan on it and cut to the right size. Then I put the waxed paper in each pan. When it comes time to remove the layers, they slip out easily. —*Mrs. Henry Glieb Lancaster, Pennsylvania*

If you want a quick frosting for applesauce or banana cake, sprinkle generously with granulated sugar, coconut and chopped nuts before baking. Comes out with a crunchy topping. —*Mrs. Ralph Mohr Breda, Iowa*

I think coffee has an improved flavor if you drop a prune into the pot while the coffee brews.
—*Mrs. Clifford Munson Oneida, Illinois*

If you butter the knife you're using, you can easily get a sharp cut through meringue pie. If you're taking a meringue pie to a church social or somewhere else, butter the waxed paper or foil used to cover the pie. This will prevent it from sticking to the meringue.
—*Mrs. N. Dagerin Levy County, Florida*

When making graham cracker crumbs or other crumbs, put the crackers in a zip-type bag, close it and then run a rolling pin over the bag until fine. Keep the bag with excess crumbs inside for future use.
—*Mrs. Ardath Effa Villa Park, Illinois*

Keep a large salt shaker filled with flour. It's handy and less messy when dusting pans or coating chicken. —*Mrs. Louis Runck Fairfax, Minnesota*

When mixing instant dry whipped topping, use half-and-half or some other creamer in place of milk. This makes the mix taste almost like real whipped cream.
—*Mrs. Don Johnston, Kent, Iowa*

Adding a ripe banana to a chocolate cake not only keeps the cake moist but also gives it good flavor.
—*Mildred Sherrer, Bay City, Texas*

I wash my pickles in cold, hard (no water softener) water in my automatic washing machine for 2 or 3 minutes. However, I don't let the washer go through the spin cycle. I

Double the amount of oatmeal you prepare for breakfast. Refrigerate leftovers. Next day, slice and brown in a skillet. Serve with syrup or butter and sugar. Doesn't this bring back memories of "way back when"? —*Mrs. Arnold Fahrenkrog*
Walcott, Iowa

have put in up to 1 bushel at a time and, surprisingly, have never lost more than three pickles by this method. —*Mrs. Russell Payne*
Bluffton, Indiana

An egg whip comes in handy for stirring up orange or other fruit juices quickly and thoroughly. I also use it to make smooth pancake batter. —*Mrs. Dean Swenson*
Grasston, Minnesota

When baking muffins, you can keep them from burning around the edges by filling one cup of the muffin tin with water instead of batter.
—*Mrs. Henry Glieb*
Lancaster, Pennsylvania

To freshen those potato chips that become soggy and stale in humid weather, place them on a cookie sheet in a 200° oven for about 30 minutes and presto—fresh chips!
—*Mrs. John Beastrom*
Ellsworth, Wisconsin

To keep salad fresh, place an inverted saucer in the bottom of the bowl before adding lettuce. The extra water will drain and accumulate under the saucer instead of soaking into the salad. —*Joan Dirkman*
Ahmeek, Michigan

For perfectly round refrigerator cookies, pack the dough into a washed can that frozen juice comes in. Cover the can; refrigerate. When ready to bake, run hot water over the sides. Push dough out and slice.
—*Mrs. James Weiland*
Zwingle, Iowa

When you freeze the fruit for pies, mix in all the ingredients called for in the recipe. Then line a pie pan with plastic wrap and pour in filling. Cover and freeze in pie pan. Remove to plastic bag when completely frozen. Filling is ready to drop into a pie shell and bake at a moment's notice. —*Iris Damkar*
Calgary, Alberta

When baking doughnuts, have an extra pan of boiling water beside the hot fat. Remove doughnut from

To substitute for cake flour, use 1 cup of sifted all-purpose flour minus 2 level tablespoons for each cup of cake flour the recipe calls for.
—*Mrs. Henry Bechthold*
Booker, Texas

fat and *quickly* dip into the water. This will remove the excess fat and will not harm the texture or flavor of the doughnut.

—*Mrs. Clarence Huss*
Hartington, Nebraska

Use a wire potato masher to decorate the top of meat loaf and for fluting the edges of pie crusts or cookies. —*Mrs. Orlin Petersen*
Utica, South Dakota

When baking a pie crust, put it on the back of a pie tin and prick well. When baked, flip it over into the tin. Baking it this way prevents the crust from bubbling.

—*Mrs. James Sylling*
Spring Grove, Minnesota

The next time you need to keep a meal warm while you take it to the field, heat some bricks in the oven at 350° to 400° for a couple of hours. Place them in a cake pan and cover with foil. Put the meal on top of this and then cover the whole thing with foil. Your meal will stay warm for 2 to 3 hours. —*Sue Ratliff*
Dumas, Texas

When I have extra peppers, I cut them into small pieces, put them in an ice cube tray, add water and freeze. (I use about 2 tablespoons peppers per cube.) When they are frozen, I put the cubes into a plastic bag and label it. These are easy to add to soup or any hot dish. This method also works for celery, onion, orange rind, etc.

—*Mrs. Albert Schuler*
Tuttle, North Dakota

Make homemade noodles simply by adding an egg to a package of pie crust. Mix, roll out, cut and let dry. They're delicious!

—*Mrs. C.R. Landphair*
Humeston, Iowa

Here's a trick for flavorful orange frosting. Combine 1 ounce package cream cheese, 2 tablespoons powdered orange drink, 2 cups powdered sugar and enough cream or milk to make the right consistency. It's delicious!

—*Mrs. Henry Bechthold*
Booker, Texas

Add a few drops of orange extract in applesauce while it is hot to greatly improve the flavor.

—*Nadine Adair*
Townsend, Montana

An enjoyable way to use up leftover mashed potatoes is to form balls of potatoes around cubes of cheese, place the balls in your broiler and broil them until they are golden brown. For an added touch, roll them in buttered bread crumbs, potato chips or Parmesan cheese.

—*Mrs. Arnold Turnis*
Hopkinton, Iowa

I've discovered a wonderful way to store my garden sweet potatoes. After washing the potatoes, I leave them outside for a day. I then wrap each potato in a piece of waxed paper. Finally, I layer the potatoes alternately with regular sand in a large

tub. If you keep the tub in the basement as I do, carry each item down before filling the tub. The tub's too heavy to carry when filled.
—*Mrs. Roger Leffel*
St. Mary's, Iowa

Keep frequently used place mats handy on the inside of a cabinet door. Fasten an office clipboard to the door and use the metal clamp to hold the mats. —*Mrs. Otto Fahning*
Wells, Minnesota

After pouring batter into your waffle iron, let it cook a bit before closing the lid. The result will be fluffier waffles.
—*Mrs. Emmett Swanson*
Hager City, Wisconsin

When opening canned goods, open the end that has been sitting on the shelf. The ingredients come out more easily, and that end is usually cleaner. —*LaVerne Nuse*
Caldwell, Kansas

I add a teaspoonful of vinegar to my boiled frosting. This keeps it soft, and it doesn't crack when the cake is cut. —*Mrs. Amos Hoover*
Denver, Pennsylvania

If you don't have enough muffin tins for a large batch of cupcakes, arrange quart-jar canning bands right side up on a cookie sheet. Insert the paper cups into each band, and fill according to directions. This prevents paper cups from spreading while baking and results in perfectly shaped cupcakes.
—*Shirley Kennell, Mode, Illinois*

I use my individual egg poacher to melt a square of chocolate. It's like a tiny double boiler.
—*Ann Zawistowski*
Coon Rapids, Minnesota

Can't get the lid off a jar? Just hold the jar upside down and pour warm vinegar around the neck at the joint between the glass and the top. Then give it another try.

Also, if you don't have one of those rubber jar openers on hand, just substitute the widest rubber band you can find. Fit it around the jar lid and it will give you a better grip. —*Relda Riley, Abilene, Texas*

When you have used a quart of sweet pickles, there is usually about a cup and a half of delicately spiced and sweetened vinegar left. Add a finely chopped medium onion and green pepper. Return to the refrigerator to marinate for a few days. It makes good dressing on lettuce salad.
—*Mrs. Lyle Cairns*
Greenleaf, Kansas

Since hash browns are a favorite at our house, I usually prepare a large batch of them at one time and then freeze some for portioning in the future. I have a method for this which you might like to try. Cook potatoes in their jackets until almost

done. Peel, grate and form into the shape you want. Package, label, date and freeze immediately. When ready to use, fry hash browns in cooking oil, using a covered pan, until potatoes are golden brown on both sides and heated through. Season to taste.
—*Josephine Nelson*
Dakota County, Minnesota

When cooking only one pizza, why not save some energy and cook it in your electric fry pan instead of lighting the oven. The results will be a perfectly done crust and soft gooey cheese. —*Dorothy Hansen*
Washington, Wisconsin

Put several drops of oil in a pan when frying with butter and you won't have to worry about the butter burning. —*Mrs. Marvin Neste*
McIntosh, Minnesota

To keep parsley fresh and crisp, store it in a covered jar in the refrigerator. Always wash it in hot water to retain its good flavor.
—*Mrs. Harold Hanson*
Flaxville, Montana

With a cake decorator, squeeze leftover dabs of colored frosting onto a cookie sheet lined with waxed paper. Freeze. You may store these little frosting decorations in freezer bags to use on cakes or cupcakes anytime. —*Joan Dirkman*
Ahmeek, Michigan

Use juice from canned fruit as a base for powdered drinks such as Kool-Aid. It gives a more fruity taste. Add more or less sugar, de-

COUNTRY TRIVIA

IN THE 1870's, a Georgia peach grower had the largest orchard in the world at that time— 350,000 trees on 2,000-plus acres.

pending on how much sugar is in the fruit juice. —*Joy Wheeler*
Summerville, Oregon

A sticky ring won't form around the cooking pot if you add a small spoonful of vegetable shortening to the water when boiling sweet potatoes. —*Wanda Leaders*
Neola, Iowa

When I have something in the oven or cooking on the stove and my husband calls me outside to help him on the farm, I no longer fret. I simply set my small timer and stick it in my pocket. When the bell rings, I run back into the house.
—*Karen Midtling*
Sheboygan, Wisconsin

While making a batch of bar cookies, I realized I didn't have any baking cocoa. I used packets of hot cocoa mix, and the cookies were delicious. —*Gretchen Howell*
Hiawasee, Georgia

I've found a way to bake potatoes that saves time and keeps the house cool in the summer. I clean and insert a new ten-penny nail through the middle of each potato before baking. The nail gets hot, and this causes the potato to bake from the inside as well as the outside. Allow about half the normal baking time.

—Mrs. J.N. Boblitt
Louisville, Kentucky

If you pinch a fold into the middle of a bacon slice, it will not curl up on the ends as you cook it. I've tried this and it works; the fold slides out as it cooks.

—Marcia Hanson, Quimby, Illinois

A very tasty and colorful relish can be made by adding a chopped onion and a cup of vinegar to a can of red kidney beans. Let stand for at least an hour; drain off the liquid. Serve cold.   —Mrs. L.E. Ford
Portland, Oregon

When preparing to bake a meat loaf, line the pan with strips of bacon before placing the loaf into the pan. (If desired, remove the bacon before serving.) You will never have a meat loaf that is overly brown on the bottom.   —Mrs. Curtis Sykora
Windom, Minnesota

Try coating the bottom of a cake pan, muffin tin or roll pan with crushed graham crackers. They prevent sticking and add an interesting flavor and coating.   —Ann Chernabaeff
Wasco, California

For a slightly different taste, try adding a cup of molasses to your pot roast. Also, a tablespoon of molasses added to vegetable soup and stews produces an excellent flavor.

—Nadine Adair
Townsend, Montana

To enhance the flavor of any tomato recipe, simply add a spoonful or two of granulated sugar.

—Mrs. Walter Peterson
Watertown, Wisconsin

When making any cream pie filling, add about a fourth of the meringue mixture to the hot pie filling. This makes the filling light and fluffy. Pour into a baked pie shell, and top with remaining meringue.

—Mrs. G.E. Parsons, Alden, Kansas

To easily and quickly frost cupcakes, put a marshmallow on top of each one a couple of minutes before you take them from the oven.

—Florence Ova
Jamestown, North Dakota

When cleaning celery, save the leaves, spread them on a paper towel-lined pan and let dry. When the leaves are crisp and dry, chop and store in a glass jar for use in soups or salads.   —Mrs. Hiebert Stoll
Wilton Junction, Iowa

You can make a layered gelatin salad easily if you know which ingredients are "sinkers" and which are "floaters". The "sinkers" are canned apricots, pineapple, peaches, pears, orange sections, grapes and prunes. The "floaters" are marshmallows, sliced bananas, grapefruit sections, mandarin oranges, raspberries, sliced strawberries, nuts, fresh peaches and pears and diced apples. The salad will make its own layers while chilling.

—*Helen Patzlaff*
Alexandria, South Dakota

I've learned that inexpensive cuts of beef need not be tough and tasteless. I simply add a tablespoon of vinegar to the water when cooking a roast. Or, you can rub it directly on the meat. Even chuck becomes tender. —*Kathleen Molencupp*
Warsaw, Missouri

My homemade doughnuts tended to be soggy until I added a tablespoon of vinegar to the frying fat. The vinegar keeps the doughnuts from being greasy.

—*Mrs. Charles Landphair*
Humeston, Iowa

One beef bouillon cube mixed with 1 tablespoon of dried onion flakes makes an inexpensive substitute for the dry onion soup mix that is so often called for in casserole recipes. —*Mrs. Samuel Griffith*
Memphis Tennessee

Keep picnic salads and relishes crisp by packing them in the top of a double boiler and filling the bottom with ice cubes.

—*Mrs. Orlin Petersen*
Utica, South Dakota

Slice cold meat loaf, dip it in your favorite batter and roll it in bread crumbs or crushed cornflakes. Saute

When serving leftover roast, try heating it up in my taste-tantalizing sauce. Simmer 1/4 cup chopped onion in 1/2 cup water with 1/4 teaspoon salt. Add 1/4 cup sugar, 1/8 teaspoon pepper, 3 tablespoons vinegar, 1 teaspoon Worcestershire sauce, 1/2 cup catsup and 3/4 cup water.

Add meat and heat through. Serve on buns. Your family will like it better than the original dish! —*Mrs. Willard Madsen*
Ruthton, Minnesota

or deep-fry at 375°-400° until crisp and warmed through.

—*Doris Riddle, Worden, Montana*

Give doughnuts added flavor by placing a few whole cloves or sticks of cinnamon in fat while frying.

—*Mrs. Lester Wolters*
Nokomis, Illinois

So many recipes call for a tablespoon of lemon juice. To keep such small amounts on hand, I purchase a half dozen lemons, squeeze the juice and freeze it in a plastic ice cube tray. I can take out a square at a time.

—*Mrs. Clifford Johnson*
Owatonna, Minnesota

If you have unexpected company and no time to fix a dessert or salad, try this. Put 1 to 2 cups orange juice in a baking dish. Place peach halves in the juice and sprinkle generously with coconut. Place a large marshmallow in the center of each peach half. Pop into a 375° oven until marshmallows are golden and peaches are hot. Serve in individual sauce dishes.

—Mrs. Don Hafer
Seward, Nebraska

To obtain nice even layers when making a layer cake, spread the batter higher around the outside of the pan. (The center usually rises more.) *—Margaret Thelen*
Fowler, Michigan

Use leftover cranberry sauce to fill the holes in baked apples for an interesting taste-teaser.

—Mrs. Orlin Petersen
Utica, South Dakota

Freeze orange segments for a refreshing, nutritious snack treat. My family loves 'em!

—Ruth Ann Giffin, Henry, Illinois

Beat frosting until it's light and creamy. Dip the top of each cupcake into the soft icing, twirl it and quickly turn it right side up to make a fancy peak. This method takes far less time and produces pretty results, too. *—Helene Levin*
Laguna Hills, California

When making chocolate curls to use as a garnish on a dessert, a swivel-blade vegetable peeler will do the trick. Make sure that the chocolate is not too soft.

—Mrs. W. Jervis
Somerville, Massachusetts

I cover all my recipe cards with clear Con-tact paper. I cut the paper twice as large as my card, allowing a small bit for a border. Cover one side, and fold the remainder over the other side. The result is quick, easy, long-lasting recipe cards. I also do this with magazine recipes.

—Mrs. Darlene Johnson
Sentinel, Oklahoma

NIP OF NATURE
How come you can't see a bird's breath?

EVEN on the coldest winter days, it's unlikely you'll see a bird's breath. That's because of a bird's fast breathing (40 times faster than humans). With these quick, short breaths, such a small volume of air is taken in that the vapor in their breath usually is gone before you can see it.

Still, some people, such as Dave Cummins of Ann Arbor, Michigan, say they have seen small puffs of air coming from birds' beaks.

"It has to be below zero, the air has to be still and you have to be within 6 feet of the bird," reports Dave. "I've seen the breath of mourning doves at our feeder when the light is behind them."

Frozen or canned whole kernel corn has a fresh summertime flavor when milk is substituted for cooking water and a teaspoon of sugar is added. Cook on top of the stove as usual, or place in a baking dish, cover tightly and bake at 350° for about 30 minutes. *—Joan Dirkman Ahmeek, Michigan*

I've found that sprinkling confectioners' sugar on the cake plate will prevent the cake from sticking when you serve it later.
—Mrs. N. Dagerin Levy County, Florida

Are you tired of spilling toothpicks or having someone handle them all? Empty spice bottles make excellent holders for round toothpicks. The picks come out of the holes when the bottle is inverted.
—Catherine Lang Kidder County, Nebraska

If you ever let your meringue get too brown or slightly burnt, just peel off the burnt top, sprinkle coconut generously over the meringue and brown again.
—Mrs. John Isakson Beresford, South Dakota

If brown paper grocery bags seem to be filling up all of your kitchen cupboards, cut them into good-sized pieces for draining bacon and other fried foods. They are very absorbent. *—Mildred Sherrer Bay City, Texas*

For a delicious crust for fried chicken, crush 2 cups of cornflakes very fine. Mix with flour and other seasonings. Roll the chicken in the mixture, and fry until golden brown in hot fat. *—Mrs. Amos Hoover Denver, Pennsylvania*

My husband and I love to fish. We do it whenever farm work allows, even through ice in the wintertime. So, whenever I want to freeze some of the fish from our most recent excursion, I simply put the cleaned fish in half-gallon milk cartons, fill them with water and freeze.
—Mrs. I. Dentinger Lee County, South Carolina

When making instant iced tea, use a small amount of hot water to dissolve tea and sugar before filling with cold water and ice cubes. The hot water brings out the flavor of the tea.
—Mrs. James Hickman Canonsburg, Pennsylvania

Store cooking oil in an empty, thoroughly washed liquid detergent bottle. No more dripping or waste when you squeeze out as much as you need! *—Orlean Agnes Trail, Minnesota*

To fill plastic bags quickly and easily, I place the food into a quart jar, slip the bag over the jar and invert. The bag is quickly filled, and the top is clean for sealing. It's also a good way to measure the amount correctly. *—Joan Dirkman Ahmeek, Michigan*

When making hamburgers, mix a little flour with the meat. They will stay together nicely.
—Mrs. Amos Hoover Denver, Pennsylvania

Use your French fry basket for boiling potatoes. When they are ready to be drained, all you have to do is lift the basket out of the boiling water. They are quickly drained without any burned fingers.
—Mrs. Orlin Petersen Utica, South Dakota

Try grating orange rind into your devil's food cake batter. It will give it a deliciously different flavor. *—Mrs. Clarence Huss Hartington, Nebraska*

To help stabilize whipping cream and to add flavor, sprinkle instant vanilla pudding mix on cream before whipping. Use about 4 tablespoons for each cup of cream to be whipped. *—Mrs. Walter Peterson Watertown, Wisconsin*

To prevent a poached egg from spreading in the pan when placed into the water, add 1 teaspoon of vinegar to each pint of water.
—Mrs. Leo Johanns, Paulding, Ohio

When I open a new package of sliced bacon, I slice a 1-inch strip off each end. This yields small pieces just right for a recipe that calls for

The next time your popcorn doesn't want to pop, try replacing the cover with a wet cloth. This will also help keep the corn from burning.
—Marlyce Schamens Sparta, Wisconsin

diced bacon. I just slip the pieces into a plastic sandwich bag and store in the refrigerator or freezer until needed. We never miss those ends and welcome them in other dishes.
—Mrs. Keith Herrman Connell, Washington

Before chopping raw meat, cut it into small pieces and freeze slightly. The meat will go through the chopper without clogging, and the juice lost will be minimal.
—Joan Dirkman, Ahmeek, Michigan

You can open a 1-pint container of frozen whipping cream and, with a knife, cut the cream in half. Whip one half, and seal the other half in the carton to use another time.
—Mrs. Ed Fahey Farmington, Minnesota

When I need crisp lettuce cups, I cut the core from the head of lettuce and fill it with cold water. In a very short time, the outer leaves are crisp. *—Mrs. George Knop Campbell Hill, Illinois*

Pour scalding water over oranges and let them stand 5 minutes. It makes them peel easily and very clean. —*Nadine Adair Townsend, Montana*

When making meringue for a pie, I add about 1 tablespoon of clear corn syrup to the egg whites. This makes the meringue expand and stand higher.
—*Mrs. Terrie Mauger Baltimore, Ohio*

I found that soaking steaks in milk for at least an hour before broiling makes them much more tender.
—*Shelia Koch Glen Ullin, North Dakota*

When rolling out a pie crust to put into the pie pan, it's somewhat difficult to pick up the crust, right? Instead, I just roll the crust up onto the rolling pin, put it over the pan and unroll it again.
—*Mrs. Dean Jones Reading, Kansas*

Store fudge, cookies or other foods in empty coffee cans. If you like to do holiday or other baking well in advance, coffee cans also go in the freezer. (An extra lid over the bottom of a can prevents damage to the freezer floor.)
—*Helen Davis, Waterbury, Vermont*

When preparing that occasional meal of assorted leftovers, are you distressed at the number of kettles you have on the stove—and in the dishpan—when the meal is over?

Next time, try putting each leftover into a piece of aluminum foil that you have folded up into a bowl shape. Put these "aluminum bowls" containing the leftovers in a frying pan, add a little water, cover and steam. —*Mrs. L. Stewart Oilmont, Kansas*

Try coating fish with finely crushed onion- or garlic-flavored potato chips before frying. They give it a deliciously different taste.
—*Mrs. Leon Ross San Bernardino, California*

When maraschino cherries are all gone, fill the bottle with pineapple chunks and soak in the cherry juice. The colored pineapple makes a pretty addition to a fruit salad.
—*Mrs. Ronald Schomberg Lone Tree, Texas*

If you need to whip cream ahead of time, it will not separate if you add a touch of unflavored gelatin (about 1/4 teaspoon per cup of cream). The gelatin also speeds up whipping. —*Mrs. Lorenz Wilker Owatonna, Minnesota*

When you bake a cake but have little time to make frosting, here is a simple way to frost it. While the cake is still warm, spread it with molasses and sprinkle with coconut and/or nuts. —*Mrs. Alvin Martin Mount Joy, Pennsylvania*

If the lids on your canning jars won't seal, turn the jar upside down in a pan of boiling water and boil for 10 to 12 minutes. Remove the jar from the water, turn it upright and it will seal every time.

—Charlotte Roach
Faucett, Missouri

You can prepare a different, delicious filling for sandwiches or omelets by combining your favorite cheese with crisp bacon, avocado and chunks of canned pineapple (drained). *—Mildred Sherrer*
Bay City, Texas

In making doughnuts over the years, I have learned two tricks:

First, if you have trouble with grease soaking into doughnuts, add 1 teaspoon ginger to the hot grease or oil before frying.

Second, if you turn each doughnut over as it reaches the top of the hot grease, it will not crack. Some turn themselves, but not all. *—Mrs. Alfred Grimm*
De Witt, Iowa

Use a pizza cutter for slicing your bar cookies. It has a sharp edge and makes a nice even cut.

—Mrs. Richard Slark
Granton, Wisconsin

Place a washed whole pumpkin on a cookie sheet and bake at 300° for 1 hour. Prick the shell with a fork to allow steam to escape, then continue to bake until pumpkin is soft. It's easy to cut in half, remove seeds, scoop out pulp and blend or put through a ricer.

—Mrs. Donald Sondral
Turtle Lake, North Dakota

To make sure I always have fresh yeast on hand, I buy a pound of fresh compressed yeast from a bakery. I then cut it into 16 equal pieces, wrap it in foil and put it in the freezer where it will keep for months.

—Mrs. Paul Biermann
Winser, Nebraska

Are you wondering what to do with old fishnet stockings? Insert one into the toe of the other. Stitch both toes and tops together, and use as dishcloths. *—Dolores Lambrecht*
Grantville, Kansas

If you want to do something special with hamburgers, make patties or strips pressed very thin. Dip them into a beaten egg seasoned with salt and pepper. Roll them in flour and fry in hot oil.

—Mrs. Orlin Petersen
Utica, South Dakota

Before storing sliced meat in your freezer, spread the meat on a cookie sheet and freeze until solid. Quickly place frozen meat into a plastic bag. The slices will not stick together, so you'll be able to thaw the exact number you want.

—Mrs. W.C. Jervis
Somerville, Massachusetts

You can save time and mess by using your ice cream scoop for shap-

ing meatballs. To make hamburger patties, just scoop and press flat with a spatula. —*Pam Gansluckner*
Maiden Rock, Wisconsin

Cook shelled peas in a pot of boiling water along with the pods. Be sure to wash the pods thoroughly. When the peas are done, the pods will rise to the top and can be scooped up.
—*Mrs. M.D. Lawfer*
Stockton, Illinois

If your blender is the kind that unscrews from the base, you can screw on a regular quart or pint canning jar. How easy it is, then, to mix up salad dressings, relishes, baby foods, etc., in the containers they will be stored in. —*Jeannie Evans*
Richwood, Ohio

For an easy sauce to serve on broccoli, just thin some mayonnaise with milk, mix in a little prepared mustard and spoon over cooked broccoli. The flavor will be delicious and tangy. —*Helene Levin*
San Jose, California

When making rolled cookies, roll them out on powdered sugar instead of flour. They won't get tough, and it makes them a little sweeter, too.—*Mrs. Don Oldenburg*
Ames, Iowa

I freeze chickens in half-gallon milk cartons, covering the pieces with water and stapling the tops shut. I pack choice pieces in one car-

COUNTRY TRIVIA

AS MANY AS 200 varieties of wheat are grown in the United States, and some wheat is grown in almost every state.

ton, bony pieces in a separate carton and the gizzards, hearts and livers in yet another carton.
—*Mrs. Robert Poling*
Williamston, West Virginia

To make 1 cup of sour milk, just add 1 tablespoon of vinegar or lemon juice to 1 cup of milk.
—*Helen Svaren*
Arlington, South Dakota

You can mix your own baking powder by combining 2 teaspoons of baking soda, 1 teaspoon cream of tartar and a heaping teaspoon of cornstarch. —*Mrs. Harry Holmes*
Davenport, Nebraska

I have worked out a coding system to make it easier to match up my freezer containers with the proper lids. Whenever I get a new freezer container, I get out my permanent marking pen and put the same number on the bottom of the container and its matching lid. This sure saves me a lot of time and frustration at freezing time. —*Frankie Carrigan*
Mooresville, North Carolina

When you only have a few dirty dishes, take some seldom-used dishes from your cupboards and add them to the dishwasher to make a full load. Then, while the dishes are washing, wipe out your empty cabinets. This will help you make the most of your dishwasher's energy usage as well as keep your cabinets and dishes clean and neat.

—*Mrs. Stanley Bargar*
Meadville, Missouri

When mashing potatoes, use milk and a few drops of imitation butter flavoring to give a buttery flavor without the extra calories.

—*Mrs. Cleon Lange*
Sanborn, Minnesota

When slicing cinnamon roll dough, instead of a knife I use a double strand of sewing thread. By sliding the thread under the dough to the desired thickness and pulling the thread upward, I get a perfect, clean

cut without smashing the entire roll of dough. —*Mrs. Winston Johnson*
Hampden, North Dakota

Need a large relish tray for a buffet or picnic? Using your largest round plate, make compartments on it with stalks of celery and carrot sticks. Pile other vegetables into the sections.   —*Erma Reynolds*
Long Meadow, Massachusetts

For beautifully set pumpkin pies, add an envelope of unflavored gelatin softened in 1/4 cup cold milk for each pie.   —*Elverda Oellig*
Grantville, Pennsylvania

The secret to fluffy meatballs is to beat the mixture very thoroughly, first using a hand mixer, then a spoon. When shaping, work with greased or wet hands.

—*Mrs. Raymond Hoyer*
West Salem, Wisconsin

When baking a cake, rap your pans sharply on the countertop before

NIP OF NATURE
Why do grasshoppers make so much noise?

NO DOUBT about it, for tiny creatures, grasshoppers can sure raise a din. They do it by simply rubbing their hind legs across their wings, making a rasping sound.

Their legs have a rough edge, similar to the teeth of a comb, and their wings have ridges similar to those on corrugated cardboard.

But don't blame it on the "ladies". You see, only male grasshoppers are noisy. Female grasshoppers are good listeners, though...but they listen with ears that are on each side of their bodies rather than on their heads.

putting them in the oven. This will eliminate most of the air bubbles.
—*Mrs. Pat Yingst, Covington, Ohio*

When a pickling recipe calls for a spice bag, I use my tea ball.
—*Mrs. August Herke*
Howard, South Dakota

When the tomatoes begin to ripen faster than I can use them or can them, I run them through the blender, pour into freezer containers and freeze. They are a marvelous addition to stews, chili and soups in the winter! —*Lois Norby*
Great Falls, Montana

To save time, I always arrange my spices in the cupboard in alphabetical order, left to right. It not only saves time, it avoids mistakes, too!
—*Esther Herman*
Riverton, Nebraska

When cutting out cookies with cookie cutters in various shapes, handling the raw dough often ruins their shapes. This is remedied by rolling out the dough on a sheet of waxed paper. You cut out the cookies on the paper and peel off excess dough. Invert a cookie sheet over the cookies, and pick up the ends of the waxed paper. Flip the paper and cookie sheet over. The cookies will fall onto the sheet in perfect shape.
—*Mrs. E. McKee*
Fayette County, Iowa

Use a meat pounder instead of a fork to make a pretty design on your cookies. —*Ann Zawistowski*
Coon Rapids, Minnesota

You can revive wilted lettuce by soaking it overnight in the refrigerator in a sugar-water solution containing 2 or 3 teaspoons of granulated sugar. Works good for limp celery, too. —*Mrs. Ralph Punton*
Ayr, North Dakota

To keep crackers fresh, transfer them from the package into a large glass jar with screw-on lid. These tightly covered crackers will keep fresh until they're all used up.
—*Erma Reynolds*
Longmeadow, Massachusetts

To remove egg yolk dropped into the white of an egg, use a corner of a wet cloth. The yolk will stick to the cloth and be easily removed.
—*Mrs. Lorenz Wilker*
Owatonna, Minnesota

Add heated milk and about 1 teaspoon of baking powder to your next batch of mashed potatoes. They'll be extra light and fluffy.
—*Mrs. Norbert Miller*
Cloverdale, Ohio

To prevent boiled potatoes from turning black, sprinkle a small amount of cream of tartar in the water while they are cooking.
—*Agnes Orelan, Trail, Minnesota*

Here's a fun holiday gift idea for a cook. Bake a loaf cake or a square layer cake. Frost with light frosting, and run a brightly colored "ribbon" of frosting around the cake. Extras such as sugar bells, holly or Christmas balls may be added to the "package" of cake.

—*Mrs. William Mollett*
Greenville, Illinois

A tablespoon of lemon juice added to a carton of cottage cheese will keep it fresh right down to the last spoonful, without altering its flavor. —*Mrs. Jack Schotanus*
Mitchell, Iowa

Those of you who purchase the large tins of frozen fruit will usually end up with quite a lot of sugar and frozen juice after the fruit is used up. To avoid throwing it out, melt it down, add some pectin powder and boil a few minutes. Then store it in a jar in the refrigerator to use for pancake syrup.

—*Helen Daley, Parker, Colorado*

To skin a tomato just taken from the refrigerator, use this method. Scrape a paring knife blade over the tomato several times from bottom to top. With the point of the knife, prick the skin. The skin will

then come off easily. This is handier than scalding and never fails.

—*Mrs. Elvin Harmacek*
Dallas, South Dakota

If chilled cookie dough crumbles as you slice it, warm the blade of your knife in hot water, wipe it dry and slice. When the blade cools to the point where the dough will no longer slice easily, reheat it.

—*Mrs. Charles Landphair*
Humeston, Iowa

Prepare your own seasoned salt by filling a salt shaker with a mixture of salt, pepper, onion powder, garlic powder and other favorite seasonings. When seasoning meats, vegetables, etc., you'll only need to remove one shaker from the shelf.

—*Mildred Sherrer, Bay City, Texas*

Never add salt to frozen vegetables before cooking in the microwave. The natural salt flavor comes through more in microwave cooking than it does with conventional methods. Also, because you can cook vegetables with less water in the microwave, less nutrients are lost in the water. —*Mrs. Donald Howman*
Smithville, Ohio

Use a small amount of baking powder in your gravy if it seems quite greasy. The grease will disappear. —*Mrs. Bernard Boysen*
Firestill, South Dakota

When baking a ham, slit the rind lengthwise on the underside before placing it in the roaster pan. As the ham bakes, the rind will pull away and will come off easily without lifting the ham. —*Mrs. Orlin Petersen Utica, South Dakota*

I save electricity and a hot kitchen by "sunning" my iced tea in the summer. Just put a few tea bags in a glass jar filled with water, set it in the sun and, in about half an hour, add ice for delicious iced tea.
—*Paul Shepard, Orio, Illinois*

Put a handful of tissue paper, torn into shreds, at the bottom of the cookie jar. This allows air to flow through and keeps the cookies crisp.
—*Merle Woods Dunsmuir, California*

If your scalloped potatoes are watery when they finish baking, just lift the potatoes around the top, pour in a few instant potatoes and stir them gently into the liquid.
—*Mrs. Richard Hunter Hemingford, Nebraska*

Soak nuts in water overnight before cracking and nut meats will come out in halves. —*Ethel McSloy Havre, Montana*

You say you don't have time to make a pie for dinner tonight? Try this quick pie crust: Coat a pie pan

For a moist cake, I always put a pan of water in the oven while the cake is baking. The heat doesn't rob the moisture this way. —*Mrs. Pat Johannsen Collins, Ohio*

with butter and press in cornflake crumbs. This makes a delicious crust that is especially good with pumpkin pie.
—*Mrs. Robert Morton Baker, Montana*

When canning, place an inch square of unheated paraffin in the bottom of the canning jar. When hot food, such as jelly, is poured into the jar, the paraffin melts and rises to the top, sealing the jar. —*Helen Svaren Arlington, South Dakota*

For a change-of-pace meat stretcher, mix 1/2 cup of poultry dressing with 1 pound ground beef and a little milk. The seasoning in the dressing will add nice flavor to your meat loaf or hamburgers.
—*Mrs. Jim Pate Williamston, North Carolina*

CHAPTER 9

HEALTH & BEAUTY IDEAS THAT SAVE FACE

Warm weather always seems to bring more than our fair share of cuts and scratches from the new freedom outdoors. I save by making my own bandages. A roll of adhesive tape is inexpensive, and with a package of cheesecloth, I can make a year's supply of bandages, gauze strips and smaller patches.

—*Mrs. Helen Chartier*
Oak Lawn, Illinois

Everyone knows how miserable it is to get fiberglass insulation bits off your hands, arms and clothes. I've found that a bath in warm water with 1/2 cup of fabric softener gets rid of the itch, and all the fine little hairs slide right off. Works well on clothes and inquisitive children.

—*Mrs. Conrad Vogelgesang*
Wanblee, South Dakota

After a few days of gardening in the hot sun, my hair gets very dry. About once a month, I give myself an oil treatment. I put hair oil on my hair. (It's best to do when you'll be likely to spend the day in the house.) I leave it on all day, then wash it out and set as usual. I find that it really helps me keep shine and oil in my hair. If your hair is excessively split and dry, cover it with a towel after putting the oil on it, or leave the oil on overnight.

—*Lorna Oliphant*
Richmond, Missouri

An empty container from lemon juice is great to carry lotion in. I just wash it, fill with lotion and put it in a purse.　—*Lynne Martin*
Lefor, North Dakota

My favorite facial is plain honey smeared all over my face and neck. I leave it on for 15 minutes and wash it off with a wet washcloth. It really helps the circulation, and my skin feels very soft and smooth. I try to do this twice a week.

—*Mrs. Harold Donaldson*
Denton, Montana

For wind- or water-roughened hands, smooth on plenty of petroleum jelly before going to bed, and put on a pair of cotton gloves. You'll be surprised at how soft your hands are in the morning.

—Marjorie Ver Steegh
Oskaloosa, Iowa

Here's a remedy for dull, drab hair especially good for those who are allergic to most hair care products, as I am. Using equal amounts of black tea and sage, brew as for strong tea. When cool, use as is, or dilute with water. Use this for the last rinse when shampooing. It may be stored in the refrigerator for future use. (I learned that it will mold if kept on a shelf too long.)

—Lois Madetzke
Elmore, Minnesota

Make a paste of one package of yeast and water. Rub it on your face. Leave it on for 20 minutes, then wash it off with warm water. Rinse with cold water. It's very invigorating.

—Mrs. R.W. Kinninson
Ovid, Colorado

Rub petroleum jelly into the base of your nails to soften cuticles and prevent dry hurting hands. The bonus is that petroleum jelly is much less expensive than commercial nail products and works on lips, too.

—Antoinette Wallner
Brookfield, Wisconsin

Mix together in a pan 1 quart of warm water, 1 teaspoon olive oil, the juice of one lemon and a squirt of dish detergent. Soak your hands in this for several minutes. Then scrub the nails with a soft brush, and continue to the hands, wrists, arms and elbows. Rinse, dry and apply your favorite hand lotion. This removes all stains and leaves your skin soft.

—Christine Deakins
Jonesboro, Tennessee

Soothe skin that is burned, roughened and dried from working outside by using a mixture of 1 tablespoon cream or milk and 1 tablespoon of salad oil. I like to use this facial before I put my makeup on. It will also make your face feel smooth and refreshed.

—Charmaine Gordner
Mooreland, Oklahoma

Here's a trick to save your hairdo, especially during plowing and planting time. This trick works for me when I sleep, too. I wrap toilet tissue lightly around my hair, holding it in place with thin bobby pins. Then I tie a nylon net scarf over my head and clip the sides. It's cool because the air blows through, but every hair stays in place while being protected from dust.

—Judy Crisman
Rushville, Indiana

Before doing outside work, apply petroleum jelly generously to hands and then slip them into cotton work gloves. When working with hands in water, use the same method, but substitute rubber gloves for the cotton ones. This is especially effective when working with hot water. Hands stay soft and young-looking.

—Mrs. Jettie Clemens
Norborne, Missouri

Your bathtub will never overflow again if you time how long it takes to fill—then set your kitchen timer accordingly whenever you run a bath!

—Linda Neukrug
Walnut Creek, California

I keep a shower cap with a knit lining handy to wear outside for dirty work or cold windy days. It's easy to put on, takes a minute to pull off if someone stops by and doesn't smash down a pretty hairdo.

—Helen Humphrey
Bronson, Kansas

To keep my hair clean while plowing, I made a cap from a large circle of bright-colored tricot and put an elastic band around the edge to fit my head. The size of the cir-

cle depends on your hairstyle. My hair is backcombed, so I need a large size. The tricot is soft and pleasant to wear and is easy to wash and dry.

—Mrs. Veryl Jessen
Boyd, Montana

Before you put on moisturizing cream at night, wet your face and neck. The lotion will spread easier and will penetrate deeper to soften your skin.

—Mildred Sherrer
Bay City, Texas

To make a bath special for a child (or yourself!), scatter a few flower petals into the water.

—Sharon Jacobson
Lincoln, Nebraska

When pieces of soap get small, they're hard to use. They needn't be wasted, though. I simply make a bag by sewing two washcloths to-

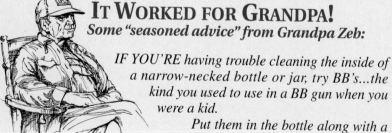

IT WORKED FOR GRANDPA!
Some "seasoned advice" from Grandpa Zeb:

IF YOU'RE having trouble cleaning the inside of a narrow-necked bottle or jar, try BB's...the kind you used to use in a BB gun when you were a kid.

Put them in the bottle along with a small amount of dishwashing detergent and hot water. Shake vigorously, pour out water and rinse. Presto, another clean neck!

I keep the BB's in a small jar in the silverware drawer so they're handy when we need them.

gether, and I keep dropping the pieces into it. When the bag is full, I just sew the top shut with my sewing machine. I then have a self-soaping washcloth. —*Carol Ulery Stites, Idaho*

I just have to give you the hint my mother always used for a dry shampoo. I have relied on it several times. Rub cornmeal into your hair, massage your head, then brush and comb it out. This really perks up the hair and scalp. —*Lois Madetzke Elmore, Minnesota*

An excellent way to stop mosquito bites from itching is to rub with a paste made from bar soap. Rub until itching stops and allow the paste to dry. Remove later.
—*Helen Chartier, Oak Lawn, Illinois*

Rinse your hands in vinegar and dry them thoroughly before going outside to work in very cold weather. The vinegar conditions your hands so that your fingers will remain limber a little longer.
—*Linda Weir San Francisco, California*

Working outside around the home is a perfect time to use the makeup that has been shoved to the back of the drawer because the color wasn't quite right for you or it was a poor purchase made one day in a weak moment. It will still form a protection for your skin.

Also, try mixing those dried-out leftovers together and thinning them with a small amount of witch hazel, astringent or baby oil. A creamy lipstick forms a barrier against sun and wind, and I use up all my old lipsticks that way.
—*Mrs. Miles Pierce, Eaton, Indiana*

No matter how carefully I guarded my fingernails, they continued to split and peel. Finally, in desperation, I got a professional manicure and asked the manicurist if she could suggest something.

When she mentioned the possibility of allergy, I was skeptical, but I decided to try eliminating one hand care product at a time. Over a period of weeks, all were tested. Sure enough, a nail-building cream was the culprit. Now my nails are almost back to normal again.
—*Mrs. C. Griffith Memphis, Tennessee*

This recipe for cough syrup is safe even for toddlers. Slice an onion very thin, and alternate layers of onion and sugar. Place a bowl or plate on top of the layers, and squish them down. Soon there will be a juice forming which is very sooth-ing for a cough. If the child likes onions, you may give him the entire sweetened onion. Best of all, there are no medication side effects to worry about. —*Loretta Wege Onaga, Kansas*

Mix cornmeal with lemon juice, and massage over the face. This cleanses the pores and refreshes the skin.

Milk is also a great facial. The

153

natural vitamins, minerals and fats all help your skin. If it's powdered milk, make a paste to pat on the skin. Let dry until it begins to pull. Rinse off.
—*Peggy Bjorkman*
Milwaukee, Wisconsin

A tomato cut in half and pressed on the elbows and heels will soften and diminish callouses and beautify arms and feet.
—*Estelle Beck*
Quincy, Illinois

Place small pieces of hand soap in a container and allow them to dry. When many pieces have accumulated, use your blender on high to completely pulverize into powder. Pour into a pretty container. This soap is the most luxurious bubble bath ever. (Of course, clean your blender thoroughly before using for any food products.)
—*Jane Gradeless*
Columbia City, Indiana

Whenever I had hiccups as a child, my mom would put a handkerchief over the top of a glass of water. I'd then slowly sip water through the handkerchief. Worked every time!
—*Sherry Ruff*
Turtle Lake, Wisconsin

Once a week, I treat my feet to a beauty bath. Near my favorite chair I place a large towel, nail clippers, file, lotion, etc. Then I fill a large pan with hot water and add a little bath oil. If I have sore, tired feet, I add 2 tablespoons Epsom salts. Next I tune in my favorite TV show and relax with my feet in this solution. I dry the feet well, apply lotion and clip the nails. It feels great.
—*Verda Diel, Kiowa, Kansas*

Drinking water out of the far side of a glass will get rid of your hiccups. The trick is to bend over far enough to drink. But be careful not to pour too fast or the water will go right up your nose!
—*Barb Danson, Dayton, Minnesota*

Put a day's dosage of pills in a separate bottle each morning. You know at a glance whether or not you have taken a pill and don't have to worry about taking more than the required dosage.
—*Mrs. Hans Leuthold*
Tillamook, Oregon

Unwrap bar soap before storing. It will harden and last longer besides giving your cupboard a pleasant fragrance.
—*Kit Thompson*
Baldwinsville, New York

Before starting any "dirty" jobs, apply hand cream liberally to your hands and put on a pair of work gloves.
While you are working, your hands are getting a beauty treatment.
—*Mrs. Einar Haaland*
Woodbury, Connecticut

Try this solution to a sticky situation! To remove tree pitch from hands, spray them with nonstick vegetable cooking spray. Rub hands together to work off pitch, then wash with warm water and soap.
—*Desoree Thompson*
Cabazon, California

I place a closed plastic bottle of my skin lotion into the water as I step into a hot tub. When my bath is finished, the lotion is warm and great to smooth on.
—*Mrs. Martin Hanson*
Quimby, Iowa

Save money by refilling liquid soap dispensers with this homemade solution: Grate a soap bar, mix with 3 cups water, melt in a microwave or on the stove, then beat with a rotary beater until smooth.
—*Joanie Elbourn*
Jamestown, Rhode Island

To clean and soften hands after gardening or fieldwork, wash them with pure apple cider vinegar (either diluted or not is fine).
—*Ethel Williams*
Lawrenceville, Pennsylvania

If your costume jewelry drop necklaces leave a tarnish spot on your light-colored shells and blouses, just paint the back of the drop with clear nail polish.
—*Mildred Sherrer, Bay City, Texas*

I've found that a diluted vinegar-and-salt rinse will do away with odors such as onion and garlic on the breath. A soda and salt mixture

in warm water is also a very good inexpensive mouthwash. In addition, these rinses are excellent germ-killing gargles when you are suffering from a sore throat.
—*Mildred Grenier*
St. Joseph, Missouri

To soothe cuts and bruises, make an ice pack for keeping at hand. Fill a zip-type sandwich bag with 2 cups of water and 1/3 cup rubbing alcohol. Zip shut and place in freezer. The slush-type ice that forms will mold perfectly to most parts of the body.
—*Mrs. Arthur Schroeder*
Manitowoc, Wisconsin

Tired of your nylons always running? What I do is put my brand-new hosiery into the freezer for 24 hours, one time only. They always last longer. —*Beverly Kearns*
Ellensburg, Washington

Do you suffer from a dry scratchy throat in winter? Add moisture to the air by putting a bowl of fresh water on your radiator or heating vent each day to act as a "humidifier".
—*Sharon Meaney*
Clearfield, Utah

A slice of onion applied to a bee sting will take the pain away.
—*Julie Klee, Streator, Illinois*

When a bar of soap gets too small to conveniently use, there's no need to throw it away. Just break the scraps into small pieces and put them into an empty squeeze detergent bottle. Fill the bottle with warm water and let it sit for at least a day. Now you have "liquid soap"—simply squeeze out the soap as needed for washing. —*Mary Stilton Bangor, Maine*

To have bath powder that matches your favorite cologne, pour about 1 cup of baby powder into an empty powder box and spray in six or seven squirts of your cologne; stir well. It's much less expensive than buying perfumed bath powder.
—*Juanita Gerlach, Granbury, Texas*

I keep an aloe vera (cactus) plant in a flowerpot near my kitchen window. Called the "medicine plant", it helps soothe and heal burns and cuts that are so common in the kitchen. Just cut off a leaf and squeeze its juice on the injury. It's a pretty plant, too!
—*Mrs. Orville Doyen, Rice, Kansas*

Get combs really clean with no effort. Just put them in the automatic washer along with a load of clothes and you'll find clean combs on top when the cycle is finished.
—*Mrs. Loren Riddle, Castana, Iowa*

When those tiny screws in your glasses won't stay tight, take them out and dab them with a drop of shellac or super glue, then put the screws back in and tighten them. It's a sure cure! —*Donna Flack Denver, Colorado*

Take seven big gulps of water without drawing a breath to eliminate hiccups. —*Pam Baumgartner Minneapolis, Minnesota*

I used to have chapped hands all winter until I discovered latex gloves (the close-fitting kind used by veterinarians). I wear them when

NIP OF NATURE
Is there anything to the weather rhyme, "Red sky in the morning, sailors take warning; red sky at night, sailors' delight"?

YES, *there may be more fact than folklore, at least the "red sky at night" portion.*

Weather patterns tend to flow from west to east. So, when a sunset appears especially red, "tomorrow's air" lying behind it is likely dry and a nice day will follow. If the sunset appears to be gray or yellowish, the sun is likely shining through a mass of wet stuff, and this forecasts rainy weather's a day away.

I milk or do other hands-on farm chores where bulky gloves get in the way. —*Marion Weigold*
McBain, Michigan

For a handy ice pack, use a bag of frozen vegetables such as peas. It's inexpensive and molds itself well to the injured area.
—*Barbara Howland*
Framingham, Massachusetts

If you burn your tongue while eating something that's too hot, put a little sugar on your tongue. Let the sugar dissolve and that will take away the burn and you can enjoy the rest of your meal.
—*Bernadette Franco*
Charlotte, North Carolina

You don't need expensive hand cleaners to remove pine tar and tree sap! Simply wet with rubbing alcohol, then follow up with soap and water. —*Tanya Kelley*
Doylestown, Ohio

Here's a sure cure for the hiccups. Pour approximately 4 to 6 ounces of water into a glass cup and place a metal teaspoon in the glass. Drink all of the water, leaving the spoon in the glass while you drink. It works every time for me!
—*Joan Kratzer*
Zolfo Springs, Florida

Put mouthwash into a plastic squeezable bottle and just squirt out the amount you need. No more mess or wasted cups.
—*Mary Ann Dwileski*
Nassau, New York

COUNTRY TRIVIA

THE smallest breed of horses is the Falabella, which grows only 30 inches high. Originally bred in Argentina, Falabellas are kept as pets.

I put a dab of vanilla extract right on cold sores. It works well and you have the vanilla right in your kitchen cabinet, saving you the trouble of going to the store.
—*Pat Thompson*
Dansville, New York

To save soap when the soap bar gets small, I simply get out a new bar and bathe with it. Then I place the small bar on top of the new one and squeeze the two together. They always meld and I never have any small pieces lying around. I have been doing this for years and wonder why anyone would throw soap away. —*Doris Powers*
Memphis, Tennessee

To remove all traces of shampoo, use a vinegar-water solution as a final rinse. It leaves your hair soft, glossy and sweet-smelling.
—*Sue Humphrey*
St. Joseph, Missouri

Even though we farm wives are always on the go, it still seems we need some spot reducing now and then. If you have small children, though, there's no need to make exercising a drudgery that you do alone. Have them join in and make a game of it.

When I'm doing toe-touches, I put the baby on the floor next to me and tickle him every time I reach for my toes. He loves it! Or I have a little one hold my feet while I do sit-ups. Exercise time has become a part of the day to look forward to!
—*Mrs. Gary Meyers*
Winslow, Illinois

If your hands burn and sting after handling hot peppers, pour rubbing alcohol on them.   —*Pat Lane*
Pullman, Washington

Arthritis in my finger joints is eased when I drink cider vinegar and honey three times a day. I mix 2 teaspoons of cider vinegar and 2 teaspoons of honey into 1/2 cup of warm water—and that makes me feel much better!   —*Duain Dohm*
Westboro, Wisconsin

There are lots of ways to get small fibers or "pricklies" in your skin…from cactus, steel wool, insulation and other things around the house or yard. One way to get these hard-to-see stickers out of your finger is to rub a thin layer of glue over the sore spot. Let the glue dry, then peel it *and* the fibers away!
—*Virginia Boyd*
Redyard, Connecticut

If you get tired standing at the kitchen sink for long periods of time washing fruits and vegetables, etc., like I do, try this—open the cabinet doors under the sink, pull up a tall stool and you'll have room to put your tired feet under the sink.
—*Lucille Annesser, Joplin, Missouri*

Save pieces of used soap, tie them tightly in a piece of soft flannel and dip in boiling water until soft. Then place in cold water until firm. Remove the flannel and you have a good ball of soap ready to use.   —*Ruby Shelton*
King, North Carolina

Here's a tip for toasty hands even on frosty days: When you go out to start up your car or pickup in the morning, turn on the heater and set your gloves on the floor. When you put the gloves on, you'll feel warm all over!   —*Marion Carter*
Gilman City, Missouri

Instead of throwing away those tiny scraps of soap, save them until you have a quart or so. Place them in a pan with water and heat on the stove, stirring until melted.

Pour the smooth mixture onto waxed paper, mold it into different shapes and add food coloring if you wish. I've saved myself from buying about eight bars of soap by doing this!
—*Janice Smith*
Cynthiana, Kentucky

To treat canker sores inside your mouth, place some powdered alum (a spice) on them. It tastes very bitter, but takes away the sting and dries up the sores after several applications.
—*Rhonda Fries*
Pittsburgh, Pennsylvania

To remove a wooden splinter, place a drop or two of iodine over the spot where the splinter entered. The iodine will turn the splinter a darker color, allowing you to see it clearly. Press an ice cube over the spot for a few seconds before probing. —*Mrs. Raymond Heintz*
Poynette, Wisconsin

Here's a home remedy for poison ivy or poison oak. Purchase some lime (the dry white powder) from the drugstore or hardware store, and mix it with shortening until you have a paste like cold cream. Spread the paste on your rash. It has worked for me! —*Reta Howell*
Grand Prairie, Texas

To easily remove thistle stickers, take a piece of wide packing tape and apply it to the affected area, then remove it. Several applications of tape should pull out the stickers. I tried this with my son, and it pulled the tiny hair-like stickers right out of his foot.
—*Joan Hamilton*
Chehalis, Washington

Eat a spoonful of peanut butter to get rid of hiccups. Works every time! —*Sandy Hathaway*
Aurora, North Carolina

Here's a home remedy for bee stings: Wet the injured area and apply meat tenderizer. It stops the pain immediately. —*Jean Kubley*
Glidden, Wisconsin

Soak panty hose in 2 cups of salt and 1 gallon of water for 3 hours, then drip-dry to prevent runs.
—*Rosemary Reiners*
Bucyrus, Missouri

To get the last of the hand lotion out of a plastic or glass bottle, warm the bottle in the microwave without a cap. After 15 seconds or so, the lotion will be heated enough so that it runs easily, and you can pour the last drops into the new bottle, thus not wasting any.
—*Kerry Bouchard*
Shawmut, Montana

CHAPTER 10

DEALING WITH PESTS & PETS

I had weevils in my cornmeal until I began storing it in the freezer. It needs no thawing to be ready to use. —*Hazel Baxter, Friona, Texas*

If crickets are a problem, just put some borax in a plastic squeeze bottle (the kind that baby powder comes in). Then sprinkle the borax in any cracks and along baseboards where the crickets are gathering. But be sure it's in areas out of reach of children and pets! —*Bill Wagner Hastings, Michigan*

Newspaper repels moths. This is most helpful when storing woolen rugs, too.
—*Mrs. Arlen Schellpfeffer Horicon, Wisconsin*

One summer, I was kept busy trying to protect my plants in the flower boxes, where our cats dearly loved to sleep. Finally I found that putting pinecones around the plants not only kept the cats out but also made the boxes prettier as the plants began to grow. Another bonus: The cones discouraged weeds!
—*Mrs. Stephen Viggers Washington County, Iowa*

My husband tried all the usual ways to get one of our calves who had been abandoned by his mother to drink milk out of a bottle or bucket. But that stubborn calf wouldn't touch it.

Then I shooed everyone out of the barn and went to work. I got a wooden spoon and some corn syrup and forced a spoonful into the calf's mouth. After I did this a few times, he was eager for more.

Next, he was drinking milk from the spoon, and by the time my husband came back in, I had him drinking from a bottle.
—*Mrs. Leland McAbee Broken Bow, Nebraska*

If you're stung by a bee, apply a slice of onion to the spot and hold it there for a minute or two. It does the trick! —*Jay Stphenson* *La Follette, Tennessee*

If you don't have a storage cupboard near your calf, lamb or pig pens, invest in a nail apron or make one. Then you can carry along scours tablets, small bottles of medicine, needles, syringes, a tape measure to use for growth checks, etc. A small notebook and pen to jot down health notes is also handy. Be sure to hang your apron from a nail placed high enough so that playful animals cannot reach it! —*Tonia Bledsoe* *North Lawrence, Ohio*

Even the most stubborn calf will be eager to learn how to drink out of a bucket…if you skip a feeding before offering him the bucket for the first time.
—*Mrs. Alfred Studer* *Sabetha, Kansas*

If you are having a problem with rabbits or other little animals eating at your plants and flowers, just sprinkle a little red pepper on the plants. —*Lori Juhl* *Luverne, Minnesota*

I have a small patch of sweet corn, eight or nine hills square, in my garden. But since I have thieving raccoons for neighbors, I was having trouble harvesting any of my crop. To put a stop to this, I set a bedrail post in the middle of the patch, ran an extension cord out to it and hung up a 25-watt flashing light bulb. When the corn starts ripening, I turn the light on about dark and turn it off when I get up in the morning.

It works; I haven't lost any more corn to coons. It scares them away from my grapevines near the corn patch, too.
—*Mrs. Harvey Muller* *Danboro, Pennsylvania*

For best results when milking your "nanny" goat, feed her some grain to keep her busy and content until you get the job done. It's also a good way for you to keep tabs on her eating habits.
—*Susie Wiedenbeck* *Del Norte, Colorado*

Hair's a help in keeping rabbits away from your garden! Just fill nylon or net bags with strands from a hair brush…then stake bags around your plot.
—*Desoree Thompson Cabazon, California*

Sprinkle moth crystals in your vegetable and flower gardens to keep animals such as rabbits, chipmunks and dogs out. It has even helped us keep birds away from our strawberries.
—*Mrs. Wilbert Zimmerman* *Ringle, Wisconsin*

Sponge your kitchen counters and cupboards with vinegar and the ants will stay away.
—*Twilla Hornickel, Ord, Nebraska*

Bothered by moths among your woolens? To keep pests away, store wearables with a few whole cloves.
—*Marie Person*
Melrose, Massachusetts

When a calf is too weak to nurse, we feed it using an old turkey baster. We're able to force-feed if necessary and the calf can learn to suck at the same time
—*Lynne Kaye Bilyew*
Assumption, Illinois

For homemade flypaper, simmer equal amounts of sugar, corn syrup and water till granules dissolve, then brush onto narrow strips cut from brown paper bags. Tack strips up by one end.
—*Wanda Smith, Rockville, Maryland*

Giving a calf a pill can be a pain for you! I've found this solution works for me: After popping the pill into the calf's throat with a balling gun, I use a regular-sized pop bottle filled with water to wash it down.

Since the mouth of the bottle is small and long, the water goes down the calf's mouth, not up its nose...*or down my leg.* —*Amy Wright*
Cataldo, Idaho

Add a mothball to the dirt when planting a tree to keep insects away.
—*Veronica O'Connor*
Stoutsville, Missouri

Plan on building a doghouse but not sure how big it should be? A good rule of thumb is to make it one-third longer and one-half taller than the dog, and make the width two-thirds of its shoulder height. In cold climates, the house should have a vestibule that should be twice the width of the dog and 2 inches taller than its shoulders.

—*Bev Albrecht, Cincinnati, Ohio*

IT WORKED FOR GRANDPA!
Some "seasoned advice" from Grandpa Zeb:

IF FLEAS are brought into the house by your dog, don't have a bird! (On the other hand, the bird might take care of the fleas.) But here's a way to get rid of fleas without expensive commercial products:

Put an inch of water in a shallow bowl and add a tablespoon of liquid dishwashing soap. Don't stir the solution. Before you go to bed, put the bowl on the floor and place a lamp with a 60-watt bulb as close to the bowl as possible. Turn out all the other lights.

Then put your dog in the room, but close off the area so he can't get near the bowl. Then enjoy sweet dreams. Have patience—it works.

Bugged by box elder bugs? Fill a plastic cup (one at least 3 inches high) half full with a peppermint mouthwash. Set in windowsills or wherever bugs are a nuisance. They are attracted to the taste and soon end up trapped in the liquid.

—*Eilene Swensen*
Mission Hill, South Dakota

To make life a little easier for the birds during extra-frigid winter weather, I hang two 40-watt outdoor lights from tree branches about 6 inches from the feeder. Even when they're not eating, some birds just sit there to enjoy the warmth that those bulbs give off. —*Ev Nugent*
Agincourt, Ontario

Bringing in bugs along with your just-picked produce? Rinse garden-fresh vegetables well, then let soak in mixture of 1 gallon water and 1 cup vinegar for about 5 minutes. Insects will be easier to pick off, and the flavor of your produce won't be affected. —*Joyce Corzine*
Scotts Hill, Tennessee

A newborn calf who is too heavy to pick up and too stubborn to go in the right direction can easily be "assisted" toward the barn by using a gunnysack as a sling under its stomach. It works best with someone lifting on each end of the sling, but even one person can lift the calf enough so it can be pulled in the right direction with little trouble.

—*Judy Studer*
Greenfield, Wisconsin

Hair spray or iodine spray can help reunite a calf with its mother. Just spray some on the calf and some on the cow's nose…you'll be surprised how fast the cow will start licking the calf. —*Mrs. Allen Curl*
Wasta, South Dakota

"Dry clean" your dog during winter by rubbing baking soda into its fur. Brush out with an old hairbrush. —*Martha Beckman*
Granada Hills, California

I've come up with this home remedy to help rid baby calves of scours. I add 1 package pectin, 1/2 teaspoon salt and 1/2 teaspoon soda to 1/2 gallon of warm water, then mix in a can of bouillon or consomme *or* some Karo syrup. I feed this mix in place of milk.

—*Sharon Thompson*
Tygh Valley, Oregon

Here's a safe way to "best" pests that bother your cabbage and broccoli plants! Dust the plants in late afternoon with baking soda. When dew settles on the soda, the mixture will form an anti-worm enzyme—but it won't harm humans, and it'll wash off easily with a little water. —*Betty Campbell*
Sparta, Georgia

Instead of using chemical spray last spring when we had an ant problem, I brushed heavy "traffic areas" with some baby oil. The ants had a tough time keeping their balance on the slick surface…and, after several applications, our "friends" vanished!

—*Margaret Shauers*
Great Bend, Kansas

It's hard to reason with a stubborn pig who doesn't want to step into a truck, right? Well, I've found that if you put a bushel basket over its head, you can lead a pig anywhere you want it to go.
—*Ruth Weis, Burchard, Nebraska*

If baby calves are too sick to eat on their own, "spoon-feed" them instead—with a turkey baster! Just dip the baster into a pail of warm milk, then slip into calf's mouth. A baster is also handy for flushing out wounds on horses or other livestock.
—*Lin Chaffey, Tofield, Alberta*

I have kept the raccoons out of my 1/2-acre sweet corn patch for 2 years now by burning a light and playing a radio all night long. I put the radio in the middle of the patch and cover it from weather.
—*Margie Finch*
Janesville, Wisconsin

Keep raccoons and other small animals out of your hair—and plants—by spreading dog hair (available at dog groomers') around the edges of your garden.
—*Toni Gween, Okeechobee, Florida*

Leave leaves out of the chicken coop! Chickens can't digest stems.
—*Sharon Nichols*
Brookings, South Dakota

Mealybugs bugging your growing things? Dip a cotton swab in rubbing alcohol and brush each bug.
—*Mildred Sherrer, Bay City, Texas*

Nasturtiums, spearmint or radishes planted near squash plants will act as a natural insecticide.
—*Veronica Seek, Kalispell, Montana*

If skunks have holed up in your garage or shed, beat them at their own game! Punch a few holes in baking powder cans and add several mothballs. The smell will disturb your unwanted visitors so much they'll soon depart.
—*Gertrude Johns*
Greenbrier, Arkansas

When we have to revive a newborn calf with artificial respiration, we use a 1-liter motor oil plastic container. To do the same, wash con-

When we first spot one of our young chickens pecking at another one, we immediately apply pine tar to the victim's wound. Then, when the attacker(s) return, and find that the taste is really awful, they soon find something else to amuse themselves with. You have to catch the pecking early, though, for this treatment to be effective.
—*Ben Wolff*
Mukwonago, Wisconsin

tainer *thoroughly*, then cut 1/4 inch off of the bottom and discard. Fit "respirator" snugly over the mouth and nose of the calf to form a tight seal as you blow into the pour spout.
—*Noreen Riviere*
Radville, Saskatchewan

Use a thick solution of baking soda and water on a dog that has gotten too "friendly" with a skunk. Allow it to dry on the dog—the baking soda stays in the coat, and it keeps right on working!
—*Carol Apple*
Schenectady, New York

When my youngsters came back from the blackberry patch one day, they were covered with seed ticks I couldn't wash off easily. So I dabbed the sticky side of masking tape onto the little critters—and quickly captured them all!   —*Betsy Rugen*
Prairie Home, Missouri

Don't plant sweet corn near tomato plants—the same worm likes to feast on both crops.
—*Jeanette Strobel*
Brainerd, Minnesota

If spiders and mites seem mighty pesty, try this "natural" insecticide. Mix 1/2 cup of buttermilk and 4 cups wheat flour in 5 gallons of water. Spray as needed to control the problem.
—*Mildred Sherrer*
Bay City, Texas

Are you up all night checking on cows about to calve or mares soon to foal? Save yourself those countless trips out to the barn (not to mention sleepless nights!) by installing a baby monitor. Put the transmitter in the barn and the speaker in the house, with the receiver beside your bed. Then "stay tuned"!   —*Barbara McCleary*
Marion, Pennsylvania

Blow up plastic bags, tie securely and attach to the tops of garden stakes with a 1-foot length of string. Drive the stakes in and around your garden and fruit areas. Also tie the bags to fruit shrubs and fruit tree limbs. They make marvelous "scarecrows" when the wind blows.
—*Alberta Hanson*
Cushing, Wisconsin

Don't forget that feathered friends count on you in the winter! When it's cold outside, they es-  pecially need suet to build up extra fat. Give this recipe a try:

Melt 1 pound lard and 1/2 cup peanut butter in a saucepan over low heat, stirring occasionally. Add 1 cup cornmeal and 1/2 cup of sunflower seeds. Pour into a pan lined with waxed paper and chill until set. Place a chunk of suet in an empty mesh onion bag and hang from a tree branch.   —*Tina Sheppard*
Ballston Spa, New York

Teaching a new calf to drink? Set the pail of milk inside an old car tire. The calf can butt its head against the pail without spilling the milk.
—*Paula White, Viola, Wisconsin*

Once sweet corn starts to form on the cob, you can keep raccoons at bay by sprinkling a little cayenne pepper or red pepper between the rows and up and down the cornstalks. If coons step in the pepper and lick their feet, they're sure *not* to like the heat! *—Ruth Schoeff Huntington, Indiana*

Since we keep a backyard flock of hens, we find ourselves occasionally with a boxful of noisy chicks that need tending. Instead of using a heat lamp to keep them warm, I put a fuzzy old teddy bear face down on a heating pad. With nooks and crannies to escape into and a cozy place to sleep, the chicks are content…and surprisingly quiet! *—Barb Meuleman Port Perry, Ontario*

If your dog gets "skunked", rub tomato juice in its hair, then bathe it. The skunk's "perfume" will disappear! If you're out of juice, substitute ketchup mixed with water. *—Mrs. L.B. Felz Throckmorton, Texas*

To get rid of bothersome slugs, sprinkle rock salt around the base of your house. *—Eleta Jones Louisville, Kentucky*

If birds feast on your fruit trees, make them feel unwelcome—by hanging plastic bags on the branches. The bags' rustling sound scares the majority of birds off, leaving most of the harvest for eating and canning. *—Barbara Tennant Potrero, California*

Sweeten pellets with a sprinkling of molasses to get very young calves to eat them. Put an older "cousin" in with the babies, too—little ones'll soon catch on from watching it eat. *—Diane Jahner Lehr, North Dakota*

To remove porcupine quills from pets, mix 2 teaspoons of baking soda with 1 cup of vinegar and pat on the quills. Wait 10 minutes, reapply, wait another 10 minutes and remove the quills. *—Karen Schieche, Alma, Wisconsin*

To make a neat cozy bed for your dog in winter, fill a burlap bag with hay or straw and place in its doghouse. *—Ethel Williams Lawrenceville, Pennsylvania*

When our mares foal, we give the babies their first haircut almost right away—by the time they're a week old. We start by trimming bridle areas and whiskers, then move on to their ears in a few months. That way, the horses are much easier to handle when they get bigger. *—June Wemlinger Tecumseh, Missouri*

Here's a way to save money on small pets' flea collars. Buy a large flea collar, cut it in half and put

snaps on the other end with no fastener. You get two collars for the price of one. Store second collar in a zip-type bag until ready to use.
—*Kris Ward, Monticello, Minnesota*

Do you have problems with dogs getting into your garbage? Spray bug spray on your garbage sacks or bags, and dogs will not come near them.   —*Maria Sills Oak Ridge, Tennessee*

To teach an orphan pig to drink, put 1/2 inch of warm milk into a flat pan and set piglet in the milk, feet and all. Push its head down until it tastes the milk. Even newborns quickly learn to drink this way.
—*Marjorie Talbert St. Ignatius, Montana*

To keep spiders out of your house, keep a few hedge apples or Osage oranges in the basement or in whichever room has spiders.
—*Mrs. Clifford Schwab Hamilton, Ohio*

Worms won't bother tomatoes if you plant dill nearby.
—*Juanita Peek, Annona, Texas*

Put an unwrapped stick of spearmint gum in your flour bin and that will keep the bugs out.
—*Carolyn Holdeman Goshen, Indiana*

If dogs run through your flower beds, stomp a few mothballs into the ground around the edges. That'll stop 'em.
—*Bernice Ausberger, Fonda, Iowa*

COUNTRY TRIVIA

WASHINGTON County, Texas has more horse ranches than any other county in the U.S.

To reduce cat hair around your house, gently run a damp paper towel over the cat. It collects both hair and dirt.   —*Drusilla Hartz West Chester, Pennsylvania*

For insect bites and bee stings, I rub a dab of toothpaste over the spot. Before long, the swelling goes down and the itch goes away.
—*L. Broadwater McHenry, Maryland*

Put cucumber peels on your kitchen windowsill to keep out pesky ants.   —*Betty Thompson Belton, South Carolina*

Instead of using insecticide spray against roaches and fleas, try this citrus solution. Put the juice from four lemons or two grapefruits in 1/2 gallon of water. Let the rinds soak in the water, too. Rub this solution on floors. Bugs don't like the smell and they will stay away.
—*Mildred Sherrer, Bay City, Texas*

Don't dispose of aquarium water when you clean out your fish tank. Instead, use it to water your plants. It doubles as an excellent fertilizer, too.   —*Ruth Hiltunen Osakis, Minnesota*

If you find a skunk in your garage or other small building, one way to get rid of him is to spray insect repellent into the building through a crack or hole in the wall. The skunk won't like the smell and will take a walk...out of the building.

—*Mylle McLean, Cheyenne, Kansas*

Keep cats out of your flower bed by sprinkling a can of cayenne pepper on the soil. One sniff and off they go!

—*Elva Pate*
Williamston, North Carolina

Trouble with bugs in your kitchen cabinets? Sprinkle cinnamon on the shelves. That will get rid of the bugs, and smell good, too!

—*Karen Work, Lompoc, California*

When mosquitoes bother you, gently rub a sheet of fabric softener on your skin. It will drive away the mosquitoes.

—*Kim Curtis*
Pickford, Michigan

To keep my trash can from smelling and make it less tempting to animals, I freeze all food scraps and then throw them out on the morning the trash will be picked up. I also rinse all food containers that I'm about to throw away.

—*Marion MacDonald*
Beacon, New York

To keep ants out of bird feeders, use a paper towel to put a small amount of vegetable oil on the plastic cap atop the feeder. It doesn't harm the birds, but it sure keeps ants away! I did this to my hummingbird feeder and didn't have ants for weeks.

—*Kathy Smedstad*
Silverton, Oregon

If you need a foster mother in the chicken house, try a little "trickery". Dust orphan chicks with talcum powder, then dust the designated hen's chicks, too. Since they will have the same scent, the hen will think the chicks are all hers.

Short a few heat lamps? To keep piglets or baby lambs warm temporarily, put them in a basket along with straw and a gallon jug of warm water (capped, of course!).

—*Aileen De Hamer, Cedar, Iowa*

To keep sweet corn from being bugged, put a drop of mineral oil on silks when they start out of the shuck.

—*Virginia Kiser*
Piedmont, Missouri

If moles have been bothering your tulips, just put a ring of gravel around your bulbs when you plant them. This discourages the moles from eating the bulbs.

—*Toni Hogenbirk*
East Stroudsburg, Pennsylvania

Use trash can bags cut in half as litter box liners. Large plastic grocery store bags work, too.

—*Marlene Mullen, Valley City, Ohio*

When we put our box fan in the window to draw in cool night air, we noticed it also sucked in tiny bugs. To avoid this, attach two or

three layers of cheesecloth—the type used in kitchens—to the screen. It'll also reduce dirt intake.
—*Kathryn Simmons*
Point Pleasant, West Virginia

You can quickly make a disposable dish for feeding your dog or cat by cutting a few inches off the bottom of a 1-gallon plastic milk jug. When you want a fresh dish, recycle the old one and cut a new one.
—*Silas Dodgen, Ithaca, New York*

Keep flies away from windows in your home by cutting 2-inch pieces of a pest strip, then attaching them with a small nail between the window and screen. —*Rosalie Sheptick*
Hayward, Wisconsin

Banish bugs from your house "naturally"—by hanging a bouquet of dried tomato leaves in all rooms. Mosquitoes, spiders and flies will flee!   —*LaFlorya Gauthier*
St. Didace, Quebec

To keep cabbageworms away, "season" your plants by mixing 1/4 teaspoon thyme, 1/4 teaspoon sage and 1 quart water. Spray on any cabbage family plants in your garden.
—*Mrs. Allen Curl*
Wasta, South Dakota

Is your pet in the doghouse because it brings mosquitoes into *your* house? Attach a plastic bag, a feed sack or other material over the door of the doghouse, then cut slits in it. When the dog walks through, mosquitoes rub right off!
—*Mrs. W.R. Stogner, Dallas, Texas*

An easy way to feed baby pigs that haven't learned to drink yet is to put a slice or two of bread in a pan of milk—the bread soaks up the milk, and the pigs will suck on the bread.   —*Margaret DeCamp*
Muscatine, Iowa

To keep birds out of your strawberry patch, place several wooden black cats found in craft shops around the plants. Glue marbles on the cats for eyes and paint on whiskers. Ours look so real that birds never come near our berries.
—*Margaret Martin*
Harrison, Arkansas

Anyone who has ever run after chickens and ducks out in the yard knows they're not easy to corner. I finally bought a *big* fishing net. No more wild chases!   —*Mary Burr*
Valley Springs, California

Pigs can be trained to come when you call! Before feeding ours, I always bang on the metal feed bucket with an old metal spoon. Then, if they escape from their pen, I do the same…and they come running every time!   —*Irma Eaton*
Tollhouse, California

Substitute small bowls for bottles when you feed piglets—they are easier for the animals to drink from and easier for you to clean! Besides, with bowls, you can add cooked potatoes to the milk when pigs are ready for solid food. —*Bev Hunter Birch Hills, Saskatchewan*

Weevils hate bay leaves! So put some of these potent leaves in your flour and cereal containers during warm weather to keep the pests out. —*Mrs. George Boettcher Polk County, Wisconsin*

Sparrows and other small birds won't take up residence under your patio awning if you tuck plastic throwaway cups in its ridges. —*Sandra Cowden, Westpoint, Utah*

The squirrels had a habit of climbing right up into my bird feeder and bothering my feathered friends—until I discovered this homemade way to "baffle" them. I cut a small hole in the center of the bottom of two empty gallon milk jugs. Then I turned them upside down and threaded them on my bird feeder pole, as far up as the base of the feeder. Two jugs are just enough to keep the squirrels from scampering past to help themselves to a free meal! —*Frieda Shannon Iowa City, Iowa*

If you're tired of your dog turning over his water dish, try this trick—it worked for me! Use an old angel food cake pan with a stake pounded through the "hole" into the ground. No matter how rough your dog plays, he'll never get all wet! —*Mildred Sherrer, Bay City, Texas*

If you can't sleep because a cricket's come calling, here's a sure cure. Put a wet washcloth in your kitchen or bathroom sink at night, and you'll find your noisy "neighbor" hiding there in the morning! —*Eilene Swensen Mission Hill, South Dakota*

While goats can get *your* goat by chewing bark off trees, I've found an effective way to stop them: Soak a shovelful of goat manure in a bucket of water for several days, then—with a large brush—"paint" the trunks and any overhanging limbs the goats might be tempted to munch on. Repeat the treatment occasionally. —*Corae Garner Jasper, Arkansas*

To give little lambs a fast start, try this milk replacer recipe: Blend together 1-1/2 pints whole cow's

NIP OF NATURE
How long is the pregnancy of a horse?

THE AVERAGE is 336 days. And as for the length of a pregnancy for some other animals, this little guide should help:
Rabbits...31 days; Swine...114 days; Sheep...148 days; Goats...151 days; Cattle...283 days; Horses...336 days; Llamas...345 days.

milk, 1 egg, 1 teaspoon of cod liver oil (or less) and 1 tablespoon dark Karo syrup; feed 2 pints per day.

And here's my home remedy for bloated lambs: Mix together 1 tablespoon baking soda, 1/4 to 1/2 teaspoon ginger and 1/2 cup warm water. —*Knalurt Kranch New England, North Dakota*

Since cats, dogs and other animals tend to urinate repeatedly in the same places, cleaning and removing the urine stain isn't the whole solution. You have to get rid of the odor, not just mask it, or the animal will likely return to the same spot.

So, use a mixture of equal parts of white vinegar and baking soda, and apply it as you would any cleaning solution. Sponge it onto the carpet or wall. This will neutralize the odor and help prevent it from happening again. —*Virginia Ratcliff Stone Creek, Ohio*

Got a snake problem? Snakes like the warmth of stone steps or a stone wall on a sunny day. To discourage them from taking their naps there, just sprinkle a bag of dried sulfur around the house. It keeps ants away, too. You can get dried sulfur at most farm and garden stores. —*Sylvia Howard Brookville, Indiana*

There's no mistaking how much your calves should get to eat—no matter who's doing the feeding—if you follow this tip.

Mark the "fill line" on the pitcher used for measuring milk or water for milk replacer with a bright color of nail polish. (If you use two measurements, use two colors.) The polish stands up well to frequent washings, too. —*Sherry Giles Plum City, Wisconsin*

To remove bats from your attic, first seal all cracks except the one that the bats appear to be using most as access to the attic. You can tell which one that is by the droppings around the opening. Then put a bright light at the peak of the attic and leave it on around the clock for a few days. Bats don't like lights. Then, after checking that all the bats are gone, seal up the entrance hole. —*Martha Pasche Escondido, California*

Before you start scratching insect bites, rub on meat tenderizer, white vinegar or lemon juice. Any of these eliminate the itch. But don't apply the lemon juice full strength if you've already scratched the area raw. —*Norma Grimsman Hastings, Michigan*

To keep squirrels off your birdfeeder, hang the feeder from a long wire suspended between two trees, but away from any low branches. Then, to keep the squirrels from "tight-rope walking" to your feeder, string a number of empty thread spools on the wire. When the squir-

To soothe nervous ewes during lambing time, play the radio continuously. The sound will help to keep sheep calm as people come and go.
—*Sonya Colvin*
Cambridge, Iowa

rel steps on the spools, they'll spin, flipping him off. It not only works, it's fun to watch. —*Tom Wheeler*
Richmond, Illinois

I grow carnivorous plants like Venus's-flytraps, pitcher plants and sundews. They act as natural insecticides in my house, helping rid us of bugs that often lurk in country homes. —*Connie Rubens*
Carter, Montana

Here's a way to get rid of spiders. Put cedar chips in the toes of old panty hose and hang the hose from the porch railing or other areas where the spiders build their webs. I don't know why, but it works.

Two other ways to get rid of spiders are to spray rubbing alcohol on windowsills, or scatter perfumed soap chips around their "working areas". —*Robert Black*
Darlington, Maryland

If woodpeckers or other birds begin pecking holes in the wooden shingles and eaves of your house, just hang some toy snakes around the eaves where the birds are both-

ering. Hang them so that the breeze will move them. —*Jean Fehl*
Angleton, Texas

Try this approach to a knotty problem! Wearing old rubber gloves, rub a little vegetable oil on cockleburs stuck in a horse's mane or tail. They will come right out!
—*Sharon Becker, Osceola, Iowa*

If your cats don't like to share a litter box, get some inexpensive shallow plastic pans so each can have its own. —*Lorraine Voken*
Beaver Dam, Wisconsin

It may be hard to believe, but skunks hate strong odors. So, to keep skunks from moving into your toolshed or whatever, hang a bar of strong disinfectant or room deodorizer in the building. —*Shirley Aust*
Cambridge City, Indiana

To get rid of skunk odor (and I hope you never have to!), you might try this method that worked superbly for me a number of years ago:

One spring evening just before dark, I decided to go out and close the chicken house door so no coyote or skunk would get at our laying hens.

Unfortunately, the skunk beat me there and when it was as surprised as I was, it sprayed me full in the face (but luckily not in my eyes)!

In panic, I remembered what one of our older neighbors had told me about how she got rid of the smell after a skunk had sprayed her. I decided to try her remedy.

I gathered a few small pieces of wood and some wood chips. I put down the chips first, then the firewood, and risked a quick trip into my kitchen to get matches and a cup of cornmeal.

I lighted the fire, and when it was blazing a little, I sprinkled half of the cornmeal over the flames, causing a heavy swirl of smoke. I stepped to one side of the fire so that the slight breeze blew the smoke onto my body.

I twisted and turned, bent down low, and encouraged the smoke to engulf my body. I continued turning and contorting myself to get the greatest possible exposure to the smoke. I blew on the fire to make it blaze again, then added the rest of the cornmeal. Bending low, I carefully lowered my head to get the smoke into my hair, turning around and around.

I felt the smell was gone, but was afraid I was no longer a good judge of that! So I put out the fire, went in and washed up, and then decided to say nothing when my husband and daughter came home.

After they told me of the evening's events, I couldn't stand it any longer. "Do you smell anything?" I asked innocently.

"No, nothing. Should we?"

Then I told them my adventure!

They came closer to me and sniffed. My daughter even smelled my hair. No odor!

My husband thought I was fooling them, so I told him to go out and check the chicken house. He didn't have to go that far, for when he got near the hen house, the smell reached him and he firmly believed me.

My neighbor's trick had really worked, bless her heart.

—*Rheba Clark, Cincinnati, Ohio*

To ward off mosquitoes or other biting insects, rub baby oil or imitation vanilla extract on your skin. Works for me!
—*Connie Simons, Gatesvillle, Texas*

Squirt lemon juice on windowsills and along the bottom of doors to discourage ants from entering the house.   —*Karen Ann Bland Gove, Kansas*

Out of insect spray? If you're bothered by bees or other insects and don't have any of the regular sprays around, just grab a can of hair spray. It stiffens their wings and they'll drop to the ground.
—*Lorraine Roppe Fargo, North Dakota*

173

CHAPTER 11

CHILD-CARE TIPS TO FIX LITTLE DISASTERS

Any dish or bowl can be turned into a spill-proof dish for a child. Just attach one of the round soap holders sold in grocery and dime stores. (These round rubber disks covered with small suction cups are for holding soap to the shower wall or sink.) Dampen one side and press it onto a plate. Then press the plate to the high chair or table.
—Mrs. Ralph Stellick
Stoddard, Wisconsin

Whenever our family goes on a car trip, each of the children brings along a covered cake pan to hold crayons, pencils, paper and coloring books. When closed, the lid makes a nice writing surface.—*Pat Rodeffer*
Ferris, Illinois

When our young son became ill with a virus, the doctor prescribed several liquid medicines that had to be taken during the day. One kind was bad-tasting to him, and it became quite a battle to get him to take

it. In desperation I gave him an ice cube to suck on for a while before taking the medicine. The ice temporarily dulled his taste buds, and he swallowed the medicine without a complaint.   *—Mrs. Eugene Meyer*
Burt, Iowa

The sugar bowl proved to be a problem with our small children. Not only did they often spill sugar, but they wasted it by putting too many spoonfuls on cereal and other foods. Finally I put the sugar in a large salt shaker and taped on a little "sugar" label. My problem was solved.   *—Mrs. Ed Ungrun*
Bedford County, Tennessee

When towels begin to look worn, convert them into soft, cuddly animal toys for children. Stuff the animals with discarded nylons. The toys are easily washed in your machine and dry quickly.
—Mrs. H.B. Haaland
Woodbury, Connecticut

174

When old socks wear out in the heels and toes, cut off the good tops and slip over baby's arms while he's in the high chair. This is great when you have the child all dressed but need to feed him. You know how messy shirt sleeves can get!

—*Mrs. William Bockting*
Morrison, Missouri

When we travel with our children, we don't have room for a suitcase for each person. To give each child a sense of responsibility and a chance to pack some of his own things, I make 12-inch x 8-inch "ditty bags". Each bag has a drawstring and holds pajamas, toothbrush, a book, a toy and maybe a jacket. The filled bags double as pillows while riding. —*Mrs. H.D. Fountain*
Iowa City, Iowa

When making bibs for small children, instead of using strings to tie the bibs, use elastic 1/4 inch wide and long enough to slip over a child's head easily. This eliminates knots and torn strings.

—*Mrs. H.O. Daley*
Parker, Colorado

To remove the handwriting on the wall—junior variety—I find that nothing is so quick and easy, even for stubborn crayon marks, as a dab of abrasive "whitening, brightening-type" toothpaste on an old toothbrush. —*Mrs. Robert Olson*
Taylor, Wisconsin

Having a family of nine children, we usually have two or three out every night baby-sitting, work-

ing or on dates. After being called out of bed several times because someone had been locked out, I decided to put the names of family members who were out each night on our blackboard. Now, as each person comes home, he crosses off his name. The last person in locks the door and turns off the light. —*Mrs. Joe Sullivan*
Macomb, Illinois

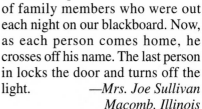

Gum in a child's hair is easily removed with some turpentine on a cloth or piece of cotton. Just rub, and the gum disappears.

—*Mrs. Robert Knapp*
Lancaster, Wisconsin

A dish rack makes a handy catchall for the playthings of a bedridden child. The rungs meant for holding dishes are perfect for holding story books and coloring books. And the silverware holder is just right for crayons, pencils and scissors. —*Mrs. Irvin Quesenberry*
Clements, Minnesota

Attach the non-slip decals, normally sold for the bottom of bathtubs, to the back and seat of baby's high chair. It will prevent baby from slipping down in his seat—a good safety precaution for the small infant.

—*Mrs. Arnold Van Huizen*
Stockton, Illinois

Do you wonder how to amuse the children on a cold or rainy day when they're "penned in"? I've found this clay recipe, which uses ingredients from your cupboard. Combine 2-1/2 cups unsifted flour, 1/2 cup salt, 3 tablespoons corn oil and 1 tablespoon powdered alum. Pour 2 cups boiling water over ingredients. Mix well. Stored in a covered container, it lasts indefinitely.

—*Mrs. Joe Holterman*
Osage County, Missouri

When my children use their bubble pipes, loops and giant hoops, they need bubble solution in large quantities. My recipe for an economical, tough bubble liquid consists of 2 tablespoons powdered detergent, 1 tablespoon glycerin, 1 cup very hot water and a few drops of food coloring. —*Mrs. Robert Olson*
Taylor, Wisconsin

Use sweetened alphabet cereal to decorate children's birthday cakes. They are cute and fun to eat, too. —*Mrs. Frank Schnuelle*
Beatrice, Nebraska

We renovated an old folding aluminum-framed camp table using paneling that had been painted with blackboard paint for the top. With chalk and erasers handy, this table amuses all ages, whether at home or camping. We use it for drawing pictures, playing games such as tic-tac-toe, keeping scores or just plain doodling. —*Mrs. Carl Cramer*
Fort Jones, California

This sounds silly, but it works. If you have children who use an awful lot of toilet tissue, squeeze the roll as you put it on the dispenser so that it's not quite round. It takes a lot more pulling to get too much.

—*Mrs. Bill Largent*
Moiese, Montana

When a small child is ill, put his food in a muffin tin with colored paper liners. He'll be interested, and you'll get him to eat at least part of his food. —*Mrs. Vernon Ambrosy*
Zwingle, Iowa

Buy discarded samples in two colors from a carpet store. Use them to make a checkerboard rug. Glue an

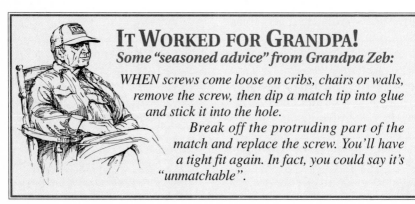

IT WORKED FOR GRANDPA!
Some "seasoned advice" from Grandpa Zeb:

WHEN screws come loose on cribs, chairs or walls, remove the screw, then dip a match tip into glue and stick it into the hole.

Break off the protruding part of the match and replace the screw. You'll have a tight fit again. In fact, you could say it's "unmatchable".

old burlap feed sack to the back of the samples, and turn the edge under. Use lids from juice or fruit jars for checkers.

—Mrs. R.C. Churnside
Ecleto, Texas

When our children were small, we kept two small jars in the car glove compartment. The lids each had a hole in the top just large enough for a drinking straw. When we went to a drive-in or traveled, there was no worry of spilled drinks.

—Mrs. Keith Littrell
Johnstown, Colorado

When grandchildren come to visit the farm in the summer, it is hard to keep the smaller ones amused when I am so busy. I found one of the children rummaging through an old box of buttons, and he asked to play with them. There weren't many, but it gave me a clue for future visits.

I bought two boxes of colored buttons of various sizes at a notions counter. I poured the buttons into a shallow pan and gave each child a large blunt needle and strong thread. Soon they were making necklaces, headbands and bracelets. They played endlessly with the buttons.

—Mrs. S.A. Fowler
Sikeston, Missouri

The top of a birthday cake can be made pretty with colored "life-savers". Stick the candles into the holes in the centers, and then "plant" the candies in the frosting. Youngsters will eat the cake and decorations, too. —Mrs. Fred Walta
Kingfisher, Oklahoma

When I want some nice treats for children who will be visiting, I make ice cream cones ahead of time, dip them in coconut and chopped nuts, wrap them in foil and put them in the freezer. Gives me more time to enjoy my adult guests and treat the kids at the same time.

—Mrs. James Pate
Williamston, North Carolina

When our toddler became an intrepid climber, I moved our medicines from the medicine cabinet, which could not be locked, to a cabinet with double doors that had loop handles. To lock the cabinet, I slipped a bicycle padlock through the handles. —Deleta Landphair
Humeston, Iowa

If you are having a birthday party, you can use cookies decorated with each child's name as place cards. Use brightly colored frosting, and write with a toothpick. The children will be delighted with these personalized cookies.

—Mrs. Orlin Petersen
Utica, South Dakota

When you want to take pillows along on your vacation or camping trip, make pillowcases for each pillow from different prints. There is never any question about whose pillow is whose. —Mrs. Louis Runck
Renville County, Minnesota

After your toddler has outgrown his use for the filled (jelly-like) teething ring, keep it in the freezer for those constant bumps on the head. Much quicker and neater than an ice cube! —*Mrs. Robert Berry Holman, Wisconsin*

I always canned several quart jars of water for traveling with our babies. It's easy to do. Just proceed as you would for putting up juices.

This way, you'll never have babies with upset tummies from a change in water. —*Elaine Jelinek Winner, South Dakota*

I've discovered a warning system to alert me when my toddler is in a drawer or cupboard that is "off limits". I fasten a bell or chime in the back of all drawers that I want to keep the little one out of. Each time one of these drawers moves, I am immediately informed.

You wouldn't believe the number of accidents and messes I have prevented using this system.

As an added plus, a child quickly learns that if a drawer chimes, it is one to stay out of.
—*Mrs. Ron Dolash, Gladbrook, Iowa*

If the girls in your family have trouble keeping barrettes in their hair, glue some strips of Velcro to the inside of the barrettes. The hair sticks to the Velcro and will keep the barrettes from slipping.
—*Mrs. Robert Roach Faucett, Missouri*

A novel way to invite children to a party is to write the information on an inflated balloon, then deflate it and send it in an envelope which reads, "Blow me up!"
—*Mrs. Irvin Quesenberry Clements, Minnesota*

If your child has outgrown the sleeves on her sweaters, turn them under up to the elbow, tack, then roll a large cuff. She will still be right in style. —*Lucille Maruskin North Olmsted, Ohio*

Here's a handy trick for keeping the little ones happy and quiet during a long car or airplane trip.

Before setting out, take some of their old small toys (or even buy

I remove all glass eyes from my children's stuffed toys and replace them with a satin stitch or cross-stitch embroidery. The toys are just as lovable and I rest easier knowing that I won't have to make an emergency trip to the hospital to have a glass eye removed from a little one's stomach.
—*Betty Hogan Greenwood, Indiana*

new ones) and wrap them individually. Or, let the children wrap the toys themselves, using paper sacks, wrapping paper or the funny papers.

Then while you are traveling, hand the gift-wrapped toys to the children one at a time. They love unwrapping the toys and seem to enjoy the toys much longer this way.

When wrapping the toys, keep in mind that the more paper you layer around each toy, the longer it will take the child to unwrap them. And if you wrap the toys in the funny papers, the wrapping paper will amuse the children, too.
—*Mrs. Paul Velsor*
Hazel Green, Wisconsin

It's much easier for little ones to zip their own coats and jackets if you attach key chains or rings to the zippers. —*Mrs. Henry Josephs*
Gardenville, Pennsylvania

Our children were always reluctant to give up their favorite games. So, whenever a board game started looking worn, I'd mount it on a piece of plywood. Saved our family some money and many tears.
—*Elsie Bauer, Greenleaf, Kansas*

Teach young cooks to separate eggs by letting them practice with eggs that are going to be scrambled. —*Shelly DeVries*
Cavour, South Dakota

When children accumulate a lot of puzzles, it's almost impossible to put them in order after several are upset at once. I've found it saves a lot of time and trouble if you number each of the puzzle boxes or trays and then put the same number on the back of each of the puzzle pieces.
—*Mrs. Pat Rodeffer, Ferris, Illinois*

I sew a strip of elastic around the bottoms of my toddler's coverall legs to prevent them from pulling out of his boots and getting wet and muddy. —*Mrs. Dale Rhodes*
Kalona, Iowa

Save yourself some hectic mornings when school's in session by keeping a bookcase or stacked shelves near the back door. Assign each child one shelf on which to assemble lunch, gym bag, homework, etc. On the way out the door, youngsters can  pick up their things quickly rather than creating a last-minute "crisis" by losing track of them.
—*Phyllis Kemper*
Julesburg, Colorado

Here's my trick to keep toddlers and mittens together: Snip a piece of 1/4-inch-wide elastic only as long as is necessary to reach from your child's wrist directly to the back of his neck to the other wrist without stretching.

Attach a mitten to each end of the elastic and use a large safety pin to secure the elastic's center to the back of the coat collar on the outside (do *not* put mitten string through coat sleeves).

When your toddler decides to take off his mittens (in the barn, as an example), they'll be up high enough to stay clean and dry…while mittens that dangle at the cuffs will get wet or dirty whenever your child reaches down. —*Paula White Viola, Wisconsin*

My children like to have cartoon characters put on their sweatshirts. I trace their favorite characters from coloring books using a transfer pencil. Then I iron the transfers onto the sweatshirts. I paint them with embroidery paint. —*Mrs. William Roth Atalissa, Iowa*

I keep track of winter gloves, hats and scarves by stashing them in a large shoe bag I hang on the kitchen door. The children just grab whatever they may need on their way out.

—*Patricia Teres Easthampton, Massachusetts*

Next time your youngsters go ice skating, send a *sled* along. They will have a dry place to sit while putting on or taking off their skates …or just catching their breath. (If lots of people use the pond, be sure to clearly mark the sled with their names.) —*Ethel Williams Lawrenceville, Pennsylvania*

If your child gets gum stuck in his or her hair, put peanut butter on the gum and work it in. The gum will come right out.
—*Marlene Mullen, Valley City, Ohio*

Your little girl will be happier wearing her brother's "hand-me-down" T-shirts if you add some iron-on patches or colorful rickrack. Or, embroider her initials on the shirt.
—*Mrs. Jas Reimann Lebanon, Illinois*

Between uses, I cover my son's wading pool with a fitted sheet. When he wants to go for a swim, I remove the sheet and the pool is clean and ready for him.

I also add a very small amount of chlorine bleach to the water to keep it clean. The chlorine in the pool also helps dry up my son's insect bites. —*Deborah Collums Marks, Mississippi*

Want to keep kids busy? When you hear "There's nothing to do", use my mother's time-tested technique: Past magazine covers to heavy cardboard, and then cut them into jigsaw puzzles. It kept us three girls busy for hours, especially when she mixed two or more picture puzzles together for us to sort out and assemble. —*Alma Hansen New Denmark, New Brunswick*

If you have crayon marks on your wallpaper, use furniture spray polish to take them off. It works like a charm! —*Kim Baumeister Rochester, Wisconsin*

Stop leaks from ice cream cones by putting a half teaspoon of peanut butter in the bottom before adding ice cream. You'll have less laundry to do—and the child will find a "treat" when they get to the bottom of the cone!

—Mrs. James Hartzell
Watertown, New York

Here's an idea for recycling broken and worn-down crayons. Melt them (in a soup can) and pour into old candy molds. My granddaughters love to color with the special shapes.   *—Rae Stearns*
Girard, Pennsylvania

When your children outgrow their sandbox, don't discard it. Fill it with soil and plant their first vegetable or flower garden.

—Barbara Carpenter
Oakboro, North Carolina

If your young chili eaters don't like beans, try this trick: Mash the beans so they thicken the soup but are invisible to little eyes. It worked for my mother...and now it works for me, too!   *—Janey Enlow*
Centralia, Missouri

To take the "ouch" out of removing bandages, saturate area with baby oil before pulling off.

—LaFlorya Gauthier
St. Didace, Quebec

Make breakfast fun for kids by using a cookie cutter to cut a shape

COUNTRY TRIVIA

AT ONE TIME in the early to mid-1900's, there were over 1,000 round barns in the Midwest.

from center of a bread slice. Dip the slice and cutout into melted butter and place side by side on preheated griddle; crack an egg into the hole in the bread. Fry until egg is set; carefully remove the egg and toast together and serve.

—Susan Lawson
Hayes Center, Nebraska

You can make sturdy economical scrapbooks for yourself or your children by recycling brown paper grocery bags.

Take the bags and cut out uniform sheets that are twice as long as the desired page size, then put them together and stitch or staple down through the middle. Fold and cover the outside with colorful Con-Tact paper.   *—Mrs. Grover Thomas*
Mt. Morris, Illinois

Do your kids get sticky fingers from playing beneath pine trees? I've found milk washes the resin right off!   *—Mrs. Jonas Troyer*
Millersburg, Ohio

CHAPTER 12

ODDS & ENDS THAT HAD TO BE SHARED

Every week I save a few labels from envelopes that are clearly addressed and have our zip code. Such labels come on business letters and advertising material sent to us. Whenever I respond to a refund offer or send in a catalog mail order, I send along one of the labels.

—Mrs. H.D. Fountain
Iowa City, Iowa

To unscrew stuck lids on ketchup or other small bottles or jars, a nutcracker makes a perfect utensil.

—Mrs. James Schewe
Danube, Minnesota

Save buttons neatly by sandwiching them between layers of cellophane tape. When you need one, just snip it off. This is a good way to keep track of snaps, too.

—Mrs. Roy Lairmore
Beatrice, Nebraska

To label a jar that will be washed often, write on a piece of adhesive tape with a ballpoint pen. Apply a coat of clear fingernail polish over it, then add another coat later. The label will last a long time even if soaked in water.

—Mrs. Adam Kissel
Poseyville, Indiana

We love catching sunfish and bluegills, but cleaning the inside of each fish was hard on my thumbnail. Now I buy a yard of nylon net and cut it into 8-inch squares. The net scrubs the insides cleaner than my finger can, and after the fish are cleaned, the net may be tossed.

—Mrs. Ray Oscarson
Wahpeton, North Dakota

Don't discard the pile lining in an old coat. Cut the lining to a size you like and stuff it into a soft cover for a toss pillow.

—Mrs. James Pate
Williamston, North Carolina

One of the nicest gifts to give a

hospital patient or shut-in is a clipboard. It is very handy for writing letters, doing puzzles, etc. A bright-colored clipboard and paper in a different color will really brighten up a sickroom. —*Mrs. Gerald Belter*
Baraboo, Wisconsin

Quart-sized plastic freezer bags are excellent shoe bags for travel and storage. One bag is the exact size for the average shoe. They are lightweight, transparent and disposable. —*Mrs. Orlin Petersen*
Utica, South Dakota

A large scrapbook makes an inexpensive file for patterns. Paste or tape every two pages together on two sides to form envelopes. Cut out the picture from the original pattern envelope and paste it onto the front of the envelope in your scrapbook. File the pattern inside.
—*Kathleen Siedschlag*
Berlin, North Dakota

If you have a zipper-fastened skirt that won't stay zipped, sew a hook onto the open end, pointing upward to the skirt waistband. When you pull up the zipper, the hole in the end of it may be slipped over the hook to hold the zipper in position.
—*Mrs. Ernest Ross*
San Bernardino, California

Cutting bias strips is simplified by pressing masking tape on the bias of the fabric and then cutting along the edges of the tape. Pull the tape off gently, and the bias strips will be straight. —*Joan Dirkman*
Ahmeek, Michigan

Use dental floss instead of thread to sew on shirt buttons that easily twist off the neckband. They'll never come off again.
—*Mrs. Fred Proctor*
Elkhorn, Wisconsin

If you're not sure if you want pockets on a garment you are making, tape them on with transparent tape first. They can be easily moved until properly positioned, too. Apply trims the same way. It's easier and neater. —*Mrs. Pat Juenemann*
Clements, Minnesota

Before discarding outgrown or worn-out clothing, I remove the zippers and buttons so they may be sewn into new garments that I make. To avoid confusion and needless expense, I jot down the length, color and type of zipper (nylon, metal, skirt- or neck-style, invisible, etc.) on a small card that I keep in my purse.

Then, when shopping for fabrics and patterns, a quick glance at this card tells me whether or not I have a suitable zipper at home.
—*Mrs. Samuel Griffith*
Memphis, Tennessee

Use discarded curtains and zippers to make no-cost garment bags.
—*Mrs. Doyle Ryan, Brooklyn, Iowa*

If your husband is like mine, he likes to have you and the children go along with him on errands, but usually serves short notice of these trips.

To avoid a lot of scurry, I keep a "go box" stocked with things the children and I always hunted for before these last-minute trips to town. Inside are grooming items such as combs and brushes, extra clothing and things to keep us occupied while we wait for my husband—a book for each of us, real and play manicure items, stationery, coloring books and crayons.

This way, we're ready to go, with just one stop at the "go box".
—*Mrs. Otto Stank, Pound, Wisconsin*

To avoid pins scattering around the table and floor while sewing, keep a large magnet nearby. The pins cling to the magnet and make cleaning up simpler—especially if the pins spill onto the floor.
—*Mrs. Orlin Petersen*
Utica, South Dakota

Use leather from old purses or gloves to reinforce the elbows of men's work jackets or children's play clothes.
—*Leah Wilke*
San Bernardino, California

To keep material from slipping when cutting out a garment, turn a felt table pad upside down over a table or cutting board.
—*Mrs. L. Friesen*
Bowsman, Manitoba

Before cutting fabric that frays easily, draw on the fabric around the pattern with a wax crayon. Cut on the waxed line. The wax will serve to keep fraying at a minimum until the sewing is completed.
—*Mrs. C.R. Landphair*
Humeston, Iowa

For no-mess Christmas tree watering, place ice cubes in the tree stand. Use a turkey baster for more accurate, no-spill water refills.
—*Mary Ellen Martin*
Lincoln, Illinois

Potato chip cans make great candle molds. The inside of the can is waxed, so the carton peels off very easily once the candle wax has hard-

IT WORKED FOR GRANDPA!
Some "seasoned advice" from Grandpa Zeb:

FOR SOME unique, budget-type bird feeders, fill empty mesh vegetable bags with apple, orange and vegetable peelings, as well as leftover lettuce.

Hang from eaves or a tree branch that's visible from your window. Then sit back and enjoy watching the many different kinds of birds that'll come to enjoy your leftovers.

ened. And the wick is easily held in place by poking a small hole in the can's plastic cover and slipping the wick through.

—*Mrs. Wilbur Saufferer*
Faribault, Minnesota

When mending the legs of jeans and trousers or the long sleeves of shirts and blouses, slide a large rolled-up magazine into the leg or sleeve under the hole. Let it unroll, and it will hold the garment smooth while you sew. —*Beatrice Boyd*
Humeston, Iowa

If you lay your pattern pieces on the material and press with a warm iron, you won't need to pin them. They will stay in place as you cut!

—*Mrs. Fred Proctor*
Elkhorn, Wisconsin

When I mail a get-well card to someone in the hospital, I always write that person's home address for the return address on the envelope. If the person goes home before my card gets to the hospital, their return address makes certain they will get the card. —*Sherry Peek*
Tyler, Texas

Grease the threads on glue and nail polish bottles and they'll open easily every time. —*Gail Anderson*
St. Ignatius, Montana

Take a plug-in night light on your next overnight trip. This will make it much easier to find the bathroom or telephone in an unfamiliar motel or guest room in the middle of the night. We have really found this helpful, especially when traveling with children or elderly people.
—*Margaret Lewis, Sioux City, Iowa*

If you have let the hem out of a dress and find you still have a crease where the old hemline was, slip a brown paper bag over your ironing board and place the dress on it.

Next, saturate a cloth with white vinegar and go across the old hemline with it. Then press with a steam iron, being sure to use a pressing cloth.

I have found this method very satisfactory. It even works well on permanent press.
—*Mrs. Bob Roach, Faucett, Missouri*

Corners cut from used envelopes make great bookmarks. They just slip over the page you wish to mark.

—*Dorothy Hofbauer*
Lincoln, Nebraska

Add a touch of glue to the knot when tying a package and the string will not loosen during shipping.

—*Carrie Schumacher*
Fall Creek, Wisconsin

Put a magnet on the dashboard of your husband's pickup to hold lists and reminders. He can then place your shopping list in a conspicuous spot, so he doesn't forget to pick up your requested bread or milk when he comes home from town. (This idea was suggested by my husband after he repeatedly forgot my lists!)

—*Mrs. Robert Popken*
Oakland, Nebraska

Use the tubing from empty paper towel rolls to prevent the horizontal crease made by hanging laundry over wire hangers. Slice the tube the long way, put it over the bottom wire of a hanger and tape the slit shut. Slacks, tablecloths, etc. will hang without picking up any unwanted creases.
— *Mrs. Ralph Stellick*
Stoddard, Wisconsin

My over-the-shoulder bag was constantly slipping off the shoulder of my coat. I sewed a big button onto the shoulder of my coat under the collar, and now I catch the strap of my purse over the button.
— *Mrs. Otto Fahning*
Wells, Minnesota

When you sew snaps on a garment, attach all the halves on one side first. The rub chalk on each one, and press them against the fabric on the side where the mates are to go.
— *Mrs. H.O. Daley*
Parker, Colorado

Slip wet mittens over your shoe rack's "prongs". It cuts drying time in half! — *Jan Christel*
Valders, Wisconsin

For safer winter driving, keep a bit of sand on hand. Sew several small sacks from portions of old pant legs, then fill with 5 to 10 pounds of sand. Sandbags add weight to your car's trunk, making it easier to maneuver on slippery roads. And, if you get stuck on an icy patch, you can shake some out for traction. — *Jinks Grazier*
Garrison, Montana

Don't sit on the floor when marking the hem for your daughter's dress. Don't make her climb on a table, either. Sit on the stairs with her a step or two above you, and you'll both be comfortable.
— *Mrs. Fred Proctor*
Elkhorn, Wisconsin

When knitting with more than one ball of wool at a time, slip the end of each color through a plastic straw to prevent tangling.
— *Mrs. Ernest Ross*
San Bernardino, California

Glue a tape measure on the front edge of your sewing machine and cover it with clear varnish. This will save many trips to the sewing box.
— *Carrie Schumacher*
Fall Creek, Wisconsin

When the tip of a shoestring comes off, dip the end of the lace in clear fingernail polish and let dry. You will have a hard-tipped shoestring again for easier lacing.
— *Mrs. Herman Helmke*
Lake Wilson, Minnesota

Use bright-colored cookie cutters (the outline shapes, not solid cutters) as napkin rings for your country holiday table settings. Let guests keep the cutters as mementos of your dinner party.
— *Mary Ellen Martin*
Lincoln, Illinois

"Brown-bag" any extra ice cubes you make for large gatherings—they won't stick together when you put them back in the freezer like they do in plastic bags.

—*Ruth Burroughs*
Maquoketa, Iowa

The cookies you mail will arrive unbroken if you wrap several in small plastic bags and pack them in a 1-pound process American cheese box. —*Jenelle Miller*
Marion, South Dakota

My husband bales straw in a "he-can" size that's too heavy for me to carry. So, before calving season begins, I take a half dozen or so of the big bales, cut the twine, halve each bale and retie. Then, when bedding is needed, I use a "she-can" bale! —*Gloria Hunt*
Kimberley, British Columbia

When you need a patch that must absolutely match a garment, such as a coat, cut it from underneath a pocket. The hole left under the pocket may be patched with another cloth, as it will not show.
—*Alice Waters, Arcadia, Wisconsin*

After purchasing a new garment that has buttons on it, brush a small amount of clear nail polish on the back of each button to keep the thread from coming loose.

—*Ruth Barron*
Lynnwood, Washington

Cleaning muddy boots is never fun, but it's somewhat easier since I found that spraying the clean boots lightly with cooking spray such as Pam keeps mud from clinging as much. Of course, don't spray the soles. —*Donna Mosher*
Augusta, Montana

Here's a substitute for costly ribbons and bows on presents. Tie them with inexpensive yarn instead. Buy a large multicolored ball, or several balls of different colors, and twist strands together.

While making bows and tying packages, keep any yarn odds and ends 2 inches or longer. Use them to make tiny pom-poms for topping off gifts, too. —*Lillian Sharman*
Knowlton, Quebec

Bargain-priced masking tape tends to tear off as you unroll it. But I found a solution. Just pop the roll in the microwave oven for 10 to 12 seconds. The tape will peel off without breaking. —*Bill Tipton*
Ashland City, Tennessee

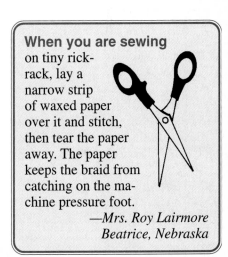

When you are sewing on tiny rickrack, lay a narrow strip of waxed paper over it and stitch, then tear the paper away. The paper keeps the braid from catching on the machine pressure foot.
—*Mrs. Roy Lairmore*
Beatrice, Nebraska

Toss two old socks in the trunk of your car. They don't take much room, but they're sure great to put over your hands when you brush snow off the windows, change a tire or whatever. —*Sharon Sellig St. Paul, Minnesota*

We save money on gift wrap and have some family fun at the same time by using the funny papers and brown grocery sacks to wrap Christmas presents.

The comics are colorful on their own. As for the sacks, we use paint, tissue paper, old Christmas cards and just about anything—the possibilites are endless. —*Betsy Buckel El Cajon, California*

Whenever I buy new rubber bathtub or sink mats, I tuck the old ones into the car trunk or truck. They give good traction on ice when slipped under the tires.
—*Adelia Habermann Calumet County, Wisconsin*

Ship cookies packed in sweater boxes layered with colored "Easter grass". Besides protecting the cookies, they make a pretty display.
—*Heather MacDonald Cornwall, Prince Edward Island*

When my husband gets a new package of black, dark blue and brown socks. I sew a few stitches

of red, pink, green or light blue thread onto the toe or heel of each pair. This makes it very easy to match the socks after washing them.
—*Mrs. Sherwood Dieter Allentown, Pennsylvania*

Cylinders that potato chips come in are handy for knitting projects— just wash and dry the empty can, place a skein of yarn in it, cut a hole in the plastic top and pull the end of the yarn through the hole. It's especially convenient for taking your knitting with you when traveling.
—*Catherine Butts, Hunter, New York*

Many fabrics today look the same on both sides. To keep them from getting mixed up, as soon as I cut a piece, I put a small piece of masking tape on the wrong side. It remains there until the garment is sewn and saves many a mix-up.
—*Mrs. Fred Proctor Elkhorn, Wisconsin*

If you have some dirty old coins that you want clean and shiny again, soak them in vinegar and water overnight. When you rinse them off the next day, they'll be just like new! —*Misti Williams Oak Hill, Ohio*

Attach small pieces of rubber to the feet of your stepladder to keep it from sliding or scuffing your floors.

Use soap or paraffin on zippers that are hard to work. Attach a small key chain to a jacket zipper to make the zipper easier to get a hold of.

When the tips of shoelaces be-

come frayed, dip them in glue, twist into a point and let dry.
—*Diane Lessig, Van Buren, Ohio*

Do you ever put a stamp on a card or envelope when you didn't mean to? Just stick the card or envelope in the freezer for a few days, and the stamp will come off easily.
—*Irene Rutkowski*
Greenfield, Wisconsin

Here's a way to remember to turn your headlights off after driving during the day. Clip a clothespin to your car's visor and when you turn your lights on, clip the clothespin onto the ignition key. Then you won't turn the engine off without remembering the lights.
—*Alicia Quadrazzi*
Escondido, California

For those of you who have trouble getting ahold of the end of a piece of masking tape, try sticking a plastic bread-tie on the end of the tape. That should provide the handle you need! —*Becky Valdez*
Vernal, Utah

Give greeting cards a "new life"—and make your own inexpensive notecards—by cutting card covers (that don't have writing on the back side) to postcard size.
—*Margaret Voitek*
Wyoming, Pennsylvania

Make your own sturdy rubber bands by recycling worn-out rubber gloves. Use scissors to cut across the width of each finger, palm and wrist. You'll have a nice vari-

COUNTRY TRIVIA

MILKWEED, used to make life jackets during World War II, is now being turned into stuffing for pillows and comforters.

ety of first-class rubber bands of just the right thickness for any need.
—*Lorine Washington*
Houlka, Mississippi

My young boys and I team up to turn plain brown lunch sacks into pretty gift bags that hold homemade caramel corn, seasoned nut mixes, etc. We draw holiday designs on the bags with paint, stencils or markers, then add the name of the person the gift's going to. After filling the bags, we tape or staple them shut and deliver! —*Brenda Mink*
Prairie du Chien, Wisconsin

I cut small squares of paper from the backs of used envelopes and keep the pieces in a small box near the telephone for notes.
—*J. Zamatti, Etna, California*

I was knitting a design with 10 different rows that then were repeated over and over. Because I kept losing my place and having to rip

189

Looking for new ways you can use "windfall" pinecones from your evergreens? Craft them into "bows" for Christmas packages! Put four or five tiny ones in a star-shaped group on top of a wrapped gift. With a tip of each cone touching another, hot-glue ends in place, making sure that you hold cones up at a 45-degree angle for a few moments until glue dries.

—Barbara Frey
Webster, New York

stitches out, I decided to tape-record the rows at my knitting speed. Now I play the tape, using headphones so as not to disturb anyone, and it helps me keep track of where I am.

—Lillian Brownell
Cambridge, New York

Make hand-sewing a snap by first running your needle and thread through a fabric softener sheet. I guarantee they will glide through the cloth like magic.*—Carol Detert*
Westchester, Illinois

Tired of dripping candles? Put them in the freezer for a few hours before you use them.

—Dawn Eckhart
Nazareth, Pennsylvania

My sister and I exchange a lot of postcards. We make them more fun and personal by using photos we've taken ourselves. The post office accepts 4- by 5-inch prints and you can put the stamp, address and message on the back. We use all kinds of photo subjects…4-H activities, vacations, school projects— you name it. It's great!

—Nancy Lane, Morral, Ohio

If you have wet shoes or boots that need to be dry by morning, put them on the floor of the kitchen near the refrigerator vent.

Refrigerators have both intake and outlet vents. If your house is like mine, the vent with no dust on it is the outlet. Put the open end of your shoes or boots next to it and they'll dry quickly. *—Nancy Everett*
Blairsville, Georgia

To avoid discarding magazines that others have not read or may have wanted to save, have each family member initial the cover when they have finished with it. And if someone would like to save the magazine, have them note that on the cover, too. *—Cathy Peterson*
Catawba, Wisconsin

Take a few spring-type clothespins along when you go grocery shopping; they're handy for clipping coupons onto the shopping cart or basket. *—Marzetta Madge*
Palm Bay, Florida

When going fishing, take along a crochet hook. Use it to free your hook when you miscast and it gets caught in bushes or clothing.

—Edward Letchman
Birmingham, Alabama

I've developed a good way to keep my shopping coupons in order. Instead of letting them pile up so that I have to shuffle through them all before going to the store, I put them in a photo album.

I put an index label on each page, so the album has an easy-to-follow order to it. Whenever I want to see what coupons I have, I can look under a particular category and quickly find out. —*Kris Ward Monticello, Minnesota*

To easily wrap newspapers or magazines for mailing, slit the ends of a business-size envelope. Then roll up the item to be mailed and wrap the envelope around it. Use the envelope's gummed area to seal it. Reinforce the seams with clear tape if necessary. —*J. James Redman Columbus, Ohio*

If you run out of colored thread or don't have the right color on hand for sewing repairs, avoid a special trip to town by using embroidery floss. Just separate one strand of floss and use it to finish your project. —*Lee McAfee Fredericksburg, Texas*

Whenever I clean my white shoes, I face the chore of also cleaning the white shoelaces. Here's a trick I've learned: Pin the laces to a towel and wash them with the rest of the clothes. The laces come out like new! —*Melba Grady Springfield, Illinois*

To salvage a postage stamp that has lost its glue, moisten the envelope flap and rub the stamp across it before sealing the envelope. —*Patricia Heflin, Springfield, Illinois*

To keep your car blanket clean, tuck it in a zippered cotton slip cover. It can double as a pillow this way, too. —*Mrs. Fred Proctor Elkhorn, Wisconsin*

Caps can be revived with a simple spin in the top rack of your dishwasher. No more scrunched brims when they come out! —*Deb Tones Branchport, New York*

Empty Christmas card boxes make nice personal-size candy containers. For make-ahead gifts, cover the boxes in foil,  fill with chunks of candy, then stack boxes in a heavy plastic bag and freeze. Later, thaw and add a bow. —*Darlene Smith, Rockford, Illinois*

Instead of letting your suitcase stand idle between your travels, why not fill it with all your letter-writing equipment—stationery, cards, unanswered letters, pens, stamps and address book.

When closed, it forms an instant, portable lap desk that can travel with you to any room in the house. In the summer, take it outside with you.

When you have finished writing, or something interrupts, you just have to close the top and all is intact and orderly. —*Mrs. Emil Lembke Sussex, Wisconsin*

My son's wallet had a habit of wandering when he was in the yard or field...until I sewed a horizontal 1-inch strip of Velcro inside his back pocket. No more missing money.

—Virginia Ricks
Gibson City, Illinois

The sleeves on my husband's denim work jacket always seem to wear out first. And when they do, I just put it to good use—as a vest for *me*. I cut off the sleeves at the shoulders, leaving about 3/4 inch of fabric that I turn under twice and stitch down.

Since it's not as bulky or warm, the vest is a nice alternative to a full coat. *—Marilyn Umble*
Atglen, Pennsylvania

We all know how frustrating it can be to try to separate stacked glasses or bowls that are stuck together. Well, I've found that if you fill the top glass with cold water and dip the bottom glass in hot water, they will come apart safely and easily.

—Sharon Finian
Buffalo County, Wisconsin

If hinge screw holes are too loose, pry a sliver of wood into each screw hole and then put the screw back in. A toothpick or matchstick usually works well; force it in, then break off the portruding head. Stuffing a bit of steel wool in the holes works, too. *—Dan Wagner*
Bridport, Vermont

Sewing on the go? A plastic tackle box makes a great portable sewing center! Small items fit nicely into the divided sections of the box; others can be taped inside the top. Place bigger items—scissors, elastic, etc.—in the bottom.

Also, try this trick for cutting sheer material. Put material over a checked plastic tablecloth, then follow checks with some sharp shears. No need to mark the material first to ensure straight lines!

—Aileen De Hamer, Cedar, Iowa

Worn-out wool socks can still provide warmth: Cut off the toes and bottom few inches and slip the remaining socks over shoes or boots before putting on overshoes. Old wool socks and sweaters also make good mittens—trace a child's hands, add enough for a seam, stitch and turn inside out. *—Jody Courtney*
Alzada, Montana

Waxed paper works fine to trace a pattern with several sizes given on the same pattern. Instead of cutting into the pattern for one size and spoiling the others, trace through waxed paper. Then cut out the size you need. *—Judy Scholovich*
Waukesha, Wisconsin

Wait! Don't throw away those wishbones! Wash them, let dry and then paint with bright-colored enamel. Tie them on top of gift packages. The recipients will love the novel touch. *—Helen Svaren*
Arlington, South Dakota

If you ever break off a key and the key stays in the lock, get a narrow saber saw blade that has large teeth. Then insert the blade into the keyhole as far as you can beside the broken key. Twist the blade to make the teeth dig into the side of the key and slowly pull it out. If it doesn't work, try it a few more times.

—Ted Carmeron, Firth, Nebraska

Here are several tips that can be used around the house:

I put my hands in plastic bags when shining shoes to keep my fingers clean.

When I bake bread, I put a small oven-proof dish of water in the oven. It helps keep the crust from getting hard.

Instead of using a regular letter opener which can injure a child, I use a plastic knife. It's safer and works just as well. *—Opel Duncan Calvin, Kentucky*

When preparing for a trip with a spouse or child, each of you should pack one of the other's outfits in your suitcase. That way, if one of you loses your luggage en route, you'll at least have a set of fresh clothes to wear. *—Melinda Neal Muncie, Indiana*

Instead of licking stamps or envelope flaps, put several ice cubes on a folded paper towel in a small dish. Slide the stamps or envelopes over the ice cubes. That makes them just moist enough to stick!

—Bernice Kerr, Petersburg, Ohio

If candles drip wax all over your glass dining table or coffee table, place a paper towel on wax, then lightly run a *cool* iron over it. The towel will "pick up" wax.

—Jennifer Johnson Big Timber, Montana

The stamp won't stick? Just dab the stamp with the white of an egg. And if you've already sealed an envelope and forgotten something, hold the flap over the spout of a boiling teakettle and it'll come open easily. Then re-glue it with egg white.   *—Mrs. Melrose Coon Hicksville, Ohio*

You'll get a lot more cans into your recycling bin if you open the bottoms of the tin cans as well as the top. Then step on the sides of the cans to squash them flat.

—Robert Goodwin Montell, Wisconsin

When tying a package with string for mailing, first dip the string in water. That will make the string shrink when it dries, resulting in a tighter and more secure package.

—Charlotte Rymph Monterey, Indiana

Keep electric cords organized by storing them in empty cardboard toilet tissue rolls. You can write on the roll what appliance the cord is used for.   *—Mrs. Allen Zimmerman Fairbury, Illinois*

If your child's plastic wading pool has a hole in it, don't throw it away. Tie rope to it and use it as a

sled or wheelbarrow to carry yard waste like grass clippings, leaves, pine needles or branches. You can pull or drag large amounts without much effort because it glides along the grass. And you can hang it up when not in use. —*Ginny Long*
Daytona Beach, Florida

My mother used to put a piece of glass from a picture frame over the recipe she was using to keep it from splatters. Today I keep recipes in a photo album with see-through protective covers to achieve the same result. —*Janet Hounsell*
Conway, New Hampshire

You can sharpen a knife by rubbing it on the bottom of a red clay flowerpot. —*Sharon Jacobson*
Lincoln, Nebraska

Wet clothes won't freeze onto the clothesline if you wipe the line first with a cloth dampened with vinegar. —*Joanne Gehman*
New Holland, Pennsylvania

To remove wrinkles from wash-and-wear clothes, place them in the dryer with a moist towel for 8 to 10 minutes. And when you're traveling, hang them on hangers over the bathtub and run the hot shower with curtains closed for 8 to 10 minutes.
—*Auton Miller*
Knoxville, Tennessee

Never hang a mirror where the sun will shine directly into it. This will soon mar the best mirror.
—*Artye Lee Scott*
Spokane, Washington

Have trouble slipping your shoe into tight galoshes? Just pull a large plastic bag over your shoe first and it will slip right in.
—*Barbara Dvorak*
Pierre, South Dakota

Applying "inch marks" with nail polish on your knitting needles provides a handy, time-saving measure.
—*Fanny Hall*
Friendship, New York

Ribbed cuffs from worn-out socks make nice wrist or ankle finish for home-sewn pajamas. White may be dyed to match the fabric.
—*Mrs. Fred Proctor*
Elkhorn, Wisconsin

Create your own "safety stickers" to post on farm equipment, tractor doors and near "danger zones". Use self-sticking white mailing labels and permanent marking pens to write messages such as "You are loved—be careful!" —*Gloria Porter*
Grandin, North Dakota

I recycle envelopes that have come in the mail and are ready to be thrown away. I often write my grocery list on the back, then insert coupons for the store inside the envelope to double its usefulness. This makes shopping trips more organized.
—*Beth Ball*
Jacksonville, Florida